BY AARON MAHNKE

Destiny: A Fairy Tale
Indian Summer
Consumed
Grave Suspicion

THE WORLD OF LORE
Monstrous Creatures
Wicked Mortals
Dreadful Places

THE WORLD OF
LORE

MONSTROUS CREATURES

DEL
REY

New York

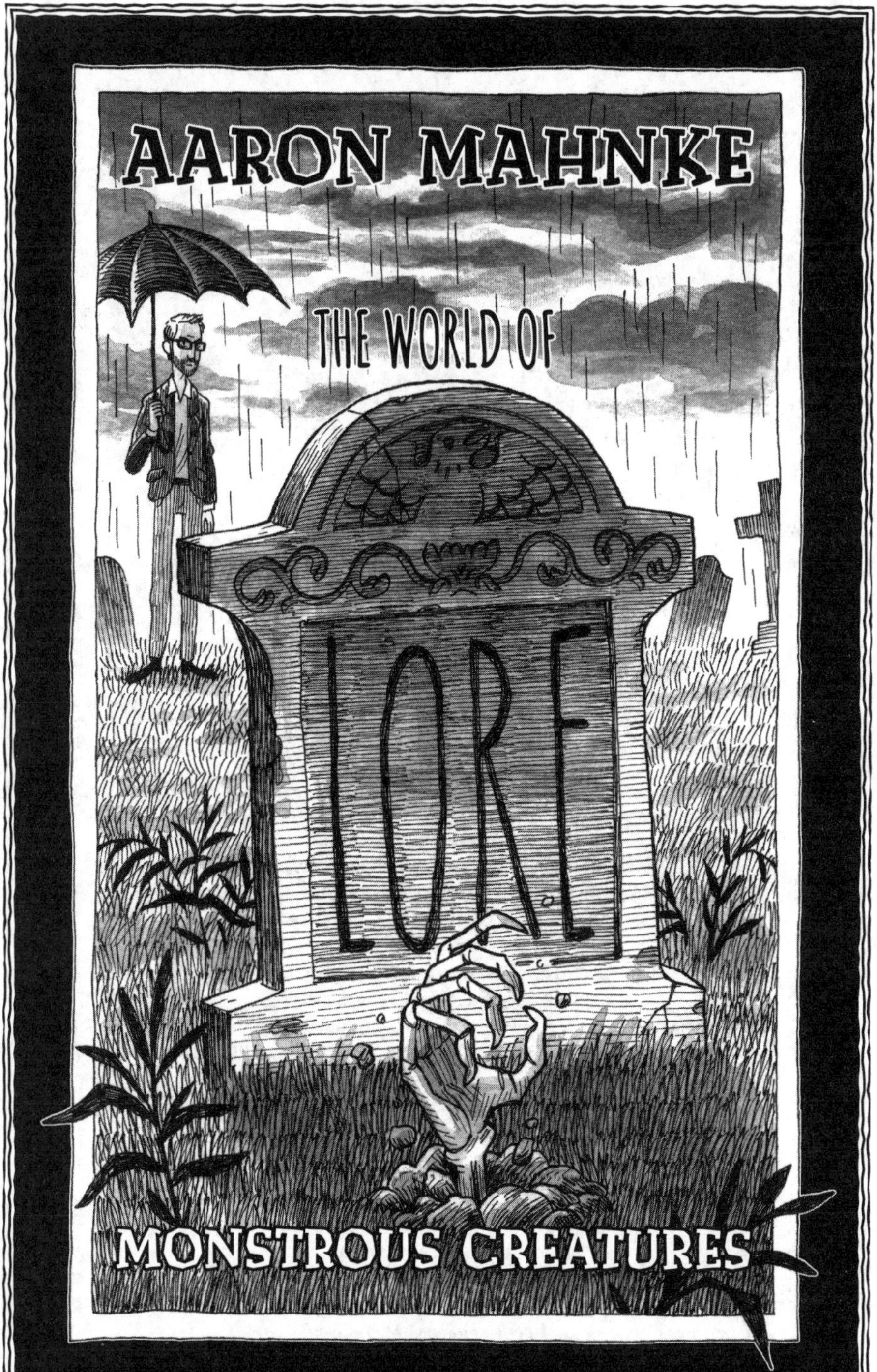
AARON MAHNKE
THE WORLD OF
LORE
MONSTROUS CREATURES

2024 Del Rey Trade Paperback Edition

Copyright © 2017 by Aaron Mahnke

Published in the United States by Del Rey, an imprint of Random House, a division of Penguin Random House LLC, New York.

DEL REY and the CIRCLE colophon are registered trademarks of Penguin Random House LLC.

Most of the text in this work is based on the author's podcast, *Lore*.

Originally published in hardcover in the United States by Del Rey, an imprint of Random House, a division of Penguin Random House LLC, in 2017.

LIBRARY OF CONGRESS CATALOGING-IN-PUBLICATION DATA
Names: Mahnke, Aaron, author.
Title: The world of lore. Monstrous creatures / Aaron Mahnke.
Other titles: Monstrous creatures
Description: New York: Del Rey, [2017] | Includes bibliographical references.
Identifiers: LCCN 2017038286| ISBN 9781524797980 (paperback) | ISBN 9781524797973 (ebook)
Subjects: LCSH: Monsters—Folklore. | Occultism. | Mythology. | BISAC: SOCIAL SCIENCE / Folklore & Mythology. | SOCIAL SCIENCE / Anthropology / General. | HISTORY / Social History.
Classification: LCC GR825 .M1835 2017 | DDC 001.944—dc23
LC record available at https://lccn.loc.gov/2017038286

Printed in the United States of America on acid-free paper

Artwork designed by M. S. Corley

randomhousebooks.com

1st Printing

Book design by Simon M. Sullivan

For Jennifer.
I'm so very glad I haven't had to walk this road alone.
I couldn't have asked for a better travel companion.

Believe nothing you hear, and only one half that you see.

—EDGAR ALLAN POE,
"The System of Doctor Tarr and Professor Fether"

CONTENTS

 THE DEAD RETURNED

They Made a Tonic 3

Deep and Twisted Roots 11

Dark Conclusions 22

Brought Back 32

The Trees 42

 A LITTLE PROBLEM

The Others 47

Under Construction 57

Tampered 64

Doing Tricks 73

 BACK TO NATURE

Trees and Shadows 87

Off the Path 98

The Beast Within 106

Hunger Pains 113

A Deep Fear 122

Lost Sheep 133

One Word 137

 OUR OTHER HALVES

Unboxed 143

Do Not Open 152

A Devil on the Roof 156

Over the Top 165

Missing the Point 175

 BEYOND THE VEIL

Passing Notes 189

The Bloody Pit 201

Dinner at the Afterglow 207

Homestead 215

Adrift 225

Take the Stand 234

The Devil's Beat 243

Mary, Mary 253

The Lump 265

Write Me a Letter 269

The Bank Job 273

Knock, Knock, Knock 277

Possessed 280

Acknowledgments 285

Bibliography 287

 THE DEAD RETURNED

They Made a Tonic

HOLLYWOOD IS OBSESSED.

Sure, we often think of obsessions like sex, violence, gigantic robots, and of course epic battles between good and evil. But another obsession of Hollywood is vampires.

You have to admit, though, that there's a lot to love about vampires. Immortality, wealth, power, and superhuman abilities such as flight and strength. Yes, they come with trade-offs, such as incredibly bad sunburns, but every movie I've seen (and I've seen a *lot,* believe me) tends to show vampires that are fairly happy with their lot in life.

My exposure to the world of vampires happened in the late 1990s when I was in college. A friend recommended the Anne Rice novel *Interview with the Vampire.* I devoured that and many of the sequels. They're fun reads, and they certainly set the tone for a decade or more of vampire-centered entertainment.

I won't touch on the vampires of the Twilight series, mostly because I haven't read any of the books. But I will say this: those books, however lambasted they have been by critics, have shown that popular culture's love of all things vampire is as undying as the creatures themselves.

When most people think of vampires, they envision something that is a purely European creature: a foreign accent, Victorian-era dress, and dark manor homes and castles. It's a common visual language for most of the Western world, so I don't blame movies and books for portraying that image. But it's one small facet of a legend that has hundreds of expressions.

The single most prominent historical figure attached to the modern notion of vampirism is, of course, Vlad III of Wallachia, otherwise known as Vlad the Impaler. Vlad ruled the small Eastern European kingdom of Wallachia from 1456 to 1462.

He was known as Vlad the Impaler because he preferred to execute his enemies by impaling them on stakes. The Ottomans called him Lord Impaler after entering his kingdom and finding "forests" of impaled victims. Vlad was a violent guy, you see. Rather bloodthirsty, you might say.

He, like his father before him, belonged to something known as the Order of the Dragon, a group established to protect Christian Europe from the invading Ottoman Empire. Vlad's father, Vlad II, was known as Vlad Dracul, or "Vlad the Dragon." When Vlad III rose to power, he took the hereditary title and was known as Vlad Draculea, "son of the dragon."

That name might sound very similar to the most famous vampire story in the world, and that's because Bram Stoker, when creating his famous creature of the night, used Vlad III as his inspiration. Well, part of it, but we'll get into that more later.

The roots of most vampire stories, however, can be traced back to superstitions founded in ancient cultures all across the world. Western Europe played host to countless stories of reanimated dead known as revenants. These were animated corpses that climbed out of the grave to torment the living. The word "revenant" comes from the Latin that means "to come back."

Come back to do what? you might ask. Well, I'm glad you did. At first, it was just to terrorize the living, but as the centuries passed, the legend became more specific. Revenants were said to return from the grave to torment their living relatives and neighbors. What was key, though, was that revenants were specific people, not anonymous zombies like the ones from our modern horror genre. These things had a past and a purpose.

In Norse mythology we can find tales of creatures known as *draugr,* "again-walkers," who would return from the grave and wreak havoc on the living. These creatures possessed superhuman strength, smelled of decay, and were pretty ugly in appearance. They could enter the dreams of the living, and they were said to leave a tangible object near the sleeping person so that, upon waking, their victims would know their dreams were more real than they feared.

Let's go back earlier than the Middle Ages, though. The legends of some ancient cultures spoke of creatures that, while not immediately similar to the vampires we know today, nonetheless shared many core characteristics.

First, we have the Greek myth of Empusa, who was a daughter of Hecate. Empusa was said to lure young men at night and then feast on their blood before moving on to the main course—their flesh. Another Greek tale involves Lamia, a mistress of Zeus who becomes cursed by Zeus's wife, Hera, and doomed to hunt children, devouring them.

Stories of undead creatures, or creatures that feed on the blood of the living, seem nearly as common as written language itself. On Madagascar, an island nation off the east coast of Africa, there are legends of a creature known as the *ramanga,* which was known to attack nobles, drinking their blood and eating their nail clippings.

Yeah, their *nail clippings.* Deal with it.

VAMPIRES IN MEDICAL SCIENCE

Are vampires real? I'll let you make the final decision on that, but what *is* clear is that most of these stories find their genesis in the human need to explain the unexplainable. For instance, early Europeans used the myth as a way of explaining why a corpse wasn't decomposing at the normal, expected rate. You can see evidence of this in Bulgaria, where graves dating back more than eight hundred years have been opened, revealing iron rods through the chest of skeletons.

And in a time when it was not unheard of to bury someone who was thought to be dead, only to find out that they really weren't, you can imagine that stories would quickly circulate that the dead were coming back to life. As a result, taphophobia, the fear of being buried alive, swept Europe and the United States. Of course, once medical science caught up, people got more practical by building alert systems into graves, just in case the person woke up and wanted out.

I realize that being buried alive sounds like a rare occurrence, but it happened frequently enough that many people were sufficiently paranoid about it to actually spend time looking for a solution. One of those people happened to be a medical doctor, a man named Adolf Gutsmuth. In 1822, and driven by the fear of being buried alive, he invented a "safety coffin" for his own interment. And he tested it out himself.

Tested it out? You bet. Dr. Gutsmuth allowed himself to be buried underground in his new "safety coffin" for several hours, during which he had meals delivered to him through a feeding tube. He enjoyed a wonderful meal of soup, sausages, and a local beer.

Sounds like a great date-night destination.

Dr. Timothy Smith of New Haven, Vermont, was another paranoid inventor. He created a grave that can be visited to this day if you happen to be passing by Evergreen Cemetery. It was a crypt buried in the usual manner, but it had a cement tube positioned over the face of the body. A glass plate was affixed to the top of the tube, at ground level.

Dr. Smith died a real, natural death, and was buried in his fancy "coffin with a view." He never woke up, but early visitors to his grave reported that they had a clear view of his decomposing head until condensation obscured the glass.

Side note: Vampires no longer scare me. Waking up inside a small box buried six feet below the surface of the earth is what true fright looks like to me.

Another culprit in humanity's use of the vampire label was porphyria, a rare blood disorder, but modern science has pretty much closed the case on that one, saying that it's too far of a stretch to connect the two topics. Rabies, of all conditions, has also been used as an explanation for the rise of vampire mythology. Surprisingly, there are a lot of commonalities between victims of rabies and vampires, such as sensitivity to light and garlic, as well as altered sleep patterns.

The most recent medical condition with a strong connection to vampire mythology was actually tuberculosis. Those who suffer from TB had no vampire-like symptoms, though, and that makes this connection harder to explain. It's also, incidentally, where one of my favorite New England legends comes into the picture.

Ladies and gentlemen, meet Mercy Brown.

Lena Mercy Brown was a young woman who lived in the latter half of the nineteenth century in the rural town of Exeter, Rhode Island, and she was a major player in what is now known as the Great New England Vampire Panic.

Stories like hers can be found all across Rhode Island, Massachusetts, New Hampshire, and Vermont, echoed in the lives of others in similar situations. And the results have surprising connections to both the modern idea of vampires and the ancient stories, as we will see.

The first person to die was Mercy's mother, Mary Eliza. That was December 1882, and she fell victim to what was then known as "consumption," so called because as the TB ravaged the body, the person would appear to waste away—consumed, if you will, by the illness. She, of course, was buried, because that's what you do with a loved one who passes away.

The next year, though, Mercy's sister Mary Olive died at the age of twenty. Same illness, same symptoms. I'm not sure when the people of Exeter, Rhode Island, started to wonder if the deaths were connected, but it might have been then, or it might have been a few years later when Mercy's brother, Edwin, took ill.

Edwin, though, was smart. He packed up and moved across the country to Colorado Springs, which had a great reputation for the healing properties of its dry climate. When he returned from the West some years later, he was alive but not doing well. And in December 1891, he took a turn for the worse.

That was also the month that Mercy herself became ill. Her tuberculosis moved fast, though. They called it the "galloping" kind, and it moved through her body quickly. By January 1892 she was dead, and the people of Exeter were more worried than ever. You see, they suspected something supernatural.

Now, this was surprising, considering how close Exeter is to Newport. That's the seaside city known for the "summer cottages" of the wealthy—folks like the Vanderbilts, the Astors, the Wideners, and the Wetmores. It was the pinnacle of educated society. Yet just a handful of miles away, one small town that should have known better was about to do something very, very creepy.

Edwin was still alive, you see. And someone got it in their mind that one of the women who died before him, either his mother or one of his sisters, was somehow draining him of his life from beyond the grave. They were so convinced of this, you see, that they wanted to dig them all up.

Yes. All of them.

Once they received the father's permission to do this horrible thing, a group of men gathered in the cemetery on the morning of March 17 and began to dig up the bodies.

What they were looking for was any evidence of an unnatural state. Blood in the heart, blood around the mouth, or other similar signs. The first body, that of Mary Eliza, the mother, was satisfactorily decomposed, though, so they ruled her out. Of course she was, you might say; she had been dead and buried for a decade.

Mary Olive was also in a normal state of decomposition. Again, being dead ten years usually helps convince people you're really dead. But when they examined Mercy's body—a body that had not been buried because she died in the middle of winter, but instead had been stored in a stone building that was essentially a walk-in freezer—they discovered a remarkable state of preservation.

Shocking, I know.

So what did they do? Well, these superstitious townsfolk did what they learned from their ancestors: they cut out Mercy's heart and liver (within which they found red, clotted blood), burned them on a nearby stone (which is still there, by the way, near her headstone in the cemetery), and then mixed the ashes with a tonic. That tonic was then given to Edwin to drink.

Yes, Edwin Brown drank his own sister's liver and heart.

Did it work? Nope. Edwin died less than two months later. What it did do, however, was set up Mercy Brown to be the "first American vampire." I suppose it's not important to mention that she wasn't really a vampire, because you are an intelligent person, but it doesn't hurt to say it.

As unusual as an event like this must sound, you might be surprised to learn that it happened quite frequently. In 1817, nearly a century before Mercy Brown's exhumation, a Dartmouth College student named Frederick Ransom died of TB. His father, so worried that the young man would leave the grave and attack the family, had him dug up. Ransom's heart was cut out and burned on a blacksmith's forge.

Even Henry David Thoreau heard tales of these types of events, mentioning one in his personal journal. He wrote on September 26, 1859:

The savage in man is never quite eradicated. I have just read of a family in Vermont who, several of its members having died of consumption, just burned the lungs, heart, and liver of the last deceased, in order to prevent any more from having it.

So, of course, word spread about what happened to Mercy Brown, as it usually did when a body was dug up and carved into pieces like that. Mercy's case actually made it into a newspaper called the *New York World,* and it made quite an impression on the people who read it.

How do we know? Because a clipping of that article was found in the personal papers of a London stage manager after his death.

You see, his theater company had been touring America in 1892. He evidently found the story inspiring, so much so that he sat down a few years later and wrote a book.

The man? Bram Stoker. The book? Oh, I'm sure you guessed that already. It was *Dracula,* published in 1897.

Deep and Twisted Roots

IN THE EARLY 1990s, two boys were playing on a gravel hill near an abandoned old mine outside of Griswold, Connecticut. Kids do the oddest things to stave off boredom, so playing on a hill covered in small rocks doesn't really surprise me. And my guess is that they were having a blast.

That is, until one of them dislodged two larger rocks. But when the rocks tumbled free and rolled down the hill, both boys noticed something odd about them. They were nearly identical in shape, and that shape was eerily familiar. They headed down the hill one last time to take a closer look, and that's when they realized what they'd found: skulls.

At first, the local police were brought in to investigate the possibility of an unknown serial killer. That many bodies all in one place was never a good sign. But it became obvious very quickly that the real experts they needed were, in fact, archaeologists.

They were right. In the end, twenty-nine graves were discovered in what turned out to be the remnants of a forgotten cemetery. Time and the elements had slowly eroded away the graveyard, and the contents had been swallowed by the gravel. Many skeletons were still in their caskets, though, and it was inside one of them—marked with brass tacks to form the initials of the occupant—that something odd was discovered.

Long ago, it seems, someone had opened this casket shortly

after burial and had then made changes to the body. Specifically, they'd removed both femurs, the bones of the thigh, and placed them crossed on the chest. Then, moving some of the ribs and the breastbone out of the way, they placed the skull above them. It was a real-life skull-and-crossbones, and its presence hinted at something darker.

The skeleton, you see, wasn't just the remains of an ordinary early settler of the area. This man was different, and the people who buried him knew it. According to them, he was a vampire.

That Which Was Buried

While it might be a surprise to some people, graves like the one in Griswold are actually quite common. Today we live in the Bram Stoker era of vampires, so our expectations and imagery are highly influenced by his novel and the world it evokes. Victorian gentlemen in dark cloaks. Mysterious castles. Sharp fangs protruding over blood-red lips.

But the white face with red lips started life as nothing more than stage makeup, an artifact from a 1924 theatrical production of the novel, called *Count Dracula*. Another feature we associate with Dracula, the high collar, also started there. With wires attached to the points of the collar, the actor playing Dracula could turn his back on the audience and drop through a trap door, leaving an empty cape behind to fall to the floor moments later.

The true myth of the vampire, though, is far older than Stoker. It's an ancient tree with deep and twisted roots. As hard as it is for popular culture to fathom, the legend of the vampire—and of the people who hunt it—actually predates Dracula by centuries.

Just a little further into the past from Bram Stoker, in the cradle of what would one day become the United States, the people of New England were identifying vampire activity in their towns and villages, and then assembling teams of people to deal with what they perceived as a threat.

It turns out that Griswold was one of those communities. According to the archaeologists who studied the twenty-nine graves, a vast majority of them were contemporary to the vampire's burial, and most of those showed signs of an illness. Tuberculosis is the most likely guess. Which goes a long way toward explaining why the people did what they did.

The folklore was clear: the first to die from an illness was usually the cause of the outbreak that followed. Patient Zero might be in the grave, sure, but they were still at work, slowly draining the lives of the others. Because of this belief, bodies all across the Northeast were routinely exhumed and destroyed in one way or another. In many ways, it was as if old superstitions were clawing their way out of the depths of the past to haunt the living.

The details of another case, from Stafford, Connecticut, in the late 1870s, illustrate the ritual perfectly. After a family there lost five of their six daughters to illness, the first to have passed away was dug up and examined. This is what was recorded about the event:

> *Exhumation has revealed a heart and lungs, still fresh and living, encased in rotten and slimy integuments, and in which, after burning these portions of the defunct, a living relative, else doomed and hastening to the grave, has suddenly and miraculously recovered.*

This sort of macabre community event happened frequently in Connecticut, Vermont, New York, New Hampshire, Ontario, and—of course—Rhode Island, where the family of Mercy Brown exhumed her body after others died.

Mercy Brown wasn't really the first American vampire, though. As far as we can tell, that honor goes to the wife of Isaac Burton of Manchester, Vermont, all the way back in 1793. And for as chilling and dark as the exhumation of Mercy Brown might have been, the Burton incident puts that story to shame.

Captain Isaac Burton married Rachel Harris in 1789, but their marriage was brief. Within months of the wedding, Rachel took sick with tuberculosis and soon died, leaving her husband a young widower. Burton married again in April 1791, this time to a woman named Hulda Powell. But again, within just two years of their marriage, Burton's new bride also became ill. Friends and neighbors started to whisper, and as people are prone to do, they began to try and draw conclusions. Unanswered questions bother us, so we tend to look for reasons. And the people of Manchester thought they knew why Hulda was sick.

Although Isaac's first wife, Rachel, had been dead for nearly three years, the people of Manchester suggested that she was the cause. Clearly, from her new home in the graveyard, she was draining the life from her husband's new bride. With Burton's permission, the town prepared to exhume her and end the curse.

The town blacksmith brought a portable forge to the gravesite, and nearly a thousand people gathered there to watch the grim ceremony unfold. Rachel's heart, liver, and lungs were all removed from her corpse and then reduced to ashes. Sadly, though, Hulda Burton never recovered, and she died a few months later.

This ancient ritual, at least as far as the people of Manchester, Vermont, were concerned, had somehow failed them. They did what they had been taught to do, as unpleasant as it must have been, and yet it hadn't worked.

Which was odd, because that hadn't always been the case.

IF THE SHOE FITS

As we've seen, a lot of what we think we know about the vampire legend is thanks to Bram Stoker's *Dracula,* which is set in Romania. But Stoker never traveled there, and the castle that he describes as the home of Dracula was based on an illustration of Bran Castle he found in a book. The image of this Romanian castle may have captured the mood he was aiming for, but as far as historians can tell, the castle has no connection to the historical Vlad III, or Vlad Draculea.

The notion of a vampire, or at least of an undead creature that feeds on the living, *does* have roots in the area, though. Stoker was close, but he missed the mark by a little more than three hundred miles. The real roots of the legend, according to most historians, can be found in modern-day Serbia.

The Serbia of today sits at the southwestern corner of Romania, just south of Hungary. Between 1718 and 1739, the country passed briefly from the hands of the Ottoman Empire to the control of the Austrians. Because of its place between these two empires, the land was devastated by war and destruction, and people were frequently moved around in service to the military. And, as is often the case, when people cross borders, so do ideas.

Petar Blagojevich was a Serbian peasant in the village of Kisilova in the early 1700s. Not much is known about his life, but we do know that he was married and had at least one son. And Petar died in 1725, at the age of sixty-two, of unknown causes. In most stories, that's the end. But not here. You probably knew that, though, didn't you?

In the eight days that followed Petar's death, other people in the village began to pass away. Nine of them, in fact. And all of them made startling claims on their deathbeds—details that seemed impossible to prove but were somehow the same in each case. Each person was adamant that Petar Blagojevich, their recently deceased neighbor, had come to them in the night and attacked them.

Petar's widow even made the startling claim that her dead husband had actually walked into her home and asked for, of all things, his shoes. She believed so strongly in this visit that she moved to another village to avoid future visits. And the rest of the people of Kisilova took notice. They needed to take action, and that would begin with digging up Petar's corpse.

Inside the coffin, they found Petar's body to be remarkably well preserved. Some noticed how the man's nails and hair had grown. Others remarked at the condition of his skin, which was flush and bright, not pale. It wasn't natural, they said, and something had to be done.

They turned to a man named Frombald, a local representative of the Austrian government, and with the help of a priest he examined the body for himself. In his written report, he confirmed the earlier findings and added his observation that fresh blood could be seen inside Petar's mouth.

Frombald described how the people of the village were overcome with fear and outrage, and how they proceeded to drive a wooden stake through the corpse's heart. Then, still afraid of what the creature might be able to do to them in the future, the people burned the body. Frombald's report details all of it, but he also makes the disclaimer that he wasn't responsible for the villagers' actions. Fear, he said, drove them to it, nothing more.

Petar's story was powerful, and it created a panic that quickly spread throughout the region. It was the first event of its kind in history to be recorded in official government documents, but there was still no explanation for what had been observed.

Just a year later, though, something happened, and the legend has never been the same.

CARGO IN THE BLOOD

Arnold Paole was a former soldier, one of the many men transplanted by the Austrian government in an effort to defend and police their newly acquired territory. No one is sure where he was born, but his final years were spent in a Serbian village along the Great Morava River, near Paracin.

In his postwar life, Arnold had become a farmer, and he frequently told stories from days gone by. In one such story, Arnold claimed that he had been attacked by a vampire years before, while living in Kosovo. He survived, but the injury continued to plague him until he finally took action. He said that he cured himself by eating soil from the grave of the suspected vampire. And then, after digging up the vampire's body, he collected some of its blood and smeared it on himself.

And that was it. According to Arnold, and the folklore that drove him to do it, he was cured. After he died in a farming accident in 1726, though, people began to wonder, because within a month of his death, at least four other people in town complained that Arnold had visited them in the night and attacked them.

When those four people died, the villagers began to whisper in fear. They remembered Arnold's stories of being attacked by a vampire, of taking on the disease himself, of his own attempt to cure himself. But what if that hadn't worked? Out of suspicion and doubt, they decided to exhume his body and examine it.

Here, for what was most likely the first time in recorded history, the story of the vampire was taking on the form of a communicable disease, transmitted from person to person through biting. This might seem obvious to us now, but we've all grown up with the legend fully formed. To the people of this small Serbian village, though, this was something new, and horrific.

What they found seemed like conclusive evidence, too: fresh skin, new nails, longer hair and beard. Arnold even had blood in his mouth. Putting ourselves in their context, it's easy to see how they might have been chilled with fear. So they drove a stake through his heart.

One witness claimed that as the stake pierced the corpse's chest, the body groaned and bled. Unsure what else to do, they burned the body. And then they did the same to the bodies of the four who had died after claiming Arnold had attacked them. They covered all their bases, so to speak, and then walked away.

Five years later, however, another outbreak spread through the village. We know this because so many people died that the Austrian government sent a team of military physicians from Belgrade to investigate the situation. These men, led by two officials named Glaser and Flückinger, were special: they were trained in communicable diseases.

Which was a good thing. By January 7, 1731—just eight weeks after the beginning of the outbreak—seventeen people had died. At first, Glaser and Flückinger looked for signs of a contagious disease, but they came up empty-handed. They noted signs of mild malnutrition, but nothing deadly could be found.

The clock was ticking, though. The villagers were living in such fear that they had been gathering together in large groups each night, taking turns keeping watch for the creatures they believed were responsible. They even threatened to pack up and move elsewhere. Something needed to be done, and quickly.

Thankfully, there were suspects. The first was a young woman named Stana, a recent newcomer to the village, who had died during childbirth early in the outbreak. It seemed to have been a sickness that took her life, but there were other clues. Stana had confessed to smearing vampire blood on herself years before, as protection. But that, the villagers claimed now, had backfired, most likely turning her into one instead.

The other suspect was an older woman named Milica. She too was from another part of Serbia and had arrived shortly after Arnold Paole's death. Like so many others, she had a history. Neighbors claimed she was a good woman who had never done anything intentionally wicked. But she had told them once of how she'd eaten meat from a sheep killed by a vampire.

And that seemed like enough evidence to push the investigators to go deeper—literally. With permission from Belgrade, Glaser and the villagers exhumed all of the recently deceased, opening their coffins for a full examination. And while logic and science should have prevailed in a situation like that, what they found only deepened their belief in the supernatural.

Of the seventeen bodies, only five appeared normal, in that they had begun to decay in the expected manner. These five were reburied and considered safe. But it was the other twelve that alarmed the villagers and government men alike, because these bodies were still fresh.

In the report filed in Belgrade on January 26, 1732, signed by all five of the government physicians who witnessed the exhumations, the witnesses claimed that these twelve bodies were completely untouched by decay. Their organs still held what seemed to be fresh blood, their skin appeared healthy and firm, and their nails and hair apparently had grown since burial.

We understand decomposition much better today and recognize that these are not uncommon findings, but three centuries ago it was less about science and more about superstition. This didn't seem normal to them. And so when the physicians wrote their report, they used a term that, until that very moment, had never before appeared in any historical account of such a case: they described finding the twelve bodies in a "vampiric" condition. In the face of so many unanswered questions, this was the only conclusion they could commit to.

With that, the villagers did what their tradition demanded:

they removed the heads from each corpse, gathered all of the remains into a pile, and then burned the whole thing. The threat to their village was finally dead and gone.

But something new had been born. Something more powerful than a monster, something that lives centuries and spreads like fire.

A legend.

THE IMMORTAL ONE

Many aspects of folklore haven't fared too well under the critical eye of science. Today we have a much deeper understanding of how disease really works and what happens to the body after people die. And while experts are still careful to explain that every corpse decomposes in a slightly different way, we have a better grasp of the entire process now than at any previous time in history.

Answers, when we find them, can be a relief. It's safe to say that today we don't have to fear a vampiric infection when the people around us get sick. But still, at the center of these old stories were people, normal folk like you and me, who simply wanted to do what was right. We might handle things differently today, but it's hard to fault them for trying.

Answers don't kill every myth, though. Vampire stories, like their immortal subjects, have simply refused to die. In fact, they can still be found if you know where to look for them.

In the small Romanian village of Marotinu de Sus, near the southwestern corner that borders Bulgaria and Serbia, authorities were called in to investigate an illegal exhumation. But this wasn't in 1704, or even 1804. No, this happened just a decade ago.

Petre Toma had been the clan leader there in the village, but after a lifetime of illness and hard drinking, his accidental death in the field came almost as a relief to his family and friends. That's how they put it, at least. So when he was buried in December 2003, the community moved on.

But then individuals from Petre's family began to get sick. First it was his niece, Mirela Marinescu. She complained that her uncle had attacked her in her dreams. Her husband made the same claim, and both offered their illness as proof. Even their infant child was not well. Luckily, the elders of the village immediately knew why.

In response, six men gathered together one evening in early 2004. They entered the local graveyard close to midnight and made their way to the burial site of Petre Toma. Using hammers and chisels, they broke through the stone slab that covered the grave and then moved the pieces aside.

They drank as they worked. Can you blame them? They were opening the grave of a recently deceased member of their community, but I think it was more than that. In their minds, they were putting their lives in danger. Because there, inside the grave they had just uncovered, lay the stuff of nightmares: a vampire.

What these men did next will sound strangely familiar, but to them it was simply the continuation of centuries of tradition. They cut open the body using a knife and a saw. They pried the ribs apart with a pitchfork and then cut out the heart.

According to one of the men who were there, when the heart was removed, they found it full of fresh blood—proof, to them at least, that Petre had been feeding on the village. When they pulled it free, the witnesses said that the body audibly sighed and then went limp. It's hard to prove something that six incredibly superstitious men—men who had been drinking all night, mind you—claimed they witnessed in a dark cemetery. But to them it was pure, unadulterated truth.

They then used the pitchfork to carry the heart out of the cemetery and across the road to a field, where they set it on fire. Once it was burned completely, they collected the ashes and funneled them into a bottle of water. They offered this tonic to the sick family, who willingly drank it. It was, after all, what they had been taught to do.

Amazingly, everyone recovered. No one died of whatever illness they were suffering from, and no one reported visits from Petre Toma after that. In their mind, the nightmare was over. These men had saved their lives.

Maybe something evil and contagious *has* survived for centuries, spreading across borders and oceans. It's certainly left a trail of horrific events in its wake, and it's influenced countless tales and superstitions, all of which seem to point to a real-life cause. Far from being unique to Serbia or Romania, this thing is *global*.

And as if that weren't enough, this horrible, ageless monster is—and always has been—right inside each of us. Like a vampiric curse, we carry it in our blood. But it's probably not what you'd expect.

It's *fear*.

Dark Conclusions

T HE VAMPIRE FOLKLORE of our ancestors is as varied and textured as the countless modern versions that Hollywood presents us with each year. Most, however, still focus on some aspect of Bram Stoker's famous novel. It's fair to say that our love for the story of Dracula is just as undying as the monster himself.

One of the results of this obsession is that we often ignore or forget the other major players in the Dracula story. For example, Mina Murray is the powerful, heroic woman who spends the bulk of the story fighting to destroy Dracula, rather than wallowing in self-pity. Quincey Morris sacrifices himself to defeat the monster. And Jonathan Harker, Mina's eventual husband, strikes one of the killing blows. The novel is full of characters, but all seem to fade into the shadow cast by the vampire lord himself.

All except for Abraham Van Helsing, that is. Over the decades, his character has received a good amount of attention from fans of the book, and honestly, how can you blame them? He was intelligent, brave, and skilled in his craft. And in a lot of ways, Van Helsing represented something we all aspired to be.

It's a side effect of growing up with stories of creatures who want to hurt us. If there really is something living under the bed, or in the closet, or in that dark, damp corner of the basement, then shouldn't someone care enough to protect us? If these creatures are the antagonists of our nightmares, then surely there are also protagonists. The heroes. The champions. Those brave souls who are tasked with fighting back.

Van Helsing was a fictional construct, of course, but his character echoes an ancient, widespread belief that can be found, in some form or another, within many folktales. No matter what the monsters might be, there are always those who fight them.

Amazingly, those hunters still walk among us.

BORN TO HUNT

Some of the earliest folktales involving hunters of the supernatural can be found in Bulgaria and nearby countries. After five centuries of occupation by the Ottoman Empire, the Bulgarians finally pushed out the Turks in the 1890s. During those first few years of freedom, the country's rich folklore and traditions were gathered up and recorded for the first time, and right at the center of these records were stories of the vampire.

These tales have such power that people today still believe them and follow their prescriptions, such as the ritual exhumation of suspected vampires. It's a belief that runs deep, mostly because of intense fear and superstition. To many, though, vampires were real, and they needed to be hunted down.

As a result, there were people in these Bulgarian villages called *såbotnik,* who could detect vampires. They were called upon when a community suspected a vampire was hunting and harming them. Once the grave of a suspect was dug up and the body exposed, the *såbotnik* would determine whether or not the corpse was really a vampire. If it was, the *såbotnik* was also responsible for destroying it.

This was a power each *såbotnik* acquired at birth, according to the stories. You just had to be lucky enough to be born either on one of the days between Christmas and January 6—a time known to ancient Catholics as the Unclean Days—or on a Saturday, which sounds pretty random to me, but hey, whatever.

Another group of vampire hunters was known as the *vampirdžia.* These were more akin to the modern movie version of Van Helsing that we know today. Destined to hunt vampires from birth, they traveled the land armed with weapons and tools, looking for battle. And they did all of this while following prescribed methods, like hunting vampires on Saturdays and leading the vampires into graveyards, where they were somehow weaker.

And these *vampirdžia* were heroes, often earning a good living from the gifts and donations of fearful villagers. There are even records of a provincial capital, Veliko Târnovo, actually employing a number of them and sending them out to investigate and hunt when reports of vampires popped up. Honestly, you could film this stuff and pass it off as an *Underworld* sequel. But it really happened, and to me, that's what makes it so much more compelling.

The idea of hunting individuals who threatened society wasn't isolated to Bulgaria, though, or even limited to the concept of the vampire. Contemporary to these *vampirdžia* tales were stories that highlighted another dangerous creature, one that walked right among us: the witch. And yes, we all already know that there was hysteria and persecution. Yes, there were hangings and burnings and other superstition-fueled acts of violence. But at the center of much of it, there were hunters.

In 1486, a German Dominican friar named Heinrich Kramer wrote a book that he called the *Malleus Maleficarum*, "the hammer of the witches." Kramer was more than a friar, though; he'd served for years as an inquisitor with orders from Pope Innocent VIII. After his retirement, he wrote what he believed to be the gold standard for understanding and identifying witches.

The Catholic Church condemned the book just three years after it was published, but it was too late. The *Malleus Maleficarum* acted like an accelerant, thanks in part to Gutenberg's printing press, and spread across Europe, where it fueled the flames of religious hysteria and social unrest. The book was used for centuries to teach others about witches—where they came from, how to detect them, and what to do when you found one.

And this was the world that Matthew Hopkins was born into in England in 1620. The son of a Puritan minister, he was raised to fear the Devil and lash out at what he saw as heresy. By the age of just twenty-four, Hopkins had set up shop in Sussex under the title of Witchfinder General, and began a short but devastating career in the discovery and conviction of witches.

In the 350 years that spanned the early 1400s to the late 1700s, it's estimated that less than five hundred people in total were executed for witchcraft in all of England. That's less than two executions per year, right? During their short two-year operation, though, Hopkins and his team were responsible for three hundred of those deaths.

This is the man who invented the "swimming" test for witchcraft, which most people have heard about. The accused would be tied to a chair and tossed into a pond or lake, and then Hopkins would wait to see if the person floated. If so, that person was a witch and would be killed. If the accused sank . . . well . . . they still died, but with a clear name. It doesn't make sense to us, I know, but in the 1640s, Hopkins could do no wrong. Everyone trusted him. His book, *The Discovery of Witches,* went on to fuel witch trials in the American colonies in the late 1600s, and some of his interrogation methods were even used in the Salem, Massachusetts, trials. Don't get me wrong, the man was a monster. But he clearly left his mark as a witch hunter.

One last thing: according to the Bulgarian folklore surrounding vampire hunters, there was one big risk for those in the profession. Anyone who served as a *sàbotnik* or *vampirdžia* was most at risk of becoming a vampire themselves. Even in England, Hopkins didn't die a hero. Instead, he was viewed as a monster and bogeyman. Rather than going down in history as some sort of heroic hunter, he acquired a reputation of having been evil himself.

Because sometimes, whether the creature is a thing of our own invention or simply the focus of a personal obsession, the hunter is always at risk of becoming the very thing they pursue.

Jumping at Shadows

In 1968, Paramount released *Rosemary's Baby,* based on the hit novel from a year before. And 1973 saw the release of the original

Exorcist, followed by *The Omen* three years later. There was a satanic craze sweeping through America—a mixture of fear and fascination—and Hollywood wanted to capitalize on it. But it's often overlooked that this craze was preceded by an earlier wave of fear across the Atlantic, in England, that began when Londoners began to notice graffiti and vandalism inside the historic Highgate Cemetery.

Highgate is an old cemetery, established in 1839. While it was initially one of the city's most fashionable burial places, with elaborate funerary architecture, over the years it became less popular. In World War II, German bombs damaged some of the vaults, and during the following decades it fell into disrepair, with trees and brush beginning to overtake the property. Youth and vandals began to spend more time inside the cemetery, and reports circulated of occult symbols, open graves, and bodies that had been moved for unknown reasons.

In 1969, a group calling itself the British Occult Society sought to investigate the unusual phenomena taking place in the cemetery, and they also listened to those in the neighborhood who had stories of their own to share. Which is where they first encountered the rumors of something—maybe a person, or maybe something else—that prowled the graveyard at night. The stories described it as a tall, dark figure that could paralyze those who encountered it.

A man named David Farrant was intrigued, and so on December 21, 1969, he camped out in the cemetery overnight. It was the winter solstice and he was a paranormal investigator, so it all sort of lined up, at least in his mind. And according to him, the night was a huge success. The way he described it, at some point during the hours between dusk and dawn, Farrant encountered a creature that stood over seven feet tall, with eyes that glowed brightly. But when Farrant looked away for a moment, it vanished. He wrote to the local paper and asked if others had seen the same figure. Amazingly, for about two months, letters flooded in from others who described similar experiences.

About the same time, though, another man who was interested in the same goings-on in the cemetery, Seán Manchester, made further discoveries—bloody ones. Manchester believed the stories of the mysterious, dark figure, but he also found numerous animals in the cemetery that had been drained of blood. Upon inspection, he reported that each of them had small holes in its neck. When the local papers asked him if he had a theory, he told them he did. The figure, according to Manchester, was clearly a vampire.

And not just any vampire. This was what he called a "King Vampire," brought over from Wallachia in the 1700s by a curious noble, and then buried on the estate that eventually became Highgate Cemetery. All of the satanic activity, according to him, was the work of local occultists trying to resurrect this creature.

So Manchester offered to hunt it down and exorcise it. He acknowledged that the law made it a bit . . . ah . . . *difficult* to go around plunging wooden stakes into corpses, but he'd already done it twice before. According to him, he was willing to put his life on the line to track down and destroy the King Vampire.

Few people bought it. They did believe that something was going on inside the cemetery, though, so the police began to patrol the area, watching for anything out of the ordinary. Over the next few months they chased a number of vandals out of the graveyard, but none of them turned out to be anything more than teenagers pretending to be vampire hunters, just out looking for a thrill.

And then, on August 1, 1970, something happened that changed all of that. That night police were called to Highgate Cemetery and directed to one particular crypt that was deep inside the property. When they arrived, they found the tomb door standing wide open, and inside, stretched out on the cold stone floor, was a body. Not particularly odd, given the location, but it was the condition of the body that alarmed them.

It had been charred beyond recognition, and then decapitated.

DARK FORCES COLLIDE

The police went public with the discovery and admitted that this, of all the things they'd found in Highgate so far, could actually be the work of occultists. And that was all the public needed. The papers were filled with headlines. People couldn't help but jump to conclusions. And both Seán Manchester and David Farrant were right there in the middle of it, examining the clues and trying to make sense of it all.

They weren't on the same side—each man had his own methods of investigation, some of which were a bit unorthodox. Two weeks after the burned body was discovered, Farrant was discovered by police to be wandering the cemetery at night. When they arrested him for trespassing, he was found to be carrying a large crucifix and a sharp wooden stake.

His group didn't stop, though. They began to camp overnight in the graveyard on a regular basis, finding more peculiar clues, all of which pointed—to them, at least—to the work of a group bent on resurrecting the King Vampire.

One night Farrant took a reporter from the *Evening News* into Highgate with him, and together they discovered a crypt with an eerie scene. The body had been removed from the coffin inside the crypt and placed in the center of a large pentagram that had been drawn on the stone floor. Farrant and his group also claimed to find bodies with voodoo dolls placed next to them, bodies with missing heads, skulls placed in odd locations, and symbols that hinted at rituals from previous nights. All of it, they said, pointed to a dark evil that needed to be stopped. Their efforts, as risky as they seemed, were aimed at doing just that.

Months later, Farrant was arrested a second time, along with his girlfriend. The police apparently thought the couple was transporting marijuana, but it turned out to be a plastic bag of chamomile, of all things. They claimed it was an ingredient in one of their rituals. According to them, they had found a crypt that showed signs of a recent black magic ceremony, and so their group had gone there to cleanse it. Once they had all gathered inside the open tomb, they stood in a circle around the perimeter of the room, reading passages from the Bible along with spells they claimed had been lifted from ancient books of magic. Some of the women in the group even stripped to dance naked in the center of the room. They were symbols of purity, according to Farrant.

Manchester publicly disapproved. He preferred to conduct his exorcisms in broad daylight, which allowed him to be safer, and—as some critics pointed out—also made it more likely that there would be an audience around to watch him. But that didn't mean his rituals were any less entertaining. At one point, Manchester claimed that he was led to a tomb by a young woman possessed by a demonic spirit named Lusia. Inside the tomb, he claimed, was an ancient coffin with no nameplate. He had opened the coffin and was about to plunge a wooden stake into the corpse when another member of his group stopped him. Instead, Manchester simply sprinkled the body with holy water and cloves of garlic. According to witnesses, as he did this, loud rhythmic booms could he heard, growing louder the deeper into the ritual they went.

Events in Highgate seemed to end shortly after January 1974. On the twelfth of that month, local police were called to inspect the car of a local resident, parked near the cemetery. Inside, they found an embalmed corpse seated at the wheel, its head removed and nowhere to be found.

Farrant was interviewed as a suspect, but in the end it turned out to be a prank put on by a group of local teenagers. One of them had actually taken the head home and kept it on his mantel—until it began to smell, that is.

Manchester found a way to make a career out of his adventures in Highgate, and over the past few decades has become known as a "vampire expert," appearing in many television documentaries on the subject. He's written two books: one about the Highgate Vampire, and a handbook for would-be hunters.

David Farrant experienced less success in the wake of the events. He was arrested in 1974 for vandalizing property within the cemetery. He denied any involvement, of course, but the police were hungry for a real suspect after nearly five years of activity. He was sentenced to four years in prison, but was paroled after just two years when it was determined that his rights had been violated. He went back to heading up the British Occult Society, where he still works today.

Newspapers at the time featured photos of Farrant with his

vampire-hunting tools. He was referred to as the "Graveyard Ghoul" by one local paper, and another called him a "wicked witch." In a book written in 1991, Manchester refers to him as "a wayward witch who dabbled in the black arts."

In the eyes of some, at least, David Farrant seemed to suffer a fate similar to Matthew Hopkins's. Rather than succeeding, it seems, the young man became the thing he hunted.

THE PURSUIT

Halloween is one of my favorite times of the year, and I bet you feel the same. It's one of the few moments when we stop and acknowledge the shadows—the mystery and the unknown. Because life without mystery is stale and flat, and days like today help to add texture to our lives.

Each year, millions of children dress up and walk through their neighborhoods. They each have a favorite creature, something they want to become for the one night of the year when it's expected and normal. And they'll do all of this like hunters on a mission.

Interestingly, the teens who live near Highgate still creep into the graveyard every year. Each Halloween, they find a way inside, gather together, and go on their own vampire hunts. And that's no easy task these days. The cemetery has been cleaned up, its gates have been locked, and it's opened to the public only for paid, guided tours. Still, the youth of the area manage to celebrate Halloween there each and every year.

Twenty years before the events in Highgate Cemetery, though, there was another gathering of youth farther north. Glasgow, the second-largest city in Scotland, straddles the river Clyde. South of the river, just north of the M74 motorway, is a neighborhood known as Gorbals. It's an area of the city that has a rough history. The industrialization and overpopulation of the late 1800s led to the construction of tenement slums throughout the first half of the twentieth century. It's gone through some attempted redevelopment, but in the 1950s it was probably at its lowest point.

One night in September 1954, a police constable named Alex Deeprose was called to investigate a disturbance at the Southern Necropolis, a burial ground as old as Highgate and just as creepy in its own way. When the officer got to the cemetery, he found that some of the neighborhood children had gathered there. Hundreds of children, in fact, ranging in ages from four to fourteen. And they were armed. Deeprose managed to gather them all together and lead them out of the graveyard, but the following night they were back. Each of the children carried something dangerous—knives, sticks, metal bars. Some even brought dogs along. And Deeprose wanted to know why.

Some of the children told him that two local boys had been killed, and they had come to the graveyard for revenge. The constable didn't know of any murders in the area, but then again, there was a lot that went on in Gorbals that went unreported. But he was concerned about the gatherings, so he spoke with some of the parents. Some were worried about the safety of their children; others were troubled by the stories and what it said about their children's fascination with violence and danger.

Yet hundreds more children arrived at the cemetery the very next night. Constable Deeprose dispersed them once more, but he also wanted to know what it was they were hunting. Who were these two mysterious boys who were said to have been killed, what had killed them, and why did the children think they could find the suspect here, in this particular graveyard?

The killer, he was told, was a *vampire*. A vampire that stood over seven feet tall, with sharp teeth and glowing eyes.

Brought Back

No one wants to die. If the human design was scheduled for a revision, that's one of the features that would get an overhaul. Our mortality has been an obsession since the dawn of humanity itself. Humans long for ways to avoid death, or at least make it bearable.

Some cultures have practically moved heaven and earth doing so. Thousands of years ago, the Egyptians built enormous stone structures in order to house their dead and ensure them a place in the afterlife. They perfected the art of embalming so that even after death, their bodies might be ready for a new existence in a new place.

Death, though, is a reality for all of us, whether we like it or not. Whether we're young or old, rich or poor, healthy or sick, life is one long journey down a road, and we walk until it's over. Some think they see light at the end of it all, while others hope for darkness. And that's where the mystery of it all comes in. No one knows what's on the other side; we just know that the proverbial walk ends at some point.

And maybe that's why we spend so much time guessing at it, building story and myth and belief around this thing we can't put our finger on. What would be easier, some say, is if we just didn't die. If we somehow went on forever. It's impossible, but we dream of it anyway.

No one returns from the grave . . . do they? Most sane, well-adjusted people would say no. But stories exist that say otherwise, and these stories aren't new. They've been around for thousands of years and span multiple cultures.

And like their subject matter, these stories simply refuse to die. One reason for that—as hard as it is to believe—is because some of those stories appear to be *true*. Depending on where you look and whom you ask, there are whispers of those who beat the odds.

Sometimes the journey doesn't end after all. Sometimes the dead really do walk.

THE RETURNED

The quintessential zombie movie—the one that all the commentators say was responsible for putting zombies on the map nearly fifty years ago—was George A. Romero's classic *Night of the Living Dead*. The creatures that Romero brought to the big screen managed to influence generations of filmmakers, giving us the iconic zombie that we see today in television shows like *The Walking Dead*.

The trouble is, Romero never used the word "zombie" to describe the creatures from his landmark film. Instead, they were "ghouls," a creature borrowed from Arabian folklore. According to the mythology, ghouls are demons who eat the dead, and because of that, they're usually found in graveyards.

But Romero's film was not the first story featuring undead creatures that hunger for the flesh and blood of the living. Some think that that honor falls to the *Odyssey*, the epic Greek poem written by Homer nearly three thousand years ago. In the story, there's a scene in which Odysseus needs to get some information from a long-dead prophet named Tiresias. To give the spirit strength to speak, Odysseus feeds him blood.

In a lot of ways, the creatures we think of today as zombies are similar to the European tales of the revenant. They've gone by many names. The ancient Irish called them *neamh mairbh,* meaning "the undead." In Germany there is the *Wiedergänger,* "the one who walks again."

The word "revenant," if you remember, is Latin, and means "the returned." The basic idea is pretty easy to guess from that: revenants were those who were once dead but returned to haunt and terrorize their neighbors and family.

It might sound like fantasy to our modern sensibilities, but some people really did believe that this could happen. Historians in the Middle Ages wrote about revenant activity as if it were fact. One man, William of Newbury, wrote in 1190:

> *It would not be easy to believe that the corpses of the dead should sally from their graves, and should wander about to the terror or destruction of the living . . . did not frequent examples, occurring in our own times, suffice to establish this fact, to the truth of which there is abundant testimony. Were I to write down all the instances of this kind which I have ascertained to have befallen in our times, the undertaking would be beyond measure laborious and troublesome.*

Newbury goes on to wonder why the ancient writers never mentioned events like these (though he doesn't seem to take that as proof that revenants are pure fantasy). In fact, he was wrong about that. The ancient Greeks *did* have certain beliefs surrounding the dead and their ability to return to haunt the living. But to them, it was much more complicated, and each revenant came back with its own unique purpose.

You see, in the Greco-Roman world people believed that there was a gap between the date of someone's actual death and the *intended* date of their death. Remember, this was a culture that believed in the Moirai—the Fates—who had a plan for everyone. So, for example, a farmer might be destined to die in his eighties from natural causes, but he might instead die earlier in an accident at the market or in his field. People who died early, according to the legends, were doomed to wander the land of the living as spirits until the date of their intended death arrived.

Still with me? Good. So the Greeks believed that it was possible to control those wandering spirits. All you needed to do was make a curse tablet, something written on clay or tin or even parchment, and then bury it in the person's grave. Like a key in the ignition of a car, this tablet would empower you to control the wandering dead.

It might sound like the world's creepiest Martha Stewart howto project, but to the Greeks, magic like this was a powerful part of their belief system. The dead weren't really gone, and because of that, they could serve a purpose.

Unfortunately, that's not an attitude that was unique to the Greeks. And in the right culture, at the right time, under the right pressure, that idea can be devastating.

THE CRUCIBLE

In Haiti, the vast majority of the people—up to 95 percent, according to some studies—can trace their roots to West Africa. It's a remnant of a darker time, when slavery was legal and millions of Africans were pulled from their homes and transported across the Atlantic to work the Caribbean sugar plantations that filled European coffers. And while African slaves were shipped to the New World with no possessions besides the clothing on their backs, they did come with their beliefs—with their customs and traditions, and with centuries of folklore and superstition. They might not have carried luggage filled with precious heirlooms, but they held the most important pieces of their identity in their minds and hearts, and no one could take that away.

There are a few ideas that need to be understood about this transplanted culture. First, they believed that the soul and the body were connected, but also that death could be a moment of separation between the two. Not always, but it *could* be. I'll explain more about that in a moment.

Second, they lived with a hatred and fear of slavery. Slavery took away their freedom. It took away their power. They no longer had control over their lives, their dreams, or even their own bodies. Whether they liked it or not, they were doomed to endure horribly difficult labor for the rest of their lives. Only death would break the chains and set them free.

Third, that freedom wasn't guaranteed. While most Africans enslaved in the Caribbean dreamed of returning to their homeland in the afterlife, there were some who wanted to get there quicker. Suicide was common in colonial Haiti, but it was also frowned upon. In fact, it was believed that those who ended their own life wouldn't wind up back in Africa at all; instead, they would be punished. The penalty, it was said, was eternal imprisonment inside their own body, without control or power over themselves. It was, in a sense, just like their life. To the slaves of Haiti, hell was just more slavery, but a slavery that went on forever.

These bodies and trapped souls had a name in their culture: the zombi. It was first recorded in 1872, when a linguistic scholar recorded the word "zombi" and defined it as "a phantom or ghost," noting that the term was "not infrequently heard in the Southern States in nurseries and among the servants." The name, it turns out, has African roots. In languages spoken in west central Africa, where many of the Africans enslaved in the New World were captured, there are similar-sounding words that refer to divinities, ghosts, and objects that get their power from ancestors or spirits.

The walking dead, at least according to Haitian lore, are real.

What did these zombies look like? Well, thanks to Zora Neale Hurston, we have a firsthand account. Hurston was an African American author, known for her novel *Their Eyes Were Watching God*, and regarded as one of the pillars of the Harlem Renaissance. And it was while researching folklore during a trip to Haiti in 1936 that she encountered one.

In her book *Tell My Horse*, Hurston recounts what happened:

> *I had the rare opportunity to see and touch an authentic case. I listened to the broken noises in its throat.* . . . *If I had not experienced all of this in the strong sunlight of a hospital yard, I might have come away from Haiti interested but doubtful. But I saw this case of Felicia Felix-Mentor which was vouched for by the highest authority. So I know that there are Zombies in Haiti. People have been called back from the dead.*
> *The sight was dreadful. That blank face with the dead eyes.*

The eyelids were white all around the eyes as if they had been burned with acid. . . . There was nothing you could say to her or get from her, except by looking at her, and the sight of this wreckage was too much to endure for long.

Wreckage. I can't think of another word with as much beauty and horror as that, in that context. Something was happening in Haiti, and the result was wreckage. Lives broken and torn apart by something. But what?

The assumption might be that these people had all attempted suicide. But suicide is common in many cultures, not just in Haiti. When you dig deeper, though, it's possible to uncover the truth. And in this case, the truth is much darker than we'd like to believe.

Zombies, it turns out, *can* be created.

NARCISSE

On the night of April 30, 1962, a man walked into the Albert Schweitzer Hospital in Haiti. He was sick, complaining of body aches, a fever, and—most recently—coughing fits that brought blood up from his lungs. Naturally, the medical staff was concerned, and they admitted him for tests and treatment. This man, Clairvius Narcisse, was seen by a number of medical doctors, but his condition quickly deteriorated. One of his sisters, Angelina, was there at his bedside, and according to her his lips turned blue and he complained to her of a tingling sensation all over his body.

Despite the hospital's best efforts, Narcisse died the next day. Two doctors, one American and the other American-trained, each confirmed his death. Angelina signed the death certificate after confirming the man's identity. Because she couldn't read or write, she did so by pressing her thumbprint onto the paper. And then his family began the painful process of burying their loved one and trying to move on. Death, as always, is a part of life. Never a pleasant one, but a part nonetheless.

More than eighteen years later, in 1981, Angelina Narcisse was walking through the market in her village, something she did nearly every day. She knew the faces of each vendor; she knew the scents and the sounds that filled the space there. But when she looked down the dirt road toward the small crowd of people, something frightened her, and she screamed.

There, walking toward her, was her brother Clairvius. He was, of course, older now, but it was him. She would have recognized him anywhere. And when he finally approached her and named himself with a childhood nickname, any doubt she might have had melted away.

What followed was a whirlwind of revelations as Clairvius told his sister what had happened to him. And it all started, he said, in the hospital room. According to him, his last moments in the bed there were dark but fully aware. He could no longer see anyone, and he couldn't move. But he remembered hearing the doctor pronounce him dead. He remembered the sound of his sister weeping. He even remembered the rough cotton sheet being pulled up and over his face. That awareness continued on to his funeral, where he claimed to have heard the procession. He even pointed to a scar on his face and said that it was the result of one of the coffin nails cutting him.

Later, the family brought in a psychiatrist, who performed a series of tests on Clairvius to see if he was a fraud, but the man passed with flying colors, answering questions that no one but Clairvius himself could have known. In addition, more than two hundred friends and family members vouched for the man's identity. This, all of them confirmed, *was* Clairvius Narcisse.

So what happened to him? According to Clairvius himself, he was poisoned by his brother over a property dispute. How, he wasn't sure. But shortly after his burial, a group of men dug his coffin up and pulled him free. That's a thought worth locking away deep in the back of your brain, by the way—the man was trapped inside a coffin beneath the earth, blind and paralyzed, cold and scared. It's a wonder he didn't go insane.

The men who dug him up were led by a priest called a *bokor*. The men chained Clairvius and then guided him away to a sugar plantation, where he was forced to work alongside others in a similar state of helplessness. Daily doses of a mysterious drug kept all of them unable to resist or leave.

According to his story, he managed to escape two years later, but, fearing what his brother might do to him if he showed up alive, he avoided returning home. It was only the news of his brother's death many years later that coaxed him out of hiding.

The story of Clairvius Narcisse has perplexed scientists and historians for decades. In the 1980s, Harvard sent an ethnobotanist named Wade Davis to investigate the mysterious drug, and the result of his trip was a book called *The Serpent and the Rainbow,* which would go on to be a *New York Times* bestseller as well as a Hollywood movie. But few agree on the conclusions.

Samples of the drug that Wade collected have all been disproven. No illegal sugar plantation staffed by zombie slaves has ever been discovered. And the doctors have been accused of misreading the symptoms and prematurely declaring the man dead. There are so many doubts.

To the people closest to him, though, the facts are solid. Clairvius Narcisse died. His family watched his burial in the cemetery. He was mourned and missed. And more than eighteen years later, he came back into their lives. The walking dead.

Medical mishap or the result of Haitian black magic? We may never know for sure.

EMPTY

We fear death because it means the loss of control, the loss of purpose and freedom. Death, in the eyes of many people, robs us of our identity and replaces it with finality. It's understandable, then, how slavery can be viewed through the same lens. It removes people's ability to make decisions for themselves and turns them, in a sense, into nothing more than machines for the benefit of another person.

But what if there really are individuals out there—the *bokor* or evil priests—who have discovered a way to manufacture their own walking dead? Maybe there are people who have perfected the art of enslaving a man or a woman more deeply than any slave owner might have managed before, robbing them of their very soul and binding them to an afterlife of tireless, ceaseless labor.

In February 1976, Francine Illeus was admitted to her local hospital in Haiti. She said she felt weak and light-headed. Her digestive system was failing, and her stomach ached. The doctors there treated her and then released her. Several days later, she passed away and was buried in the local graveyard. She was only thirty years old.

Three years later Francine's mother received a call from a friend a few miles away. She needed her to come to the local marketplace there, and it was urgent. Francine's mother didn't know what the trouble was, but she made the journey as quickly as she could.

Once there, she was told that a woman had been found in the market. She was emaciated and catatonic, and refused to move from where she was squatting in a corner, head down and hands laced over her face. The woman, it turned out, was Francine Illeus.

Her mother brought her home and tried to help her, but Francine seemed to be gone. She was there in body, but there was very little spirit left. Subsequent doctors and psychiatrists have spent time with Francine, but with very little progress to show for it.

On a whim, Francine's mother had the coffin exhumed. She had to see for herself if this woman—little more than a walking corpse—truly was her daughter. Yes, the woman had the same scar on her forehead that her daughter had. Yes, they looked alike. Yes, others recognized her as Francine. But she needed to know for sure.

When the men pulled the coffin out of the earth, it was heavy. Too heavy, they murmured, to be empty. More doubtful by the minute, Francine's mother asked them to open it. And when the last nail had been pulled free from the wood, the lid was lifted and cast aside.

The coffin wasn't empty after all. It was full of rocks.

The Trees

I T WAS THE walk through the trees that reminded him of his dream. Stuckley was used to trees, as was Caleb, who walked beside him. After all, he tended an orchard for a living, so trees were, in a very real sense, his life. But walking through them now, for this reason, with this purpose . . . didn't feel right.

Again, though, his mind drifted back to the dream that had started it all. The dream from which he awoke with a start, a feeling of panic in his belly and a sense of dread so overwhelming it might as well have been a sack of field stones tied to his shoulders.

His dream was one of devastation, of loss and tragedy. Half his orchard had withered and died. Half his livelihood. Half his purpose. Half his worth. Sitting there on his straw cot, covered in sweat and heavy with foreboding, he had tried to tell himself that it was all just a dream.

But it hadn't been, in the end. Had it?

He and Caleb worked their way through the trees, and this time his mind wandered to Sarah. She had been the first to go, more than eighteen months before. One afternoon she had wandered over to the old graveyard, as she had done so many times before. She would read books there, and daydream there. She would recline on the old stone slabs and become lost in her thoughts and books of poetry.

The fever had moved through her like a wildfire, and before

Stuckley knew it, she had gone back to the graveyard. But she would stay there this time. No books of poetry. No daydreams. No reclining in the cool spring air. Sarah was gone and would never return.

The trees around Stuckley and Caleb began to thin. So had his family, actually. One by one, each of the children had taken ill. Never two at once; no, that would have been too easy. One night of anguish and grief for half a dozen sons and daughters would have been hard, but bearable for most.

But for him, the loss had been spread out. First a daughter, then a son. Then another. And another. One by one, his orchard was withering away. Fever and a heavy chest. Pale skin that looked more like bone than flesh. Each had been consumed in turn. And each death had consumed another piece of him.

There were no more trees now. Those were behind them. Before them now lay the clearing, and then the low stone wall. But as they walked slowly across the grass, Stuckley couldn't help but think of his wife, who lay dying back at their home. She was all he had now, and she too was slipping away.

But he knew what to do. He knew how to help her. He learned it by listening to the trees. Each one whispered as they passed. Each child spoke the same words from behind a veil of fever and wasting. It was always the same . . . always the same.

"I see her," each of them told him. "I see her there, waiting for me. She sits on the edge of the bed and watches me. She's come back for me."

And Stuckley asked them all, "Who? Who's come for you?"

Caleb stepped over the low stone wall first, then took the shovel from Stuckley's hand and helped the older man climb over to join him. Of course, he had known the answer before he'd even asked.

Sarah. She'd come back for the others. Each one admitted it. Each one believed it to be true. Each one of his children had wept with fear as the fever consumed their body, as they lay helpless in a bed, each watched over by their dead sister.

And now she was back for his wife.

Stuckley walked to the corner of the graveyard he knew far too well and plunged the blade of the shovel into the soil. She had always come back from here, after all. She had always ended her daydreaming and poetry reading by returning home. Why should now be any different?

But now *was* different. Now *this* was her home. *This* was where she needed to be. Not in *his* home. Not at the bedside of his wife. Not laying waste to his orchard one sibling at a time. No, Sarah was in the graveyard, and that was where she needed to stay.

Caleb helped him pry off the lid of the coffin, and then he walked away. Stuckley needed to do the rest on his own. She didn't look dead. She didn't look like a corpse more than eighteen months in the ground. She looked well rested. She looked peaceful. She looked beautiful.

But the hunting knife in his hand was already doing its work. Her heart bled as he pulled it free from her chest. It bled as if it had just stopped beating. It bled dark, and red, and slick.

And then he set it on fire. That's what you do, isn't it? When you need to cut down a tree, you burn the stump. You burn the roots. You take away its foothold in the orchard so it won't come back again.

He wanted nothing more than for Sarah to come back again. For all his children to come back again. But he knew it wasn't possible. All he knew was that his wife could be saved, and so he watched the flames blacken the heart of his oldest daughter there on the stone slab where she once had reclined in the springtime sun.

And he wept.

 A LITTLE PROBLEM

The Others

N O ONE LIKES to be alone. Even introverts need to come up for air every now and then and experience human contact. Being around others has a way of calming our souls and imparting a bit of safety, if only in theory. But sometimes, even crowds of people and scores of friends can't fight the crippling feeling that we are, in the end, isolated and alone.

Humans have become very good at chasing away that feeling, though. When darkness threatened to cut us off from the world around us, we discovered fire, and then invented electric lights. We use technology today to help us stay connected to friends and relatives who live thousands of miles away, and yet the feeling of loneliness grows deeper every year.

We've learned to harness tools to fight it, though. In ancient cultures—in the days before Facebook and even the printing press, if you can fathom that—society fought the feeling of being alone with story. Each culture developed a set of tales, a mythology and surrounding lore that filled in the cracks. These stories explained the unexplainable, filled the dark night with figures and shapes, and gave people—lonely or not—something else to talk about. Something "other."

Some tales were there to teach. Some preached morals through analogy. Others offered a word of warning or a lesson that would keep children safe. In the end, though, all of them did something that we couldn't do on our own: they put us in our place. They offered perspective. It might seem like we're at the top of the food chain, but . . . what if we're not?

From the ancient hills of Iceland and Brazil to the blacktopped streets of urban America, our fascination with "the others" has been a constant, unrelenting obsession. But while most stories only make us smile at the pure fantasy of it all, there are some that defy dismissal. They leave us with more questions than answers. And they force us to come to grips with a frightening truth: if we're not alone in this world, then we're also not safe.

A LITTLE HISTORY

In Greek mythology, we have stories of creatures that were called *pygmaioi,* a tribe of diminutive humans, smaller than the Greeks, who were often encountered in battle. Similar stories of pygmies have been around for thousands of years. We even have images of pygmy battles on pottery found in tombs dating back to the fifth century BCE.

First-century Roman historian Pliny the Elder recorded that the pygmies were said to go on annual journeys from their homeland in the mountains. They would arm themselves for battle, climb onto their rams and goats, and ride down to the sea, where they would hunt the cranes that nested at the shore.

In South America, there are tales of creatures called *aluxes.* A figure of Mayan mythology, an *alux* was said to be between three and six feet tall, hairless, and dressed in traditional Mayan clothing. Like the *pukwidgies* of Native American tribes, *aluxes* are said to be troublemakers, disrupting crops and wreaking havoc.

According to tradition, an *alux* will move into the area every time a new farm is established. Mayan farmers were said to build a small two-story house in the middle of their corn fields, where the creature would live. For the first seven years, the *alux* would help grow the corn and patrol the fields at night. Once those seven years were up, however, it would turn on the farmers, who would seal the windows and doors on the little house to trap the creatures inside.

The ancient Picts of the Orkney Islands, off the northeastern tip of Scotland, spoke of a creature they called the trow (or sometimes drow). Trows were small humanoid beings, described as being ugly and shy, who lived in the mounds and rock outcroppings in the surrounding woods. As in many of the other legends of small people around the world, the trows were said to be mischievous. In particular, they were said to love music. So much, in fact, that it was thought that they kidnapped musicians and took them back to their homes so that they could enjoy the music there. It was common for the people of Shetland to bless their children on Yule day each year as a way of protecting them from the trow.

Nearby in Ireland there are tales of a similar creature, small and hairless, called the pooka. The pooka is said to stand roughly three feet tall, and like the trow, it too lives in large stone outcroppings. According to legend, these creatures can cause chaos and trouble within a community, so much so that the local people have developed traditions meant to keep them happy. In County Down, for instance, farmers still leave behind a "pooka's share" when they harvest their crops. It's an offering to the creatures, to keep them happy and to ward off their mischief.

But the pooka isn't unique to Ireland. In Cornish mythology, there's a small, human-like creature known as the bucca, a kind of hobgoblin. Wales is home to a similar creature with a reputation as a trickster goblin. It was said to knock on doors and then disappear before the people inside opened them. And in Normandy, France, just across the English Channel, whose inhabitants share a common background with the people of Cornwall and Wales, the creature is called a *pouque,* and a common term for stone outcroppings and megalithic structures is *pouquelée.*

Oh, and if you are a fan of Shakespeare's play *A Midsummer Night's Dream,* you might remember the character Puck, the clever and mischievous elf. The name Puck, it turns out, is an Anglicization of the word "pooka" or *pouque.*

I'll stop, but I think you get the point: there doesn't seem to be a culture in the world that *hasn't* invented a story about smaller people, the "others" who live on the periphery of our world. It's not surprising, either. Many of these cultures have a deep history of invading nations, and that kind of past can cause anyone to spend a lot of time looking over their shoulder.

These stories are deep and often allegorical. They mean something, sure, but they aren't rooted in reality. No one has ever captured a pooka, or taken photographs of an *alux* stepping out of its tiny stone building. But that doesn't mean there's no evidence.

In fact, there are some legends that come a lot closer to the surface than you might have thought possible. And that might not be a good thing.

THINGS GET REAL

The Shoshone tribe of Native Americans historically lived in what is now Idaho, Nevada, Wyoming, and Utah. Their land spanned much of the countryside around the Rockies, but they also built seasonal homes high up in the mountains, sometimes ten thousand feet above sea level.

One of the Shoshone legends is that of a tribe of tiny people known as the *nimerigar*. One story tells of a man who rode up a small trail into the Wind River Mountains to check on his cattle. While he was traveling the narrow path, one of these creatures stepped out and stopped him. This was his trail, the little man said, and the rancher couldn't use it anymore. The man ignored the tiny person and continued on toward his cattle, and this angered the *nimerigar*. The tiny creature took aim with his bow and fired a poisonous arrow at the man's arm. From that day on, the story goes, the rancher was never able to use his arm again.

The *nimerigar* are just myth. Or, at least, that's what most people think. But in 1932, that perception changed when two prospectors, Cecil Main and Frank Carr, found a mummy in a cave in the Pedro Mountains of Wyoming. They said it had been sitting upright on a ledge in the cave, as if it had been waiting for them.

This mummy was small. Honestly, it was only about six inches tall in its seated position, but it appeared to have all the proportions of an adult. It had been mummified by the dry Wyoming climate. After its discovery, the mummy changed hands a number of times. Photographs were taken, as well as an X-ray, but it vanished after 1950, never to be seen again.

In 1994, after an episode of *Unsolved Mysteries* asked viewers to help locate the missing mummy, a second mummy came to light. This one was a female with blond hair, but it was roughly the same size, and also from a mountain cave. This time, medical experts were able to study it, and what they discovered was shocking. It wasn't an adult after all. It was an infant that had been born with a condition known as anencephaly, which explained the adult-like proportions of the body and head. Like the first mummy, this second one disappeared shortly after the examination, and the family who owned it vanished with it.

Halfway around the world in Indonesia, there are stories of a small, human-like creature called the *ebu gogo*. Even though the name sounds a lot like a Belinda Carlisle cover band, these creatures were said to strike fear in the hearts of the neighboring tribes. According to the story, the *ebu gogo* had flat noses and wide mouths, and they spoke in short grunts and squawks. They were known to steal food from the local villagers, and sometimes even children. And apparently, one of these incidents in the 1800s led to an extermination.

The Nage people of Flores, Indonesia, claim that generations ago, a group of *ebu gogo* stole some of their food, and the Nage chased them to a cave, where they burned them all alive—all but one pair, male and female, who managed to escape into the forest.

The stories are full of imagination and fantasy, but in the end, they might hint at something real. In 2003, archaeologists discovered human remains in a Flores cave. The remains—dubbed *Homo floresiensis*—weren't ordinary, though; they were small adults. Very small, actually, at just over three feet tall. They were nicknamed "hobbits," if that helps you picture them.

Small people, found in a cave, near the Nage people of Flores . . . it seemed like the stories were proving true. The trouble was the age of the remains. The oldest skeletons clocked in at about thirty-eight thousand years old and the youngest at about thirteen thousand. In other words, if the Nage actually *had* attacked a tribe of tiny people, it had happened a lot more than a handful of generations ago.

Unless you believe them, that is. In that case, the stories hint at something darker: that the *ebu gogo* are real, that they might still inhabit the forests of Flores, and that, ultimately, the stories were true.

It sounds enticing. In fact, I think anyone would be fascinated by such a notion. Unless, that is, those stories were about something in your own backyard.

DOVER

On the night of April 21, 1977, a man named Billy Bartlett was driving through the town of Dover, Massachusetts, with two of his friends. On Farm Street, they began to drive past a low, rough stone wall that was well known to the locals. As they did, Billy noticed movement at the edge of his vision, and turned to see something unlike anything he had ever seen before.

It was a creature with a body the size of a child's; long, thin limbs; elongated fingers; and an oversized, melon-shaped head. Billy claimed it was hairless and that the skin was textured. He even reported that it had large orange-colored eyes.

Billy later sketched a picture of the thing he had seen, and then added a note to the bottom of the page: "I, Bill Bartlett, swear on a stack of Bibles that I saw this creature."

A whole stack of Bibles, you say? Well, all right, then.

Something like this probably happens every year somewhere in the world. Someone sees something weird, their mind twists their memories, and all of a sudden they think they encountered Abraham Lincoln in a hot tub. But Billy's story had some added credibility.

You see, just two hours after he saw whatever it was that he saw, fifteen-year-old John Baxter was walking home from his girlfriend's house, about a mile from Farm Street. He claimed that

he saw something walking down the street toward him. According to him, it was roughly the size and shape of a small child. When the figure noticed him, though, it bolted for the woods.

John, being a highly intelligent teenager with powerful decision-making skills, decided that midnight was the perfect time to chase something strange into the woods, and so he followed it. What happened next was a literal "over the river and through the woods" chase. When Baxter finally stopped to catch his breath, though, he looked up to see that the creature was standing beside a tree just a few yards away from him—watching him.

That's the moment when common sense took over, and John ran for his life. Later that night he drew a sketch of what he had seen. He also told the police about it. He described a creature that had the body of a child, a large oval-shaped head, thin arms and legs, and long fingers.

On their own, each of these sightings easily could have been dismissed by the authorities, but together they presented a powerful case. Still, any chance of their similarity being labeled a coincidence vanished less than twenty-four hours later.

Fifteen-year-old Abby Brabham and eighteen-year-old Will Taintor were out for a drive on Springdale Avenue when they saw something at the side of the road near a bridge. It was on all fours, but both of them claimed they got a very good look at it. Each of them described the creature as hairless and child-sized, with an overly large head and long, thin limbs.

Three separate events spanning two nights. Three unique sightings. One seemingly impossible description, each captured in eerily similar sketches. There were small discrepancies regarding the color of the creature's eyes, but outside of that, the consistency was astounding. Each of these eyewitnesses had seen something they couldn't explain. And each of them seemed to have observed the same thing.

What I find most fascinating, though, is that nearly thirty years later, in 2006, *The Boston Globe* interviewed Billy Bartlett, and he's never wavered from his story. He's experienced embarrassment and ill treatment because of it over the years, of course. But though he's now a responsible, middle-aged adult, that maturity hasn't chased his testimony away, no matter how fantastical it might sound.

They've called it the Dover Demon ever since that week in 1977. Others have come forward with similar sightings. One local man, Mark Sennott, has said there'd been a rumor in his high school in the early 1970s of something odd in the woods. Sennott even claimed that he and some friends observed something odd near Channing Pond in 1972 that fits the description from the later reports. Channing Pond, mind you, is right beside Springdale Avenue, where Taintor and Brabham said they saw their Dover Demon. Clearly, something was in those woods.

Like most legends, this one will continue to cause debate and speculation. There have been no further sightings since 1977, but even so, the Dover Demon has left an indelible mark on the town and surrounding area.

SHIFTING THE BLAME

We don't like to be alone. But I think in the process of creating the stories that have kept us company for centuries, humanity has also invented convenient excuses. All of these human-like creatures have acted as a sort of stand-in for human behavior and accountability. In an effort to absolve ourselves from the horrible things we've done, we seem to instinctively invent other beings on which to set the blame.

But what if the "others" really were there, long before we wove them into our stories? What if they were less an invention and more a co-opting of something we didn't fully understand? Perhaps in our effort to shift the blame, we altered the source material a bit too much, and in doing so, we buried the truth under a mountain of myth.

There've been countless theories surrounding the 1977 sightings in Dover. Some think it was a type of extraterrestrial known as a "gray." Others have actually suggested that it was just a baby moose. I know, that does seem like an odd way to explain it. Only two moose sightings were recorded in Massachusetts in 1977, and both of those were out in the western part of the state, far from Dover. Add in the fact that a yearling moose weighs more than six hundred pounds, and I think it's clear that this theory just won't hold up.

But there is a different, more textured theory to consider. If you remember, Billy Bartlett saw the Dover Demon sitting on an old stone wall on Farm Street. Well, just beyond that wall is a large stone outcropping that the locals have always called the Polka Stone.

Some think that the stone's nickname is a mispronunciation of a different word, though. The original name, they say, was the Pooka Stone. It could just be folklore, perhaps the tall tales of an early Irish settler, told to a group of children around the foot of an enormous stone. Unfortunately, we'll never know for sure.

But if you really want to see for yourself, you're always welcome to head to Dover and take a drive down Farm Street. The wall and the woods beyond are still there, still dark, and still ominous. Just be careful if you travel there at night.

You never know what you might see at the edge of your headlight beams.

Under Construction

ON THE SOUTHWESTERN corner of Iceland, just to the south of the city of Reykjavik, is a small peninsula that juts out into the cold waters of the North Atlantic. It's known as the Álftanes peninsula, and although few people live there, the local government recently decided to connect the small stretch of land to the town of Gardabaer, a suburb of Reykjavik.

Last year, however, construction on the new road was brought to a halt. Standing in their way was a massive rock, twelve feet high and weighing an estimated seventy tons. According to highway department employee Petur Matthiasson, the rock has presented an *unusual* challenge to his department's construction project.

Now, you have to understand something about Iceland. Much of the region is a vast expanse of sparse grass and large volcanic rock formations. The ground boils with geysers and springs, and the sky seems to be eternally gray and cloudy. So it's important to recognize that there are hundreds—maybe thousands—of volcanic stones along the construction route.

So what could possibly be so important about this one particular stone? Why would the highway department go to such lengths, even covering the expense of hiring a crane, just to move one stone to a safer location?

The stone, they say, is inhabited. It is—as it has been for many long centuries—home to *huldufolk,* the "hidden people." They are the size and shape of humans, and live in much the same way. Except, of course, they are invisible.

THE HIDDEN FOLK

In the late 1930s, another road construction project in the same area of Iceland was planned to cut straight through a hill known as Alfholl. From the beginning, though, the project was met with challenges. First, the money for the project ran out, and when funding resumed a decade later, construction encountered even more snags.

The machines that were used to cut through the hill started to break at an uncommonly rapid rate. Tools were damaged and lost. In the end, the road was simply built around the hill to avoid the digging altogether.

When the road was due for updating in the 1980s, the notion of demolishing the hill came up again, and more machinery was brought in to drill through the hill. After the first drill broke, another was brought in, but it too stopped working. After that, the workers refused to bring any of their tools near the hill out of fear that they would be lost or broken by the *huldufolk* who guard the place.

Iceland is a culture teeming with references to this invisible society of human-like creatures. In a recent survey, more than half of all people in the country—54 percent—said they believed in the existence of these creatures. But who are the *huldufolk*?

According to one Icelandic folktale, the hidden people can be traced back to Adam and Eve. The legend says that Eve had a number of children whom she hid from God. But God, being omniscient and aware of everything that happens, found them anyway.

In the story, God declared, "What man hides from God, God will hide from man." As a result, these children of Adam and Eve vanished from sight and have lived alongside humans ever since, hidden from our eyes.

Wherever they came from, Iceland is apparently filled with them. They are described as being the same size as humans and usually clad in simple nineteenth-century Icelandic clothing, often green-colored.

The people of Iceland have another term for these creatures, though. They don't use it as often, because they feel it's not as respectful as "the hidden folk." But it's a word we all know, and its history and meaning run deep.

They call them elves.

THE ELVES OF THE WORLD

When we think of elves, most of us imagine the little people who help Santa Claus in his workshop at the North Pole. We picture tiny people with pointed ears who wear tall pointed hats. But that vision of elves is actually new, dating back only to Victorian-era fairy tales, when French stories of fairies were mixed and confused with more ancient tales of elves from the Celtic, Germanic, and Scandinavian peoples.

The oldest records of something resembling elves are from Anglo-Saxon England and medieval Iceland, though some records do exist in Germany as well. The characteristics are consistent across the continent, though: elves were described as human-like, they were said to be formerly divine creatures of some unknown origin, and they are portrayed as very, very dangerous.

In Norse mythology, elves were mainly thought of as females who lived in the hills and mounds of stones. The Swedish elves were said to be beautiful girls who lived in the forest with their king. And Scandinavian folklore describes them as fair-haired, dressed in white, and dangerous when offended.

In fact, in many folktales, elves were given the role of disease spirits. Elves could inflict horrible skin rashes on anyone who offended them, and this was called an "elven blow." The only way to calm and satisfy them was to actually visit their homes—often large stones in the forest—and leave them an offering of food.

ELVES GONE WILD

Early on, elves were simply thought of as mischievous pranksters. Anything odd that happened during a person's day could be blamed on the elves. A tangle in a person's hair was called an "elf lock," and birthmarks were referred to as "elf marks."

Over time, however, the elf developed a darker reputation. Much like their cultural counterparts in other countries, such as hobs, leprechauns, hobgoblins, and trolls, elves came to be seen as highly dangerous. A deeply common thread through all cultures is how easy it is to offend them, and how terrible the consequences might be if that happened.

One such tale was that of the changeling. According to legend, elves would invade the home of new parents and swap out their infant child for a small elf. While the human baby would be wonderfully cared for back in the home of the elves, the surrogate that was left behind, the changeling, would be fussy and unhappy.

In Iceland there are tales of *huldufolk* kidnapping adults, who are then taken back to the hills to work for the little people. In their place the *huldufolk* leave emotionless, hollow copies of the ones who are taken. It was said that if someone you knew underwent a severe personality change—becoming depressed and listless—it was because he or she had been replaced by the elves.

It was also believed that elves could enter the dreams of a sleeping person and inflict nightmares upon them. In fact, the German word for nightmare is *albdrücken,* which literally means "elf pressure."

You see, if it was horrible, unexplainable, or tragic, there was always one easy explanation that dominated medieval minds: blame it on the elves.

THE VILLAGES

But what if these were more than just folktales? If so, that might explain the incredibly similar stories that exist among the native tribes of the American Northeast.

In 2011, a nonprofit housing developer in the United States began the final stages of its plan to build a $19 million, 120-unit construction project known as The Villages. Everything about it looked promising. It would generate roughly $1.5 million in tax revenue for the town of Montville, Connecticut; it would create more than a hundred construction-related jobs; and once completed it would provide affordable housing to scores of local families.

Because The Villages was a nonprofit endeavor, the development company applied for federal funding to offset the costs. As a requirement for the funding process, the developer had to complete an archaeological survey of the 12.2-acre parcel of land.

That's when things hit a snag.

The proposed building site, it turns out, encroached on Mohegan tribe property. The Mohegan people were an offshoot of the Pequots, originating in the seventeenth century in Connecticut. They have deep roots in the area there, and naturally, parts of their historic past are still present today.

Among the sensitive archaeological sites that the Mohegan tribe claimed were at risk were Mohegan Hill, Fort Shantok, and Moshup's Rock, among others. None of those historic sites is unusual in any way, but when the Tribal Historic Preservation Officer for the Mohegans presented their case to the federal Housing and Urban Development department, there was one complaint that stood out among all the others. Creatures, they claimed, lived inside Mohegan Hill. The construction project threatened their very lives, and unless it was stopped, the "little people," as they called them, would disappear, leaving the tribe unprotected from outsiders.

The Mohegan tribe has long believed in the existence of creatures whom they call the *makiawisug,* the "little people." The stone piles on Mohegan Hill were said to have been built by them long ago, and served as protection from the outside world. These *makiawisug* have remained inside the hill ever since, guarding the stones and protecting the tribe.

These were powerful creatures that could protect and preserve the tribe, but if ignored or treated poorly, they could also bring great harm and chaos. Naturally, the Mohegan people became very good at managing their relationship with them.

One of the most prominent Mohegan tribe members of the last century was a woman named Gladys Tantaquidgeon, who passed away in 2005 at the age of 106. She was a tenth-generation descendant of the Mohegan chief Uncas, a prominent colonial-era leader, and was also a tribal medicine woman. Her role included maintaining her tribe's knowledge of the *makiawisug* and how to interact with them.

According to Tantaquidgeon, there were four non-negotiable laws for dealing with the "little people." First, serve and protect their leader and matriarchal deity, Granny Squannit. Second, never speak to them in the summer months, when they are the most active. Third, never stare directly at one, or else the creature will become invisible and steal your belongings. And finally, leave them offerings from time to time.

And so to this day, the Mohegans continue to make offerings to these creatures in hopes that they will continue their role as protectors and guardians. It is traditional to leave them an offering of cornmeal and berries, and sometimes even meat.

Sound familiar?

A CONNECTION TO THE PAST

The vast majority of people in the world don't really believe in the existence of elves or hidden people living in the bones of the earth. One explanation as to why Iceland is different, though, has to do with the Vikings.

When they conquered a city, the Vikings had real-life enemies to focus their hatred on. When they settled Iceland, however, no one else was there to be defeated. Perhaps the *huldufolk* provided the excuse they needed to feel like conquerors in a land with no native inhabitants.

Other scholars believe that elves represent our connection to the earth of old. They are a sort of primitive environmentalism, a reminder of the way life used to be before urban sprawl and manufacturing left their marks on our world.

Whatever the reason, our ancestors firmly believed in these otherworldly beings who could bless or curse them at will. Elves served as an excuse for the unexplained, as solid ground when nothing else seemed to make sense. We might laugh it off today from our modern point of view, but centuries ago, elves gave people an opportunity to hope, or a reason to be afraid.

And remember Petur Matthiasson, the highway department employee in Reykjavik, Iceland? He's made it very clear to journalists that he doesn't believe in elves. But that doesn't stop him from telling an odd story to those who ask.

Apparently his family came from the northern side of Iceland long ago. There, in the wild north country, the family claimed to have had a protective elf who brought good fortune to them. When they moved south, the family elf remained behind.

Petur recalls going on a camping trip in the north some years ago. Before he left, his father asked him to go and pay his respects to the elf and to thank her for the help she had given to his family.

Not being one to believe in the old stories, Petur forgot the request. The next day, despite an overcast sky and wet drizzle, he woke up sore and blistered by what he described as something like a sunburn. He could barely stand, in fact.

Did Petur experience some random, mysterious dermatological episode, or was he the victim of an elven blow from an angry family patron? As it was for his ancestors, the easiest explanation might just be the most otherworldly.

Tampered

I GREW UP WATCHING a television show called *MacGyver*. If you've never had the chance to watch this icon of the 1980s, do yourself a favor and give it a try. Sure, the clothes are outdated, and the hair . . . oh my gosh, the hair. But aside from the bits that didn't age well, MacGyver and his trusty pocket knife managed to capture my imagination forever.

Part of it was the adventure. Part of it was the character of the man himself. I mean, the guy was essentially a spy who hated guns, played hockey, and lived on a houseboat. But hovering above all of those elements was the true core of the show: this man could make anything if his life depended on it.

We humans have an innate drive to make things. This is how we managed to create things like the wheel, or stone tools and weapons. Our tendency toward technology pulled our ancient ancestors out of the stone age and into a more civilized world. Maybe for some of us, MacGyver represented what we wanted to achieve: complete mastery over our world.

But life is rarely that simple, and however hard we try to get our minds and hands around this world we want to rule, some things just slip through the cracks. Accidents happen. Ideas and concepts still elude our limited minds. We're human, after all. Not gods.

So when things go wrong—when our plans fall apart or our expectations fail to be met—we have this sense of pride that often refuses to admit defeat. So we blame others, and when that doesn't work, we look elsewhere for answers. And no realm holds more explanation for the unexplainable than folklore.

Four hundred years ago, when a woman refused to follow the rules of society, she was labeled a witch. When Irish children failed to thrive, it was because they were changelings. We're good at excuses. So when our ancestors found something broken or out of place, there was a very simple explanation: someone—or some*thing*—had tampered with it.

An Old Excuse

The idea of meddlesome creatures isn't new to us. All around the world, we can find centuries-old folklore that speaks of creatures with a habit of getting in the way and making life difficult for humans. It's an idea that seems to transcend borders and background, languages and time.

Some might say that it's far too coincidental for all of these stories of mischief-causing creatures to emerge in places separated by thousands of miles and vast oceans, and so there must be something to these legends. But others would say it has nothing to do with either real creatures or coincidence, and that these tales are merely a product of human nature—we want to believe there's something out there causing the problems we experience every day. A scapegoat, as it were.

Many European folktales include this universal archetype in the form of nature spirits. And much of it can be traced back to the idea of the daemon. It's an old word and concept, coming to us from the Greeks. In essence, a daemon is an otherworldly spirit that causes trouble. The root word, *daiomai*, means "to cut or divide."

In many ways, a daemon is an ancient version of an excuse. If your horse was spooked while you were out for a ride, you'd probably blame it on a daemon. The ancient Minoans believed in them, and in the day of the Greek poet Homer, people would blame their illnesses on them.

The daemon, in many ways, was fate. If it happened to you, there was a reason, it was probably one of these little things that caused it. Across history and cultures, the daemon took on a variety of names. Arab folklore has the *jinn*. Romans spoke of a personal companion known as the *genius*. In Japan they tell tales of the *kami,* and Germanic cultures mention the *fylgja*. The stories and names might be unique to each culture, but the core of them all is the same: there's something interfering with humanity, and we don't like it.

For the majority of the English-speaking world, the most common creature of this type in folklore, hands down, is the *goblin*. It's not an ancient word, most likely originating in the Middle Ages, but it's the one that's front and center in most of our minds. And from the start, it's been a creature associated with bad behavior.

A legend from the tenth century tells of how the first Catholic bishop of Évreux in France faced a daemon known to the locals there as Gobelinus. Why that name, though, is harder to trace. The best theory goes something like this: There's a Greek myth about a creature called the *kobalos* who loved to trick and frighten people. That story influenced other cultures prior to Christianity's spread across Europe, creating the notion of the *kobold* in ancient Germany. That word was most likely the root of the word "goblin." *Kobold, gobold, gobelin*—you can practically hear it evolve.

In German, the root of *kobold* is *kobe,* which literally means "beneath the earth" or "cavity in a rock." We get the English word "cove" from the same root. And so, naturally, *kobolds* and their English counterparts, the goblins, are said to live in caves underground. If that reminds you of dwarves from fantasy literature, you're closer than you think.

The physical appearance of goblins in folklore varies greatly, but the common description is that they are dwarf-like creatures. They cause trouble, are known to steal, have a tendency to break things, and generally make life difficult for humans. Because of this, people in Europe would put carvings of goblins in their homes to ward off the real thing.

In fact, here's something really crazy: medieval door knockers were often carved to resemble the faces of daemons or goblins. And it's most likely purely coincidental, but in Welsh folklore, goblins are called "coblyn" or, more commonly, "knockers."

My point is this: for thousands of years, people have suspected that their misfortune could be blamed on small, meddlesome creatures. They feared them, told stories about them, and tried their best to protect their homes from them. But for all that time, they seemed like nothing more than stories.

In the early twentieth century, though, people started to report actual sightings. And not just anyone. These sightings were documented by trained, respected military pilots.

Over and Under

When the Wright brothers made their first controlled flight in December 1903, it seemed like a revelation. It's hard to imagine it today, but there was a time when flight wasn't assumed as a method of travel. So when Wilbur spent three full seconds in the air that day, he and his brother Orville did something else: they changed the way we think about our world.

And however long it took humans to create and perfect the art of controllable, mechanical flight, once the cat was out of the bag, it bolted into the future without looking back. Within just nine years, someone had managed to mount a machine gun onto one of these primitive airplanes. Because of that, when the first World War broke out just two years later, military combat had a new element.

Of course, guns weren't the only weapons a plane could utilize. The very first airplane brought down in combat was an Austrian plane that was literally rammed by a Russian pilot. Both pilots died after the wreckage plummeted to the ground below. It wasn't the most efficient method of air combat, but it was a start. Clearly, we've spent the many decades since getting very, very good at it.

Unfortunately, though, the reasons for combat disasters go beyond machine gun bullets and suicidal pilots. One of the most
unique and mysterious of those causes first appeared in a British
newspaper. In an article from the early 1900s, it was said that in
1918

> the newly constituted Royal Air Force . . . appear[ed] to have
> detected the existence of a horde of mysterious and malicious
> sprites whose whole purpose in life was . . . to bring about as
> many as possible of the inexplicable mishaps which, in those days
> as now, trouble an airman's life.

The description didn't feature a name, but that was soon to follow. Some experts think that we can find roots of our word
"gremlin" in the Old English *germ*, which meant "to vex" or "to
annoy." It fits the behavior of these creatures to the letter.

Before we move forward, though, it might be helpful to take
care of your memories of the 1984 classic film by the same name.
I grew up in the 1980s, and *Gremlins* was a fantastic bit of eye-
candy for my young, horror-loving mind. But the truth of the
legend has little resemblance to the version that you and I witnessed on the big screen.

The gremlins of folklore—at least the stories that came out of
the early twentieth century, that is—described the ancient, stereotypical daemon, but with a twist. Yes, they were said to be
small, ranging anywhere from six inches to three feet in height.
And yes, they could appear and disappear at will, causing mischief
and trouble wherever they went. But in addition, these modern
versions of the legendary goblin seemed to possess a supernatural
grasp of modern human technology.

In 1923, a British pilot was flying over open water when his engine stalled. He miraculously survived the crash into the sea, and
was rescued shortly after that. When he was safely onboard the
rescue vessel, the pilot was quick to explain what had happened.
Tiny creatures, he claimed, had appeared on the plane. Whether
they appeared out of nowhere or smuggled themselves aboard
prior to takeoff, the pilot wasn't sure. However they got there, he

said that they proceeded to tamper with the plane's engine and flight controls. Without power or control, he was left to drop helplessly into the sea.

These reports were infrequent in the 1920s, but as World War II began and the number of planes in the sky began to grow exponentially, more and more stories seemed to follow of small, troublesome creatures who had an almost supernatural ability to hold on to a moving aircraft, and while they were there, to do damage and cause accidents. In some cases, they were even sighted inside planes, among the crew or cargo.

Stories, as we've seen so many times before, have a tendency to spread like disease. Sometimes it's because there's some truth to them, but oftentimes it's just because of fear. The trouble is in figuring out where to draw that line. And that line kept moving as the sightings were reported outside the British ranks. Pilots on the German side also reported seeing creatures during flights, as did some in India, Malta, and the Middle East.

Some might chalk these stories up to hallucinations, or maybe a bit of pre-flight drinking. There are certainly a lot of stories of World War II pilots climbing into the cockpit after a night of "romancing the bottle." And who could blame them? In many cases, these pilots had a 20 percent chance of never coming back alive.

But there are far too many reports to blame them *all* on drunkenness or delirium. Something unusual was happening to planes all throughout the war. And with folklore as a lens, some of the reports are downright eerie.

INVADERS

In 2014, a ninety-two-year-old World War II veteran from Jonesboro, Arkansas, came forward to tell a story he had kept to himself for seven decades. During the war he'd piloted a B-17, one of the legendary "Flying Fortresses" that helped Allied air forces carry out successful missions over Nazi territory. And it was on one of those missions that this man experienced something that he couldn't explain.

The pilot, who chose to identify himself with the initials L.W., spoke of how he was a twenty-two-year-old flight commander on the B-17 when something very strange happened on a combat mission in 1944. He described how, as he brought the aircraft to a higher altitude, the plane began to make strange noises. That wasn't completely unexpected, as the B-17 was an absolutely enormous plane and sometimes turbulence could rattle the airframe. But he checked the instrument panel out of habit.

According to his story, the instruments seemed broken and confused. Looking for an answer to the mystery, he glanced out the right-side window and then froze. There, outside the glass of the cockpit window, was the face of a small creature. The pilot described it as about three feet tall, with red eyes and sharp teeth. The ears, he said, were almost owl-like, and its skin was gray and hairless.

He looked back toward the front and noticed a second creature, this one moving along the nose of the aircraft. He said it was dancing and hammering away at the metal body of the plane. He immediately assumed he was hallucinating. I can picture him rubbing his eyes and blinking repeatedly, like in some old Looney Tunes cartoon. But according to him, he was as sharp and alert as ever.

Whatever it was that he witnessed outside on the body of the plane, he said that he managed to shake them off with a bit of "fancy flying"—his term, not mine. But while the creatures themselves might have vanished, the memory of them would haunt him for the rest of his life. He told only one person afterward, a gunner on another B-17, but rather than laugh at him, this friend acknowledged that he, too, had seen similar creatures on a flight just the day before.

Years prior, in the summer of 1939, an earlier encounter had been reported, this time in the Pacific. According to the account, a transport plane took off from the air base in San Diego in the middle of the afternoon and headed toward Hawaii. On board were thirteen marines, a mixture of crewmembers and passengers.

About halfway through the flight, while still over the vast expanse of the blue Pacific, the transport issued a distress signal.

After that, the signal stopped, as did all other forms of communication. It was as if the plane had simply gone silent and then vanished. Which made it all the more surprising when it reappeared later outside the San Diego airfield and prepared for landing.

But the landing didn't seem right. The plane came in too fast. It bounced on the runway in a rough, haphazard manner and then finally came to a dramatic emergency stop. Crew on the runway immediately understood why, too. The exterior of the aircraft was extensively damaged. Some said it looked like bombs had ripped apart the metal skin of the transport. It was a miracle, they said, that the thing even landed.

When no one exited the plane to greet them, the land crew opened it up and stepped inside, only to be met with a scene of horror and chaos. Inside, they discovered bodies everywhere. Each seemed to have died from the same types of wounds: large, vicious cuts and injuries that almost seemed to have originated from a wild animal.

Added to that, the interior of the transport smelled horribly of sulfur and the acrid odor of blood. To complicate matters, empty shell casings were found scattered about the interior of the cockpit. The pistols responsible, belonging to the pilot and co-pilot, were lying at their feet, their magazines emptied.

Twelve men were found dead, but there was a thirteenth. The co-pilot had managed to stay conscious, despite his extensive injuries, long enough to land the transport at the base. He was alive but unresponsive when they found him, and he was quickly removed for emergency medical care. Alas, the man died a short while later. He never had the chance to report what had happened.

BEYOND BELIEF

Stories of gremlins have stuck around in the decades since, but today they are mentioned more like a personified Murphy's Law, muttered as a humorous superstition by modern pilots. I get the feeling that the persistence of the folklore is due more to its place as a cultural habit than anything else.

We can ponder why, I suppose. Why would sightings stop after World War II? Some think it's because of advances in airplane technology—stronger structures, faster flight speeds, and higher altitudes. The assumption is that maybe gremlins could have held on to earlier planes, but the newer ones are so fast that it's become impossible for them to cling.

The other answer could just be that the world has left those childhood tales of little creatures behind. We've moved *beyond* belief now. We've outgrown it. We know a lot more than we used to, after all, and to our thoroughly modern minds these stories of gremlins just sound like so much fantasy.

Whatever reason you subscribe to, it's important to remember that many people—people we would respect—have believed with all their being that gremlins are real, factual creatures. In 1927, a pilot was over the Atlantic in a plane that, by today's standards, would be considered primitive. He was alone and had been in the air for a very long time, but was startled to discover that there were creatures in the cockpit with him.

He described them as small, vaporous beings with a strange, otherworldly appearance. The pilot claimed that these creatures spoke to him and kept him alert in a moment when he was overly tired and past the edge of exhaustion. They helped with the navigation on his journey, and even adjusted some of his equipment.

It was a rare account of gremlins who were benevolent, rather than meddlesome and hostile. Even still, this pilot was so worried about what the public might think of his experience that he kept the details to himself for more than twenty-five years.

In 1953, this pilot included the experience in a memoir of his flight. It was a historic journey, after all, and recording it properly required honesty and transparency. The book, you see, was called *The Spirit of St. Louis*. And the man was more than just a pilot. He was a military officer, an explorer, an inventor, and, on top of all that, a national hero because of his successful flight from New York to Paris. The first man to do so, in fact.

This man was Charles Lindbergh.

Doing Tricks

ON THE NORTHERN slope of a hill in southern England, near the village of Woolstone, is an artifact from another era. It's a drawing of an enormous horse, made at least three thousand years ago. Thanks to the white chalk that fills in the artwork, which is more than 350 feet long, it's been known for centuries as the White Horse of Uffington.

In April 2017, the National Trust in southern England announced that it had made a new, exciting discovery on the hill—a second chalk figure, nearly as large, that depicted another regional animal: the duck.

Now, I love Uffington. I've been there twice in the last decade, and it's one of my favorite places in all of England. So I felt compelled to read the full article, but when I did, I was surprised by what I found. While the article and accompanying video were published on March 31, they were promoted on social media the following day: April 1.

The duck, you see, was an April Fools' Day joke. Now, I'll admit I was more than a bit relieved. The White Horse is special, after all. But every year on the first of April, countless jokes are played out on the local and national level all around the world, taking our expectations and assumptions for a ride. Google might just be the biggest perpetrator of the last few years, spending what some think is millions of dollars to create fake product videos, elaborate prototypes, and full websites.

It's not a new thing, though. Humans have always been easily fooled by—and prone to create—trickery. Ancient mythology is full of characters known as tricksters, and modern media has added a plethora of new names to that list: the Joker from *Batman,* Q from *Star Trek,* even Bugs Bunny and Bart Simpson. And we love them all for it.

But it's not always fun and games. Many trickster legends are far darker than modern cartoons and movies. In fact, some of them are a lot more frightening than you'd think.

SHIFTING SHAPES

If you've come anywhere within ten feet of a comic-book-inspired movie in the past decade, you've probably been exposed to a number of modern spins on a very old idea. In fact, nearly all of the Marvel movies include one character lifted straight out of ancient mythology and brought to life by Tom Hiddleston: the Norse god Loki.

Loki does a great job of living up to the true definition of a trickster. Across the globe and the pages of history, nearly all ancient tricksters have stuck to the same small list of characteristics. They're morally ambiguous, bouncing between acts of good and evil with surprising flexibility. They have the power to create and destroy. They're often a messenger, bringing bad news or tragedy to a community. And they excel at taking any situation and flipping it on its head.

Writing about Loki nearly nine hundred years ago, Icelandic poet and historian Snorri Sturluson described him as being

> *handsome and fair of face, but [he] has an evil disposition, and is very changeable of mood. He excelled all men in the art of cunning, and he always cheats. He was continually involving the Aesir in great difficulties, and he often helped them out again by guile.*

But Loki isn't alone in the trickster space. Greek mythology has Hermes, who was—among other things—the god of thieves. West African folklore has the spider Anansi, although some stories tell of trickster rabbits as well. Many scholars think those are the roots of the more modern tales of Br'er Rabbit, a supposition that might very well be true. Folklore, as we've discussed so many times before, has a way of growing and adapting over the years.

We can see that evolution in European folklore. Those old ideas of tricksters who break the rules and make life difficult found fresh expression in new tales and legends. These stories are different but also the same, if you know what I mean. Because underneath all the cultural dress and decoration, every trickster is a shape-shifter, whether in practice or just metaphorically. Tricksters adapt and shift and change. Sometimes they're the ones doing the transformation, but oftentimes it's the status quo that gets reinvented. If there's a rule, whether social or moral or legal, the trickster is there to bend or break it.

In Europe, the concept of one single trickster god transformed into the idea of trickster creatures, plural. Their details vary from place to place, but most of their names are just as familiar to us now as Loki. Leprechauns, brownies, hobgoblins, pooka, elves, gnomes . . . each name conjures a unique picture in your mind, I'm sure, but for centuries they've all just been multiple expressions of the same trickster archetype.

These creatures are united by some common physical traits, too. Sure, they're troublesome and morally fluid, but they're also almost universally described as small humanoid beings. Dwarves, elves, tiny men and women—small enough to be overlooked or unseen by humans, but large enough to get into trouble.

Leprechauns are a great example. Their name literally means "small body," and while that's not a quality of the most ancient trickster ideas, it certainly lines up with most modern interpretations. And, of course, they're morally sketchy. One scholar describes them as "not wholly good nor wholly evil."

Second, trickster creatures were often described as red or black in color. Some stories say it's a skin color, others say it's fur, but the reasons behind the colors had to do with superstitions about evil powers. Black and red, for a very long time, were considered bad colors, so if you wanted to describe something as evil, of course it was black or red or both.

In Celtic folklore we have the pooka, who are viewed as dangerous bringers of bad luck. I mentioned them earlier, but in addition to being small, they're also usually described as covered in black fur. Oh, and they're shape-shifters, frequently transforming themselves into black horses—a fact that I'll need you to file away for later reference.

There are many more cultural variants, but I want to mention just one more: the *lutin*. These are a distinctly French version. Like the others, they're said to be small people—typically men—who are prone to mischief and prank-like fun. And like the pooka, they can shape-shift into animals.

But the *lutin* is unique in that it likes to take the form of a black cat, something most people recognize as having some element of power in various superstitions. And because of that, they are often seen as companions to witches and sorcerers, capable of cursing anyone who crosses their path. You know what? File that one away, too, okay?

The notion of tiny tricksters is clearly embedded in European folklore. They seem to pop up everywhere, from the works of Shakespeare to the Harry Potter stories and everywhere in between. All of them are small in size, are morally ambiguous, and need to be appeased to avoid negative consequences.

What's truly fascinating about folklore, though, is just how portable it is. You can take a person out of their culture, but it's much more difficult to take that culture out of them. So when Europeans began to settle in the New World, it's no surprise that they brought their superstitions and beliefs with them.

Many of those stories were meant to be entertaining. They were benign and harmless stories of morality. But three centuries ago, one settlement experienced something that shined a whole new light on the meaning—and power—of trickster mythology.

And what it revealed was beyond frightening.

FAIR WARNING

Antoine Laumet experienced the stereotypical meteoric rise that all of us dream about. He came to the New World at a time when New France extended the full length of the Mississippi River, from modern-day Canada to Louisiana in the south. At the beginning Antoine was nothing more than a fur trapper and explorer. He walked thousands of miles, spent far too many nights in the cold, and owned nothing more than what he was able to carry on his back.

But he was dependable and smart, and had a brilliant grasp of the French territories in the New World. That skill didn't go unnoticed, coming to the attention of not just the governor of New France but even the king himself, Louis XIV. Which is why by 1694, at the age of thirty-six, Laumet found himself in command of the French troops at Fort de Buade, in what is now northern Michigan.

By then he had bestowed upon himself a fancy new title and was known as Antoine Laumet de la Mothe, sieur de Cadillac, but since that takes me about fifteen minutes to pronounce, let's just stick with Antoine, shall we? Antoine, you see, was about to experience a significant boost to his reputation and power, and it's a journey we need to follow him on.

In 1701, Antoine was given permission to establish a new fort about three hundred miles south, on a patch of land situated on a narrow channel that connects Lake Erie and Lake St. Clair. The colonial minister had granted him fifteen square miles there to build the fort and settlement around it, and he was eager to get started.

On March 10 of that year, the governor of New France held a celebration for Antoine, to congratulate him on his new mission and title. The room was full of people with great power and position. There was food and drink, crystal and silver, and more ceremony than most of us will ever experience in our modern lives. And at the center of it all was Antoine.

Hours into the celebration, a door on the far side of the room swung open, and in stepped an old woman. She wasn't dressed in her finest. She didn't hold a title that matched the other guests. In fact, she was—in their eyes, at least—less than significant. But she walked in with more authority and poise than any of them could have mustered.

As she drew closer it became clear that she wasn't alone. There, upon her shoulder, sat something dark. It was a cat—a *black* cat. She told them her name was Mother Minique, and she was there to tell their fortunes. The men, cheerfully drunk out of their wits, welcomed the offer, and almost immediately all of them held their hands out to her, waiting to have their palms read.

She went down the table, hand by hand, describing in great detail the past of each person she touched. Every time she paused to examine a new one, the cat on her shoulder would lean in toward her head. Some thought it was licking her ear, but others swore it was whispering things to her.

Finally she came to Antoine, but before she could speak, he shook his head. "See what you can tell me about my future," he told her. "I care not for the past."

The woman nodded and took out a small metal bowl and a vial of thick silver liquid, almost like mercury. Then she poured the liquid into the bowl, took Antoine's hand again, and began to speak.

"Your future is strange," she told him. "You will soon go on a dangerous journey and found a great city. Someday that city will be home to more people than all of New France right now."

Antoine nodded with approval and asked her to continue, which she did . . . reluctantly.

"Your future is also dark," she continued. "It's cloudy, and your star is difficult to see. Your policies will cause trouble and bring about your ruin. The city you found will become home to war and bloodshed. The English will try to take it away. And then one day, many years from now, it will finally prosper under a flag we've never seen before."

And then she uttered one final warning: "Your name will be forgotten, even in the very city you've founded. But know this: you can change it all. Your future is still yours to decide. Just remember not to offend the one thing with the power to bring it all crashing down."

The woman paused, and everyone in the room seemed to pause with her, holding their breath to hear just what being had the ability to destroy the life of such a powerful man. When she spoke again, it was barely a whisper.

"Whatever you do, do not offend the *nain rouge*."

THREAT LEVEL RED

Even though the words themselves are French, there's no record in Europe of a creature by the name of *nain rouge*, the Red Dwarf. It seems to be a purely North American tale, although we could make the argument that the core elements of the legend borrow heavily from European folklore: dwarf-like, red coloring, easily upset. But hold on—I think I'm getting ahead of myself.

Let's just say this: by this point Antoine had lived in the territory of New France for a very long time, as had the others in the room that night. And none of them questioned the witch over that name. They were clearly very familiar with it, although how or why is still a mystery.

While the others might have felt the weight of significance at the mention of the *nain rouge*, Antoine seemed unfazed. He was confident in his future and continued his preparations for the journey south. He had a great city to found, after all. It's hard to fight the pull of destiny when it's so sweet and bright, like a siren song.

His expedition left in early June 1701 and arrived at their destination about six weeks later, on July 24. They called it Fort Pontchartrain, in honor of the French statesman. And things immediately took off. They built a friendly partnership with the local Native American tribes and set to work building all of the things an eighteenth-century military outpost would need: the tall fence of the stockade, a storehouse, a church, and—of course—the fort structure itself.

After that, life settled into a wonderful period of growth and prosperity for several years. The community was growing, and so was Antoine's reputation. He was gifted with a large plot of land by the Crown, and soon had a home built there.

Then in May 1707 the community held their annual celebration around the maypole. And it was that night that Antoine had a bizarre and frightening encounter.

He and his wife were walking back from the celebration to their new home, talking about their good fortune and bright future, when two other locals passed them. Antoine and his wife could overhear their conversation—they were essentially complaining about the wealth and position of Antoine and others, with their fine silver and nice clothing.

Then the stranger told his companion that his wife had recently seen "the little red man." Just as he was about to say more, they moved farther away, and the words were swept up into the wind. But Antoine's wife had heard enough, and pointed it out to her husband.

"The *nain rouge* is what the witch warned you about," she told him. But he shrugged it off. It was nonsense. Superstition. Nothing to be concerned about. No point in wasting time discussing it. So they walked on.

And that's when a small figure stepped out of the darkness and into the middle of their path. As it was later described, this figure was a dwarf, with a red face and shimmering eyes. When it saw them, the creature pulled its face into a wide, vicious grin, revealing sharp, animal-like teeth.

Antoine's wife stepped back and shouted out in fear. Her husband, though, moved forward. He swung his cane at the creature, striking it right in the head. "Get out of the way, you imp!"

As the cane connected with the creature's skull, the creature vanished into thin air. Even as it did, though, the shrill echo of its laughter could still be heard in the darkness. Antoine's wife, still shaking from the surprise of it all, turned and reminded her husband of the witch's warning.

"You offended him," she said. "You were supposed to appease him, but now you've made him angry. Your future—*our* future—is now at risk."

Again Antoine shrugged it off, but a few days later, after visiting Montreal, he was arrested as a result of a secret scheme by his political enemies, and quickly put on trial. Subsequently, he was forced to sell his claim to the new settlement. The rest of his life was a series of failures, and his wife never forgot why: Antoine had dared to cross the *nain rouge*.

I'd like to say that the curse ended there, but it didn't. In fact, it seems to have grown worse as the years have passed. In 1763, long after Antoine and his contemporaries had passed away, a battle was fought near the fort, at that point under British control. A group of Native American tribes, united under a leader named Pontiac, had gathered to lay siege to the fort, pinning the British down for months.

On July 31, two hundred and fifty British soldiers tried to strike at Pontiac's camp but failed horribly. Today it's known as the Battle of Bloody Run, and it comes with an interesting bit of legend attached to it. Multiple eyewitnesses claim that after the battle was over, a small red man was seen dancing on the sandy banks of the river. He was laughing as he lightly stepped over and around the piles of corpses.

Forty-two years later, in 1805, more tragedy struck the community. Fire broke out on June 11 in the building of a local baker, John Harvey. Within hours, the entire town was engulfed in flames, leveling it to the ground. They say all you could see afterward was a forest of chimneys where the buildings had once stood.

Now, large fires were common in those days, especially in cities built almost entirely of wood. But what set this fire apart from others was the multiple sightings of something incredibly odd in the days before it happened. Something that, without context, might not make sense at all.

There were sightings, people claimed, of a small red dwarf.

SYMBOLS AND CLUES

We all have plans. We have expectations and hopes and a picture in our minds of the way something is supposed to play out. Tricksters exist to shatter those plans. They are a tool of folklore to explain why things don't always go our way—why plans fail or tragedy befalls a community.

If things had gone according to Antoine's plans, the city he founded would bear his name to this day, Cadillac. Instead, he fell from grace, and the settlement took on a different name, the generic French word for a strait: Detroit.

Of course, he's not completely forgotten, though. When William Murphy and Henry Leland created their automotive company in 1902, they looked for a local name to lend the brand some class. So they called it Cadillac, and for a very long time they used Antoine's coat of arms as their company emblem.

Of course, it's easy to chalk all of this up to the power of folklore, to say that this legend was simply part of the superstitions of the French settlers who found themselves far from home in unfamiliar territory. Every immigrant brings stories with them on their journey, so why should this be any different? But as I said before, there's no mention in European folklore of a creature called the *nain rouge*.

The story is highly detailed and clearly rooted in something, though. So it should come as no surprise that the Native American tribes of the area around modern-day Michigan and southern Ontario have their own tales of a trickster god named Nanabush, described as red, small, and able to shift into other shapes. And I wouldn't be doing my job if I didn't point out how similar the name Nanabush sounds to *nain rouge*.

Detroit hasn't forgotten the little red trickster, though. In fact, he's more popular than ever. If you travel around the city, you can find local beer called Nain Rouge. There's also a wine that came out a couple of years ago. It is, of course, a red wine.

And then there's the parade that started in 2010. Each year, thousands of people dress up in costumes and march through the city. At the end of the route, they destroy a large effigy of the *nain rouge* as a way of banishing the evil from the city for another year. But maybe attacking him isn't the best of ideas. Time will tell.

One last note: Back in March 1976, a major storm hit Detroit. Several inches of ice coated trees and power lines, snapping limbs and knocking out power all over the city. A tornado was even sighted north of the city. It was one of those storms so devastating and powerful that even forty years later, people still speak about it with a bit of awe in their voices.

The day before the storm arrived, though, two utility workers were out inspecting a power line when they saw something odd. Something was climbing one of the nearby poles, and it looked an awful lot like a child, which wasn't good.

So they shouted and ran toward the pole to help the child down. As they did, the small shape reached the top and actually stood up on the tip of the pole. A moment later, it jumped off into the air and vanished from sight, but not before the workers got a better look.

It wasn't a child after all, but a tiny bearded man.

 BACK TO NATURE

Trees and Shadows

SOME OF THE things we see aren't what they appear to be. Heather Bowey and her cousins learned that lesson back in 1989. She was eleven at the time, and according to her mother, Karen, it was a bright winter day. The sort of day where the sun reflects off the snow, which always has a way of making dark objects like houses and trees stand out.

Heather and her cousins were walking along a small country road that ran between their town and the next when they saw a dog sitting in a stream near the roadside. Well, "stream" might be too strong a term. It was just a small bit of runoff, the sort that passes beneath roads through those big metal culverts, you know? It was a drainage ditch, basically.

But kids love dogs, so Heather and the others veered off the roadside and into the snow to walk toward it. They assumed it was a local pet that had wandered a bit too far from home, so they planned to check its collar and see what they could do. But even from a distance, it looked a bit odd. To be specific, it looked too *big* to be a dog.

They took one more step toward it, and then stopped. They stopped because that's when the dog turned to look at them. And as it did so, it did something they weren't expecting: it stood up on its hind legs like a human. Obviously frightened, the girls ran home as fast as they could.

Humans have always had a connection with animals. We live with them in our homes. We depend on them for food and resources. We identify with them, sometimes even treating them more like people than beasts. We speak to them, we name them, and we project human personalities onto them. For thousands of years, we've treated them as if they're more than animals. But of course, that's just our imagination.

If we believe the stories, though, it might be more true than we expected. As I said before, some things aren't what they appear to be. Sometimes they're *worse*.

A WORLDVIEW

Our connection to animals is nearly as old as humanity itself. We've almost always treated them as important parts of the world around us, although different cultures have expressed that importance in a variety of ways. The common thread, though, is that animals have always helped us to better understand our world.

Some cultures have revered them as gods. Others have seen them as valuable sacrifices to offer to whatever deity they wanted to please. In many cultures, animals have served as our companions through daily life; in others, they've journeyed with the dead into the afterlife.

Just think about what we know of ancient Egyptian culture. There were entire cults built around specific animals, such as bulls and cats. Their dead were frequently buried alongside animals that held personal or spiritual significance. And many of the Egyptian gods and goddesses were represented through simple animal symbolism. Anubis, for example, was part man and part jackal. Sekhmet was a woman with the head of a lion.

Ancient Hindu teachings, for thousands of years, have demanded deep respect for the animals around us. In China, the ancient philosophies of Confucianism and Taoism both stress the same thing. For the Hindus, that respect is founded on the idea of reincarnation. In China, it's rooted more in moral responsibility.

But the result is the same. Animals are, and always have been, important to us.

And yes, I know that ancient cultures focused a lot of their religion and practice on the sun and moon and stars, but they often framed those complex systems with simple animal-related language. That's why so many cultures have their own zodiac system, where the major constellations are represented by animals. The Greek root of the word "zodiac," by the way, literally means "circle of little animals."

(As an aside: the ancient Egyptian word for "cat" was *myw*, which sounds a lot like the noise that cats actually make. And that classic, stereotypical dog name, Fido? It comes from the Latin word *fidelis*, which means "faithful and loyal.")

It's easy to see, then, how animals have helped us understand our world a little better. They help us find our bearings and keep us company in a big, wild world. More significantly, though, they've helped us understand *ourselves* by giving humans a sense of identity and purpose—a theme or a banner to unite around, in a sense.

Sometimes those themes took the form of religion, as was the case in Egypt with the bull cult. Sometimes it's more of a totem thing, where an entire tribe or community builds their identity around a significant animal from their environment. Sometimes they did it for a feeling of safety; sometimes the animal was a symbol of power.

In Icelandic folklore, the Norse warrior class known as berserkers were members of the bear cult. *Berserker*, in Old Norse, literally meant "bear shirt," but it also embodied the fierce, powerful nature that they wanted for themselves as warriors. They were often depicted wearing bear skins, and sometimes even bear *heads* as head coverings. That's a tradition that still survives, by the way. You can see it in the ceremonial military caps worn by some personnel in multiple European countries.

The most common tribal animal, though, has always been the wolf. It's a global fascination seen in cultures in Mexico, the United States, Canada, India, Mongolia, and many countries of the Middle East. This is probably because wolves represented so much of what early humanity identified with: they move in packs, they hunt their food, and they have a distinct social hierarchy. Any hunter-gatherer community would instantly admire those qualities.

And like bears, wolves were also seen as brave and powerful warriors. Ancient Persian and Hittite warriors were known to dress in wolf skins for battle. Interestingly, though, they also had a reputation for tossing their weapons aside and just jumping on their enemies, literally biting them like animals. For a very long time, humans have wanted to *be* animals.

Which of course led to stories in which that was the case. Animals that became people, people who became animals—it's an idea so powerful that we can find it hiding inside the folklore of dozens of cultures. The Native American skin-walker. The *nagual* of Central America. And then, throughout much of Europe there's the werewolf.

They're all stories, of course. Artifacts from another time, when animals were gods and humans desperately wanted to imitate the divine. And yes, these stories also address our dual nature, because we are—in *many* ways—nothing more than animals ourselves, right? But those moral lessons have a way of distracting us from the plot: for thousands of years, people have told stories of mysterious beasts.

And, it turns out, those stories might be more real than we care to believe.

ROADKILL

In 1989, a woman was driving along the same country road that Heather Bowey and her cousins had just walked along weeks before when they'd sighted that strange creature. In Lorianne Endrizzi's case, it was well after sunset, so she was doing the responsible thing and scanning the road for wild animals. Wisconsin has plenty of deer, after all, and deer don't mix well with windshields and front ends.

Lorianne worked as a manager at one of the local bars in Elkhorn and had just wrapped up a very long, very tiring shift. All she really wanted to do was get home safely. But when she *did* notice something unusual, it wasn't in the periphery of her headlight beams; it was right on the road in front of her.

Seeing it early enough gave her the chance to slow down and swerve to avoid hitting it, but it also helped her get a good look at it. From a distance, it looked as if there was an animal hunched low to the pavement in the opposite lane. Its head was gently bobbing at an irregular rhythm, too. She couldn't tell for sure, but it almost seemed to be eating.

Then, as she slowly passed it, she claims she saw that it was eating, all right. Whatever it was, the creature was hunched over a pile of roadkill, pulling big chunks of flesh off a dead animal. Lorianne said she could clearly make out what appeared to be long, white fangs that protruded from a gray snout. Together with the pointed ears, she couldn't help but think of it as a wolf.

The trouble was, this wolf was kneeling on the road. Like a human.

It's one story, I know. And stories that are born in the middle of the night after an exhausting day of work are often full of flaws. That might very well be the case here. I think we've all had moments when we've seen things that don't make sense. So Lorianne's story could just be a bit of midnight confusion, I suppose . . . if it wasn't for the *other* stories.

Two years later—on Halloween night, in fact—it was Doris Gipson's turn. She was just eighteen at the time, and had been driving out to pick up a friend for some trick-or-treating back in town. Like Lorianne before her, she was driving that same stretch of country road, named for the old Bray family farm that it passed.

According to the story Doris later told to a local reporter, she'd briefly taken her eyes off the road to switch stations on the radio when she felt the car lurch. It was as if, she said, she'd run something over. Frightened by the possibility of what had just happened, she stopped her car, put it in park, and then got out for a look.

Doris, it seems, wasn't a big horror movie fan. Because anyone who knows anything about horror films knows that you never, *ever* get out of the car. *Ever.*

Still, there wasn't a scratch on her car. The bumper was spotless, with no sign of blood or fur or anything else that might hint at fresh roadkill. And even more convincing, there was nothing on the road. No dead animal, no unlucky farmer out for an evening walk. Not even a pothole. There was no clue anywhere that could explain the bump she'd felt.

She was about to turn and head back to her car when movement caught her attention. There was something in the trees and shadows along the roadside. According to her, it was a large figure that stood upright like a man but seemed hairy and very muscular. Which, as you might imagine, was a pretty shocking thing to see on a dark, lonely country road.

So Doris did the smart thing and bolted for her car door. As she did, the thing—whatever it was—chased after her. Doris said she could hear the heavy thud of the creature's feet on the pavement behind her and the sound of deep, panting breaths.

Thankfully, she managed to get into the car, and quickly shifted back into drive. But as she pulled away, she felt her car shudder once more. When she looked into her rearview mirror, all she could see was the dark silhouette of the creature filling her back window. It had jumped onto the trunk.

Whatever her attacker was, she claims that it fell off once she got her car moving quickly enough, but she wasn't willing to stop for another look. She *did,* however, continue on to her friend's house, and eventually they both headed back to town for some Halloween fun.

Later that night, on her way back along Bray Road to drop her friend off at home, Doris swears she saw the figure one more time. It was far off in the distance, at the edge of the light cast by her headlights, but it was the same unmistakable shape: tall, thick, and very animal-like, but standing upright on two legs.

It wasn't until the next day, in the safety of her own driveway and by the light of the noonday sun, that she took another look at the car. There, on the trunk, she found evidence that something very peculiar, and very *dangerous,* had taken place the night before: long, vicious scratches . . . all grouped together as if they were made by claws.

Claw Marks

This is the point in the story where you would probably expect me to clarify what the creature was. All of the physical descriptions certainly point toward the folklore regarding werewolves, but almost no one in Elkhorn made that connection.

Maybe that's because there were never any stories of humans transforming into the monster. Or perhaps it's because the sightings weren't limited to full moons. In the end, whatever it might have been, the people of the area took to calling it the Beast of Bray Road. But there were other theories, of course.

One common suggestion was rooted in the Native American folklore about a giant wolf known as the *shunka warakin,* which was described as sort of a hybrid between a wolf and a coyote. Others have made comparisons to the Inuit stories of the *amaroq* or the *waheela,* both of which were enormous, monstrous wolves. But honestly, there are far too many human characteristics attributed to the Bray Road creature to make the comparisons stick.

And that's without taking into account the additional sightings. Because Lorianne and Doris weren't the only ones to see something strange along that stretch of country road. And once they spoke to a local reporter, others found the courage to come forward with tales of their own.

Marvin Kirschnik was one of them. According to his testimony, he had his own encounter way back in 1981—a full decade before Doris Gipson's. Unlike the others, though, his sighting didn't happen in the dark. He'd been driving along Highway 11, which runs just northeast of Elkhorn, and as he approached the turnoff for Bray Road, he saw an unusual animal among the trees along the side of the road.

Kirschnik slowed down when he saw it, and then pulled over to get a better look. The way he described it, much of the creature was obscured by the underbrush, but it was clearly wolf-like. They stared at each other for a moment before the beast moved toward the car. Frightened, Kirschnik drove quickly away.

Five years later, in 1986, Diane Koenig was traveling in the same area, returning home after a day in nearby Burlington. From a distance, her headlights didn't give her a very clear view, so at first it just looked like a tall man was walking along the side of the road with something heavy in his arms.

As she drew closer, though, Koenig saw that this man had the head of a wolf. And the heavy burden it held in its arms turned out to be a full-sized deer. Unlike Kirschnik, though, Koenig didn't stop for a closer look, and instead sped up . . . just in case the creature decided to give chase. She kept the story to herself for years out of fear that she'd be considered a lunatic.

More stories flooded in. One unnamed girl told the authorities that she'd been chased up a tree by a wolf and had to stay there for over an hour while it paced around trying to find a way to climb up after her. What struck her as odd, though, was that the wolf walked on its hind legs. When she led her parents back to the tree the next day, they found large claw marks on the lower portion of its trunk.

Even Scott Bray, who lived on the family farm that gave the road its name, claimed to have seen extraordinary things, including enormous wolf tracks. Local animal control authorities were called to several homes in the area to examine and collect a large number of mutilated animal corpses. A few townsfolk tried to blame that one on satanic cults, but everyone else agreed it was the Beast of Bray Road.

There was a good amount of fear in town, as you might expect. But the sightings were also creating something else that's lasted to this day: a reputation. The bar where Lorianne Endrizzi worked eventually created a menu item called the Silver Bullet Special. A bakery in town started making wolf-shaped cookies. Think Roswell, New Mexico, and UFO collectibles, but with wolves, and you'll get the idea.

Even Chuck Coleman, a local state representative, got involved by using the Beast of Bray Road in his election campaign. He ran an ad that showed a man dressed up as the Beast casting his vote for Coleman. Perhaps proof of the popularity of the Bray Beast stories, Coleman won the election.

Doris Gipson's encounter also seems to have been the last sighting of the creature by travelers on Bray Road. After that, Elkhorn, Wisconsin, sort of became quiet. For a while, at least.

You see, in the spring of 1992, county animal control officer John Frederickson was called to a field outside of town, near Bray Road. This is a man who was used to the occasional roadkill or injured farm animal. He'd seen a lot in his career, but when he arrived at the field, he was well out of his depth.

Because there, lying in the pasture, were the bodies of five horses. Their throats had been slashed.

Trees and Shadows

We're drawn to animals. We always have been, and if the Internet's collection of cat videos and dog tricks tells us anything, it's that our passion for these animals isn't fading anytime soon. Perhaps they meet a deep, unspoken need in our soul, or maybe they just trigger the right pleasure center in our brains. Whatever the reason might be, animals are significant to us.

And every time I see someone dress up their dog in a sweater, I can't help but think of how, for a very long time, humans used to be the ones dressing up as animals. We envy their grace, their strength, and their power. And that envy has woven itself into the very fabric of global folklore.

But what if there's another reason we tell stories of animals that act human? What if, deep down, we fear the possibility? Or what if our ancestors told *just enough* stories about human-like animals that we wonder, just a little?

Whatever it was lurking in the trees and shadows of Elkhorn, Wisconsin, back in the 1980s and early 1990s remains a mystery to this day. No answers have been uncovered. No unexpected corpses have been found in the woods, or along the roadside. No nests or dens or whatever sort of dwelling a creature like the Beast of Bray Road might have lived in. All we have is story.

Sometimes all we *ever* have is story.

All of the witnesses who came forward to tell *their* stories seem to agree on the details. And, surprisingly, all of them appear to be telling the truth. When a documentary on the events was being produced in 2008, all of the witnesses agreed to take polygraph exams. And each of them passed. It's not irrefutable proof, but it's enough to make you wonder.

Sometime after the events of the early 1990s, a local who lived along Bray Road looked out his window to see a man standing in his driveway with a handgun. Obviously frightened by the sight of an armed stranger in his yard, he called the police, who quickly arrived. Jose Contreras was immediately arrested, and his handgun—along with fifty rounds of ammunition—was confiscated.

He eventually went to trial, and his lawyer attempted to build a case around self-defense. Contreras, he told the judge, was looking for the Beast of Bray Road, which he believed was a werewolf. That meant, according to his defense, he wasn't a danger to anyone else.

The judge, though, dismissed the notion and convicted Contreras anyway. His reason? None of the bullets in the gun had been silver.

Maybe it's fantasy. Maybe it's real. But it's amazing, at the very least, how parts of fantasy can become so accepted that they play a role in something as significant as a criminal trial.

Here's a final tale. One night in October 2010, six people were driving together down Bray Road. On the road ahead, they watched as a shadow seemed to move across their path. As they drew closer, they watched a shape run into the open field to their right.

What they say might seem hard to believe, so we'll have to take their word for it. They claimed it was an animal, covered in fur and similar in appearance to a wolf. Except it was running on two legs, not four. Once in the field, the beast dropped to all fours and ran off.

One detail sets this report apart from all the others, though. Because unlike every other encounter mentioned here, this one finds a way to make the Beast of Bray Road even more frightening. According to the witnesses, it wasn't a single creature.

There were *two* of them.

Off the Path

I'VE SPENT MOST of my life in the presence of troubled sports teams. Growing up in the Chicago area, I was always aware of how long the Cubs had gone without winning a World Series title. It was less a point of pain and more a numb spot in the collective conscience of everyone around me.

When I moved to Boston in the late 1990s, I discovered a similar culture, this time centered on the Red Sox. Again, here was a team that had spent decades waiting. Year after year, hope would be manufactured and piled high into the cart of expectations, only to have that cart dumped on its side at the end of each season.

Until 2004, that is. That was the year things changed. That was the year in which the tower of hopelessness and doubt—a tower that had taken eighty-six years to construct, brick by brick, year after year—came crashing down. Twelve years later, the Cubs experienced that very same change. The wait was over.

I don't plan to talk about baseball anymore here, but I *do* think the story of teams like the Cubs and the Red Sox have something valuable to teach us about how our minds work. Our ability to justify, to explain, to make sense of what seems so often to make no sense at all—that's what I find fascinating. Humans are so *very* good at finding reasons.

Lurking behind these seemingly endless droughts have been excuses. More specifically, the *curses*. How else are we to explain such droughts, such logic-defying gaps on their scorecards? Of course both of those teams had to be cursed, right?

But the Curse of the Bambino and the Curse of the Billy Goat weren't the first curses in history, and they were far from the last. And while some curses have been entertaining or even laughable, others have defied explanation long enough to make people wonder. Some, in fact, have even been deadly.

THE CURSE LESS TAKEN

The word "curse" comes from the Old English word *curs*. The original meaning isn't clear, but one of the uses of the Old English word is to denote a path or a route. I'm no etymologist, but I think the word picture is actually pretty clear: life is like a journey. Sometimes we walk along the path of our choosing, and sometimes we're pushed off and into the woods.

It's in those moments of chaos, of the unexpected and the unfortunate, that we feel like we've lost control. It's as if someone or something has knocked us off the path we were traveling. In those moments, it might be appropriate to say that we've been "cursed."

Curses as a concept, though, have been around since the beginning of humanity. In the earliest examples, a curse was a punishment handed out by a deity to misbehaving or devious human beings. The story of Adam and Eve in the Christian Bible is full of curses, doled out after their disobedience to God's instructions. Hard physical work, painful childbirth, and expulsion from paradise are all described as curses.

The Irish speak of curses as if they were birds. Once a curse is spoken aloud, they say, it can float around a place until it finds its target. If the intended receiver wasn't in the room, a curse could drift around for up to seven years. Not aimlessly, though; a curse is like a heat-seeking missile, waiting until the moment when the person arrives.

In Scandinavia, curses are like bullets. A person might utter a curse at an enemy, but the curse can be turned back or returned to the speaker, who then suffers the effects of the curse. Think Harry Potter–style wand duels, if you will.

The Moors of the Middle Ages had a very interesting tradition involving curses. It was said that if a man followed a prescribed set of rules and requirements, he was allowed to ask others to help him with something important. If, after jumping through all of the correct hoops, his request for help was still refused, a curse was said to descend upon those who refused him. Not a specific curse he made up, but a general, societal curse, as if tradition itself were punishing the unhelpful people.

According to legend, the Celtic people of Europe used curses in a powerful way. If a tenant farmer was fired and evicted from the land he had been hired to work, he would quickly go and gather stones from all over the property. Then he would put these stones in a lit fireplace, fall on his knees, and pray.

What did he pray for, exactly? Well, he prayed that for as long as the stones remained unburned, every possible curse would descend upon his landlord, the landlord's children, and all the generations after them. Then, rather than leave the stones in the fireplace where they could eventually become burned—thus ending the curses—he would gather them up and scatter them all around the countryside.

Curses have been there since the beginning, it seems. But over time, they have evolved to be more than just something you *do* to another person, as if they were weapons. Many of the stories that we tell on dark nights around campfires have more to do with the implications.

You see, sometimes the horrible tragedies of life refuse to be explained away without the mention of a deadly curse.

A Series of Unfortunate Events

When Prince Amedeo of Savoy told his father in 1867 that he planned to marry Maria Vittoria dal Pozzo, his father was enraged. Sure, she was of noble birth, but she was no princess, and she certainly wasn't worthy of the son of a king. He was said to have cursed their union.

On the morning of their wedding, Maria's dressmaker committed suicide. Maria took the hint and found a different dress to wear. Later, as the bridal party made their way to the palace church in a grand procession, one of the military leaders fell off his horse and died right there in the street.

The wedding procession continued on, though, and finally reached the palace gates—only to find them shut. A quick inspection revealed the reason: the gatekeeper was found in the gatehouse, lying in a pool of his own blood.

The death toll continued. Immediately after the wedding, the best man shot himself in the head. The wedding party headed to the train station—perhaps in an effort to outrun the curse—but when they arrived, the man who had drafted their marriage contract had a stroke and died on the spot. He was soon followed by the stationmaster, who somehow got pulled under the royal train and was crushed to death.

The king apparently saw a pattern and recalled the entire party to the palace. While they were leaving the train, though, one of the noblemen fell beneath the same train car. A medallion on his chest, most likely a gift from the king, was pushed through his skin, stabbing him in the heart.

Maria was the final victim of the curse, they say. She died in childbirth at the age of twenty-nine.

Here's another: Timur the Lame, or Tamerlane as he was known, was the great-great-grandson of Genghis Khan, taking the throne in 1369. He was a vicious Mongol warlord and was known for bloody military campaigns. He often built pyramids after his victories. Not with stone, mind you. No, he preferred to use the heads of the defeated army, sometimes tens of thousands of them.

He died in 1405, and I imagine more than a few people were elated at the news. He was buried in an area that we now know as Uzbekistan, and a large jade slab was placed over his tomb as a safeguard. The stone was inscribed with words of warning, though: "When I arise from the grave, the world will tremble." Some reports say that another message referred to a "great battle" that would be unleashed should his grave be disturbed.

You see where this is going, right?

In 1941, Joseph Stalin sent a team of Soviet archaeologists to look for Timur's tomb. When local Uzbek elders heard of the search and planned excavation, they spoke out in protest. They made reference to an old book that made it clear just how bad an idea it was to open the tomb. They spoke of a curse, but no one listened.

On June 21, 1941, the tomb of Tamerlane was opened and his skull was removed. The following day, Hitler's forces crossed into the Soviet Union, beginning the largest German military operation of World War II. If that war had a "great battle," this was it.

The body of Tamerlane was studied for over a year while the Soviet Union was torn apart and destroyed by Hitler's army. All told, the Soviet Union lost 26.6 million men and women to the invasion, more than any country in human history.

It's unclear why, but in November 1942 the Soviets decided to return Timur's body to the tomb, complete with a proper Islamic burial. Days later, the German invasion was repelled at Stalingrad, finally pushing the invaders back to the west and marking a turning point in the war—a turning point, some say, that was caused by the lifting of the curse.

A SAINTLY CURSE

The idea of the curse is common throughout folklore, and many popular stories use it as a plot device. The cursed spinning wheel of Sleeping Beauty, Snow White's cursed apple, and the cursed brothers of the Seven Ravens all come to mind. But there's another example in Irish tradition that tops them all, however obscure it might be.

There's an ancient Norse work called *The King's Mirror* that tells a fascinating story about St. Patrick. Patrick, of course, was known for his work spreading Christianity throughout Ireland in the fifth century, but he apparently did not always meet with success on his travels.

According to the account, St. Patrick once visited a clan that lived in a southern kingdom of Ireland called Ossory. Like any other visit, Patrick's mission was to bring his message of Christianity to the people there, but it appears that he struck out.

The King's Mirror goes on to describe how the people of the clan made every effort they could to insult both Patrick and the God he represented. Patrick, to his credit, carried on and tried his best. He preached the same message he always did, and followed the same protocol, meeting with the clan in their place of assembly. But the people there wouldn't hear him out.

Instead, they did something that might seem incredibly odd to our modern ears: they howled like wolves. It's not that they laughed at him and it happened to sound like howling. These people literally howled at St. Patrick.

Their reason was logical: the totem—or spirit animal—for this clan happened to be the wolf. To them, they were just responding to the message of an outside deity with the sounds of their own.

Now, this was pretty unheard of for St. Patrick. And the fact that this event was recorded in a Norse history book highlights just how remarkable it was. But even more unusual was Patrick's *response* to this stubborn, insulting clan.

Clearly upset, Patrick stopped speaking and began to pray. He asked God to punish the people of the village for their stubbornness. He wasn't specific, but he asked for some form of affliction that would be communal, that would carry on through the generations as a constant reminder of their disobedience.

According to the story, God actually listened. It was said that the people of Ossory were forever cursed to become the very thing they worshiped: wolves. And this curse followed a very specific set of rules.

Every seven years, one couple from the village of Ossory would be transformed into wolves. They would be stuck in this form day and night, year after year, until the next couple took over, transforming into wolves themselves and freeing the couple before them.

Part of the curse was said to be how the people of Ossory maintained their human minds while in the form of a wolf. But although they thought and spoke as humans, they were equally bound to the cravings of their new form—specifically, the craving for human flesh. In this way, the curse affected everyone, from the man and woman transformed to the people around them who lived in constant fear of being attacked.

Ever since that day, so the legend goes, the people of Ossory have been cursed.

ANSWERS AND QUESTIONS

There's media hype, and then there's grasping at straws. For some people, declaring someone or something to be cursed adds an air of mystery and drama. It's the sexy bit, and sex sells, right? For example, the Kennedy family story is sad and tragic, but when we add a dash of curse, we elevate it to near mythic proportions.

Other people, though, really do believe. Either they've experienced the sting of unexplainable misfortune or they've watched the lives of people around them crumble for no discernible reason. The human mind wants answers. It demands them. It seeks them out. People love stories, but only the ones with closure. That's what curses offer us.

At the end of the day, curses help us make sense of a thing, person, or place that seems to be haunted by misfortune. They act like a walking stick for people who are having a difficult time staying on the path. They prop us up and help us make sense of life.

I can imagine that life in sixth-century Ireland was incredibly difficult. And it would make sense that eventually someone would begin to tell stories that tried to explain the harshness of that life. Stories about a curse, perhaps. When someone failed to return from battle, or a hunting trip, or even travel between villages, it was hard to not have all the answers. Stories about attacks by local werewolves certainly did their part in explaining these disappearances. But they were just stories, right?

Gerald of Wales was a twelfth-century historian who recorded something interesting. He had been sent to Ireland by King Henry II to record the area's history. According to him, a local priest requested his company while he was there. This priest sat down and told Gerald an amazing tale.

According to the report, he had been traveling near the western border of County Meath, close to what would have been ancient Ossory, and had camped for the night in the woods. That night, with his fire burning low, someone approached from the darkness beyond the firelight and spoke to him.

Obviously, the priest was frightened, as he'd thought he was alone. But the voice of a man called out to him with great urgency. The man spoke of his wife, who was sick at home. He was worried, and wondered if this man of God might come and perform last rites for her.

Reluctantly, the priest agreed. He gathered up his belongings and followed the voice into the woods. They traveled a short distance until they came to a large, hollow tree. There the priest noticed two frightening things. First, there was something or someone lying inside the tree, presumably the sick wife. Second, though, he realized that the voice was coming not from a man at all, but from a wolf.

He was taken aback. How, he asked the wolf, was he able to speak like a man? The wolf's answer was simple: centuries before, his people had been cursed by a traveling priest, forever doomed to become wolves.

The priest prayed over the man's wife and tended to her illness. The couple was gone by morning, never to be seen again.

The Beast Within

ASK ANYONE IN the mental health profession about full moons, and you'll get a surprising answer, something that sounds incredibly like folklore and myth: the full moon has the power to bring out the crazy in many people.

We've believed this for a long time. We refer to unstable people as lunatics, a word that finds its roots in Latin. It's built from the root word *luna,* which means "moon." For centuries humans have operated under the conviction that certain phases in the lunar cycle can cause people to lose touch with reality.

Just ask the parents of a young child, and they'll tell you tales of wild behavior and out-of-the-ordinary disobedience during particular phases of the moon. Science tells us that, just as the moon's pull on the ocean creates tides that rise and fall in severity, so too does our planet's first satellite tug on the water inside our bodies, changing our behavior.

Today when we talk about the full moon, we tend to joke about this insane, extraordinary behavior. But maybe we joke to avoid the deeper truth, an idea that we are both frightened and embarrassed to entertain. For most of us, you see, the full moon conjures up an image that is altogether unnatural and unbelievable.

That large, glowing perfect circle in the night sky makes us think of just one thing: werewolves.

Science has tried to explain our obsession with the werewolf many times over the years. One theory is a disease called hypertrichosis, also sometimes known as wolfitis. It is a condition of excessive, unusual body hair growth, oftentimes covering a person's entire face. Think Michael J. Fox in *Teen Wolf*.

Psychologists actually had an official diagnosis in the the fourth edition of the *Diagnostic and Statistical Manual of Mental Disorders* called clinical lycanthropy. It's defined as a delusional syndrome in which the patient believes they can transform into an animal. Those changes take place only in their mind, of course.

But delusions have to start somewhere. Patients who believe they are Napoleon Bonaparte have some previous knowledge of who he was. I think it's fair to assume that those who suffer from clinical lycanthropy have heard of werewolves before. It's actually pretty easy to bump into the myth, thanks to modern popular culture. Werewolves have been featured in, or at least appeared in, close to a hundred Hollywood films since 1913.

One of the earliest mentions of something resembling the modern werewolf can be found in the two-thousand-year-old writings of the Roman poet Virgil. In his *Eclogue IX*, written in 40 BCE, he described a man named Moeris who could transform himself into a wolf using herbs and poisons.

About fifty years later, Gaius Petronius wrote a satirical novel called, appropriately, *Satyricon* (which I think is basically the equivalent of Stephen King writing a horror novel called *Frighticon*). In it, he tells the tale of a man named Niceros. In the story, Niceros was traveling with a friend when that friend suddenly took off his clothes, urinated in a circle, and transformed into a wolf before running off toward a large field of sheep.

The next day, Niceros is told by the owner of the sheep that one of the shepherds stabbed a wolf in the neck with a pitchfork. Later that day, Niceros noticed his friend had a similar wound on his own neck.

In the Greek myth of the god Zeus and an Arcadian king named

Lycaon, Zeus took on the form of a human traveler. At one point in his journey he visited Arcadia, and during his time in that country he visited their royal court. King Lycaon somehow recognized Zeus for who he truly was and tried, in true Greek form, of course, to kill him by serving him a meal of human flesh.

But Zeus was a smart guy, and he caught Lycaon in the act, throwing the mythological equivalent of a temper tantrum. He destroyed the palace, killed all fifty of the king's sons with lightning bolts, and then cursed King Lycaon himself.

The punishment? Lycaon would be doomed to spend the rest of his life as a wolf, presumably because wolves were known for attacking and eating humans. Most scholars believe that it is this legend that gives birth to the term *lycanthropy*: *lykos* being the Greek word for "wolf," and *anthropos* the word for "human."

INTERNATIONAL RENOWN

Werewolves aren't just a Greco-Roman thing, though. In the thirteenth century, the Norse recorded their mythological origins in something called the *Volsunga Saga*. Despite their culture being separated from the Greeks by thousands of miles and many centuries, there are tales of werewolves present there as well.

One of the stories in the *Volsunga Saga* involves a father-and-son pair, Sigmund and Sinfjotli. During their travels, the two men came upon a hut in the woods where they found two enchanted wolf skins. These skins had the power to change the wearer into a wolf, giving them all the characteristics that the beast was known for: power, speed, and cunning.

The catch, according to the saga, was that once put on, the wolf pelt could be taken off only every ten days. Undeterred, the father and son each put on one of the wolf skins and transformed into the beasts. They decided to split up and go hunting in their new forms, but they made an agreement that if either of them encountered a party of men over a certain number—and most translations say that number was seven—then they were supposed to howl for the other to come join them in the hunt.

Sigmund's son, however, broke his promise, killing off a hunting party of eleven men. When Sigmund discovered this, he fatally injured his son. Thankfully, the Norse god Odin intervened and healed the son, and both men took off the pelts and burned them.

So from the very beginning, werewolves were a supernatural thing. A curse. A change in the very nature of humanity. They were ruled by cycles of time and feared by those around them.

GOING CONTINENTAL

Things get interesting when we go to Germany, though. In 1582, the country of Germany was being pulled apart by a war between Catholics and Protestants, and one of the towns that played host to both sides was the small town of Bedburg. Keep in mind that in this era there were also still outbreaks of the Black Death, so this was an age of conflict and violence. People understood loss. They had become numb to it, and it would take something incredibly extraordinary to surprise them.

First there were cattle mutilations. Farmers from the area surrounding Bedburg would find dead cattle in their fields. It started off infrequently but grew to a daily occurrence, something that went on for many weeks. Cows that had been sent out to pasture were found torn apart. It was as if a wild animal had attacked them. Naturally, the farmers assumed it was wolves.

But it didn't stop there. Children began to go missing. Young women vanished from the main roads around Bedburg. In some cases their bodies were never found, but those that were had been mauled by something horribly violent. Finding your cattle disemboweled is one thing, but when it's your child or your wife, it can cause panic and fear. The community spiraled into hysteria.

When we think of historical European paranoia, we often think of witchcraft. The fifteenth and sixteenth centuries were filled with witch hunts, burnings, hangings, and an overwhelming hysteria that even spread across the Atlantic to the British colonies, where it destroyed more lives. The witch trials of Salem, Massachusetts, are the most famous example.

But at the same time, Europe was also on fire with fears of werewolves. Some historians think that in France alone, some thirty thousand people were accused of being werewolves, and some were even executed for it, either by hanging or by being burned at the stake. The fear of werewolves was real.

For the town of Bedburg, it was *very* real. One report from this event tells of two men and a woman who were traveling just outside the city walls. They heard a voice call out to them for help from the trees beside the road, and one of the men stepped into the trees to give assistance. When the man did not return, the second man entered the woods to find him, and he also did not return.

The woman caught on and attempted to run, but something exited the woods and attacked her. The bodies of the men were later found, mangled and torn apart, but the woman's never was. Later, villagers found severed limbs in the fields near Bedburg— limbs from the people who were missing. It was clear something horrible was hunting people in the area.

Another report tells of a group of children playing in a field near the cattle. As they played, something ran into the field and grabbed a small girl by the neck before trying to tear her throat out. But the high collar of her dress saved her life, and she managed to scream. Cows don't like screaming, apparently, and they began to stampede. Frightened by the cattle, the attacker let the girl go free and ran for the forest.

This was the last straw for the people of Bedburg. They took the hunt to the beast.

THE FACE OF THE MONSTER

According to a pamphlet from 1589, the men of the town hunted for the creature for days. Accompanied by dogs and armed for killing, these brave men ventured into the forest and finally found their quarry. Interestingly, though, they claimed that they had spotted a wolf, not a man, and quickly chased it down.

In the end it was their dogs that cornered the beast. Dogs are fast, and they beat the men to their prey. When the hunters did finally arrive, they found the creature cornered.

According to the pamphlet, the wolf transformed into a man right before their eyes. While the wolf had been just another beast, the man was someone they recognized. It was a wealthy, well-respected farmer from town named Peter Stubbe (whose name is sometimes recorded as Peter Stumpp).

Stubbe confessed all, and his story seemed to confirm their darkest fears. He told them that he had made a pact with the Devil at the age of twelve. The deal? In exchange for his soul, the Devil would give him a plethora of worldly pleasures. But like most stories, a greedy heart is difficult to satisfy.

Stubbe admitted to being a "wicked fiend with the desire for wrong and destruction," and he acknowledged that he was "inclined to blood and cruelty." To sate that thirst, the Devil had given him a magical belt of wolf skin. Putting it on, he claimed, would transform him into the monstrous shape of a wolf.

Sound familiar?

He told the men who had captured him that he had taken off that belt in the forest, and some were sent back to retrieve it, but it was never found. Still, superstition and fear drove them to torture and interrogate the man, who confessed to decades of horrible, unspeakable crimes.

Stubbe told his captors that he would often walk through Bedburg and wave to the families and friends of those he had killed. It delighted him that none of them suspected he was the killer. Sometimes he would use these walks to pick out future victims, planning how he would get them outside the city walls, where he could "ravish and cruelly murder them."

Stubbe admitted to going on killing sprees simply because he took pleasure in the bloodshed. He would kill lambs and goats and eat their raw flesh. He even claimed to have eaten unborn children ripped straight from their mother's wombs.

The human mind is always solving problems, even when we are asleep and unaware of it. The world is full of things that don't always sit right with us, and in our attempt to deal with life, we rationalize.

In more superstitious times, it was easy to lean on old fears and legends. The tuberculosis outbreaks of the 1800s led people to truly believe that the dead were sucking the life out of people. The stories that gave birth to the vampire mythology also provided people with a way to process the existence of a disease such as TB and its horrible symptoms.

Perhaps the story of the werewolf shows us that same phenomenon, but in reverse. Rather than creating stories that help explain the mysteries of death, perhaps we created the story of the werewolf to help justify the horrors of life and human nature.

The tale of Peter Stubbe sounds terrible, but when you hold it up to accounts of modern-day serial killers such as Jeffrey Dahmer or Richard Trenton Chase, it's par for the course. The difference between them and Stubbe is simply four hundred years of modernization. With the advent of electric lights pushing away the darkness, and global exploration exposing much of the world's fears as just myth, it has become more and more difficult to blame our flaws on monsters. The beast, it turns out, has been inside of us the whole time.

And Peter Stubbe? The people of Bedburg executed him for his crimes. On October 31, 1589—Halloween, mind you—he was given what was thought to be a fair and just punishment. He was strapped spread-eagle and naked to a large wooden wheel, and then his skin was peeled off with red-hot pincers. They then broke his arms and legs with the blunt end of an axe before finally turning the blade over and chopping off his head.

His body was burned at the stake in front of the entire town, and then his torture wheel was mounted on a tall pole, topped with a statue of a wolf. On top of that, they placed his severed head. Justice, or just one more example of the cruelty of mankind?

Perhaps in the end, we're all really monsters, aren't we?

Hunger Pains

ONE OF THE most chilling historical events of the last two hundred years—one that has fascinated me for most of my life—is the 1846 pioneer journey of the families and employees of James Reed and George Donner.

I can't think of a last name that evokes as much emotion, as much fear, and as much instant visual imagery as Donner. In the years since that fateful winter, that name has become synonymous with mountain passes, frozen bodies huddled around dead campfires, and of course cannibalism.

The Donner story has a way of stopping us in our tracks. We are morbidly fascinated with their tragic journey, but even more so, we're amazed at how far they went to stay alive. Their story forces us to look straight into the face of a fear that most people bury deep beneath the surface: people eating other people.

We can look for justification, we can research the reasons behind their situation and write sterile and safe papers about the horrible plight they found themselves in. But at the end of the day we are simply and powerfully horrified.

From the story of Hansel and Gretel to the modern television show *Hannibal,* we have always maintained a repulsive fascination with those who cross the line. We can't stand to think about it, and yet we can't look away, either. Maybe it has to do with the morbid symbolism of one body within another body. Perhaps it's the realization that, like cattle or wild game, humans can sometimes become food for something—or some*one*—else.

Or perhaps, deep down, we're fascinated with cannibalism because we believe maybe—just *maybe*—it could turn us into monsters.

A DEEP HUNGER

Humans have been confronted with cannibalism for a very long time. Archaeologists have discovered signs of the act that date back tens of thousands of years. In some instances the reasons have clearly been ritualistic, while other situations have been driven by food shortages. There's a lot we still don't know, but what we do understand has highlighted the fact that long ago it was far more common than it is today.

In the realm of ancient history, Greek and Roman historians recorded instances related to war and conquest. The Roman siege of Jerusalem in 70 CE, for example, resulted in scattered reports of cannibalism. Decades later, when the Romans attacked Numantia, historians in Alexandria recorded similar stories.

One interesting observation is that, over the centuries, the accusation of cannibalism has been a political and colonial tool. The ancient Greeks assumed that all non-Hellenistic peoples were barbarians and cannibals, and used that assumption to justify their hostility toward them. For many empires, even up through to the British Empire of the seventeenth and eighteenth centuries, it was a way to demonize a group of people and to grant themselves permission to come in and take over that group's territory. To bring the gift of civilization, so to speak.

But the assumption led to deep prejudice against these peoples. One example, from 1820, stands out. That was the year a whaling ship called the *Essex* was rammed and sunk by one of the whales it was pursuing. If that sounds familiar at all, it's because that story went on to inspire the novel *Moby-Dick*. After the accident, the captain and crew of twenty-one boarded three of their whaleboats.

They had two choices for a route to safety: sail three thousand miles against the wind to Chile, or half that distance *with* the wind to the Marquesas Islands. But the Marquesans were rumored to be cannibals, so they took the longer route. As a result, the crew spent months at sea, and eventually resorted to cannibalism to survive.

Reality can be cruel. And ironic, apparently.

But something darker sits at the center of many cannibalism stories. At the core of almost all Native American cultures across Canada and the northern portion of what is now the United States, there are stories of the supernatural effects that eating other humans can have on a person.

Each tribe seems to refer to the stories with different terms, but they are all eerily similar. Wabanaki legends speak of a man-eating snow giant, the *giwakwa*. The Cree tell tales of the *witiko*, also a giant and also a man-eater. The Micmac tribes of northern Maine up through Nova Scotia tell stories of the *chenoo*, creatures that once were human but were transformed through some horrible crime, usually cannibalism.

The most common name for these creatures among Native Americans, however, is one we already know from popular culture. This is the *wendigo*, a creature that was once human but was transformed by its hunger for human flesh into a monster that can't ever be satisfied.

One Native American description of the creature claims a *wendigo* is taller than a grown man, with a gaunt body and dead skin that seems to be pulled too tightly over its bones. Tales speak of the tangle of antlers upon its head, and the deep eye sockets that seemed to be dead inside. And it smelled of death and decay.

In Cree mythology, though, the *wendigo* was simply a human who had become possessed by an evil spirit. The spirit would take over a person—a neighbor, a friend, a sister, a son—and then turn its hunger and hatred toward the people around it. There was no hope for those who were transformed into man-eating creatures. Only one solution was available: these creatures must be hunted and killed. It's fantasy; it's a cultural meta-narrative about something else, something deeper. At least, that's what the anthropologists tell us.

But some have taken those legends at face value.

SWIFT AND HUNGRY

Swift Runner was a Native American from the Cree tribe who lived in the western portion of Canada. He was born in the early 1800s and worked as a hunter and trapper in the country north of Fort Edmonton, as well as a guide for the North-West Mounted Police.

He was a big man, standing over six feet tall, and according to the reports, he was well liked and respected among his people. He and his wife had six children. It was said that he was a loving father who cared deeply for his family. Which is why the winter of 1878 will be remembered as a tragedy.

According to the reports, Swift Runner stumbled into a Catholic mission in St. Albert sometime in the spring of 1879. He was distraught and unfocused. He told the priests there that the winter had been harsh and that his entire family had starved to death. He was, in fact, the only one to make it out alive.

But something didn't sit right with the priests. For one thing, Swift Runner didn't look like a man who had endured starvation throughout the winter months. He was a solid two hundred pounds and seemed healthy and strong. Another hint that all was not well were his nightmares, which often ended with him screaming.

In the end, the priests reached out to the Mounted Police. A group of investigators was dispatched to look into the matter, and they took Swift Runner back to his winter camp. To his credit, Swift Runner was helpful. He immediately showed the men a small grave near his campsite and explained that it was the grave of one of his boys.

They even went as far as to open the grave, and everything lined up with his story. They were the bones of a child, and it was safe to assume the child was Swift Runner's. But then the police discovered other clues that began to paint a darker picture. Around the camp in scattered locations, they began to uncover more bones. And a skull.

Not just a few, either. There were bones everywhere. Some of the larger bones were hollow and snapped in half, clearly the result of someone sucking the marrow out. They also found bits of flesh and hair. The evidence began to pile up, and they looked to Swift Runner for an explanation.

That's when he told them the truth. According to him, a *wendigo* spirit came to their camp during the winter. It spoke to him and told him to eat his family. At first he resisted, ignoring the voice, but slowly, over time, the *wendigo* took control. And then it took action.

Swift Runner's wife was the first to die. Then one of the younger boys. One by one, his family was killed and eaten. Then the creature moved on to his mother-in-law and his own brother. To Swift Runner, it was cold fact: a monster had eaten his family. The police agreed. What they disagreed on was the identity of the monster.

The mutilated human remains were collected and transported to Fort Saskatchewan, along with Swift Runner himself. His trial began on August 8, 1879, and it was about as cut-and-dried as it could be. Both the judge and jury refused to accept the story of the *wendigo*. They saw the man as a murderer and sentenced him to be hanged.

More than sixty people gathered at the fort on December 20 to watch the hanging. One witness to the execution, a man who had reportedly seen several hangings in his life, was said to have slapped his thigh and declared, "Boys, that was the prettiest hanging I ever seen."

THE HUNTERS

The Severn River in Ontario winds through the homeland of the Sandy Lake First Nation. This area of Canada is so isolated that it wasn't until the early decades of the twentieth century that the Western world really made the effort to reach out and connect with the people who lived there. It's way up in the far western corner of Ontario, in the kind of territory where lakes have islands that have their own lakes.

By the late 1800s, the Hudson Bay Company had closed down

enough of its trading posts that the closest one to Sandy Lake was more than 140 miles away. That was a fifty-hour walk across rough terrain. I'm not really sure that "isolated" is a strong enough word. This place was practically *alien*.

Jack Fiddler was born in the 1830s. Or maybe it was the 1840s—most people aren't sure. But we know he was a Cree Indian, and that he worked as a trader. He made the trek between the villages and the trading posts for a living, and in the process he met a lot of people. He was the son of the Sandy Lake people's shaman, and over his lifetime he had five wives and many, many children.

When Jack's father died in 1891, Jack took over as the leader of the Sandy Lake people. That sounds fancy, but in reality there were only about 120 people living in his community. He had influence on the wider geographical area, too, but his real power came from his role as tribal shaman.

A shaman's powers were a vital part of his leadership. When Jack became the spiritual leader of his people, he became the keeper of their ancient traditions and their guardian against the approaching darkness that was Western civilization. There are even legends that tell of Jack Fiddler curing illness.

But most important, Jack became their first and only defense against *wendigos*, often called on to hunt down and kill them. I know, this sounds like the stuff of comic books or Hollywood movies, but Jack Fiddler lives up to the hype. In fact, over his lifetime he claimed to have defeated fourteen of the monsters.

But Jack didn't go looking for a tall, monstrous creature with antlers and a bony body. No, he understood the *wendigo* to be more subtle. Some *wendigos*, Jack said, had been sent to attack his people by other shamans. Others had been members of his own tribe who seemed to have been overtaken by an unstoppable urge to eat human flesh. When it was his own people, Jack said that he and his brother Joseph were the ones called on to do the hard thing and kill the individuals.

But merely killing them wasn't enough to stop the possession. You see, it was believed that the *wendigo* spirit could actually hop from one body to the next, so those who died as a result of their possession were often burned to stop the infection from spreading.

For the Sandy Lake people, and many of the other Native American tribes that cover much of the northern half of North America, the *wendigo* stories were more than hearsay. It was an idea that was rooted in ancient tradition. Ceremonies were built around the legend. People were warned and educated constantly about the dangers this creature posed to the community.

And then, suddenly, all of that tradition and history ran headlong into the modern world, and the results were disastrous.

Sometime in 1905, Joseph Fiddler's daughter-in-law was brought to Jack's village. She was very sick, according to multiple firsthand accounts. She was in severe pain that drove her to cry out and moan constantly. Some of the women tending to her would even have to hold her down to keep her under control.

Jack and his brother Joseph were brought in. They were old men by then, both in their eighties and very frail, but they knew what was causing her illness. And they knew how to stop it. They had done this many times before. So they did what they did best: they took a thin rope, looped it around her neck, and then—slowly—tightened it.

It wasn't done in cold blood; it was a calculated decision that these men came to only after deep discussion. But it *was* driven by fear. If the *wendigo* spirit inside her had been allowed to take control, there was no telling how destructive it might have become. To them, this was preventive. It was mercy. A form of euthanasia that protected the entire community. The Fiddlers were mere instruments in the hands of a culture driven by superstition.

Witnesses testified to their quiet, dignified nature, but it didn't help. The men were brought before a six-person jury later that year. The Toronto newspapers printed sensational headlines about the trial, inveighing against devil worship and murder, and in response people around the country clamored for a conviction.

And the Fiddler brothers *were* guilty, without question. These men had killed a member of their family. It might not have been a crime of passion, but they were still murderers. So when the verdict came down, it was far from a surprise: guilty.

The Cree people of Sandy Lake lost their leader. They lost two of the most respected elders of their tiny community. And, most frightening to them, they lost their last remaining *wendigo* hunt-ers. Real or not, these men had been a wall that kept the darkness and fear at bay.

And now that wall was gone.

What We Really Fear

Superstition has often served to answer our questions and calm our fears. From the changelings of Ireland to the vampires of New England, the stories we tell have helped us explain the mys-teries we don't understand. That's not all superstition does, I know, but it makes up a lot of the examples we find. We fear the unknown, and we'll come up with something to explain it away.

Cannibalism is something that humans have feared for a very, very long time. Not because we're convinced that it could change us into supernatural monsters. No, at the root of it all, cannibalism is just a line that we don't think we should cross. And rightly so.

History is littered with examples of people who have crossed the line. It wasn't because their life was at risk, or because they had no choice, but because of something darker: deep belief in the folklore of their upbringing, mental instability, premeditated vio-lence. Whatever the reason, every example reveals humans to be the true monsters, capable of anything. Even the things we fear the most.

Maybe Jack Fiddler understood this. Perhaps he knew that he represented the final entry in a vital, ancient lineage. He saw a world ill-equipped to defend itself against the evils he had fought all his life. I have to imagine that the idea of it exhausted him.

On September 30, 1907, while on a walk outside with a police constable, Jack escaped into the woods, where he strangled him-self with the sash he wore. His brother would later die in prison from tuberculosis.

More than a century later, on July 30, 2008, a man named Tim McLean was riding a Greyhound bus along the Trans-Canada Highway in Manitoba, when one of the other passengers attacked and killed him. The man, Vince Weiguang, did more than kill

McLean, though. He stabbed him, beheaded him, and then proceeded to cannibalize the body.

Was the killer just insane? Or did he perhaps meet an evil spirit there on his trip through *wendigo* country? That's a question that would be impossible to answer for certain, but the courts ruled in favor of insanity. In the end, he was committed to a high-security mental institution in Manitoba, but he stayed there for less than a decade. In May 2015, he was released back into society.

A Deep Fear

A T THE HEIGHT of the Cold War tension between the United States and the Soviet Union, the American navy was using audio technology to detect Soviet submarines. These high-powered underwater microphones could detect unusual sounds from hundreds, even thousands, of miles away, helping the military peer far into the depths of the ocean.

After the Cold War ended, the National Oceanic and Atmospheric Administration built on to that old microphone system with the hope of gaining a new understanding of the massive unexplored world beneath the ocean waves. They studied ambient sounds, geophysical noise, and bioacoustics—the sounds that ocean creatures make.

But in 1997, they encountered a sound that defied explanation: a very low-frequency, very *powerful* sound. So powerful that it was picked up by their microphone system from more than three thousand miles away. Oh, and H. P. Lovecraft fans might get a kick out of the location they pinpointed: it's roughly nine hundred miles from the location of the mythical island city of R'lyeh, where Cthulhu is imprisoned, waiting and dreaming.

It didn't help that, at the time, NOAA deemed this sound to be neither man-made nor geological. It seemed to be organic, with a signal that varied too much to be mechanical. Today, scientists lean toward another theory: that it's the sound of icebergs scraping the ocean floor. Maybe. Many people still wonder what "Bloop," as they called it, really was.

We wonder because there's something dark and mysterious about the ocean. Even after centuries of exploration, we've mapped only about 5 percent of the ocean floor. It's crazy, but we know more about the surface of Mars than we do about roughly 70 percent of our own planet. There's so much darkness, so much that's unknown, that it leaves us feeling a bit uneasy.

We fear the unknown because it's full of questions. Questions are risky. They're dangerous. They prevent us from settling in and feeling comfortable. And the ocean is full of questions.

But according to some, there's a very good reason to be afraid.

ANCIENT DEPTHS

One of the endearing features of many early European maps is the inclusion of tiny little sketches sprinkled throughout the ocean—sketches of beastly green heads protruding from the waves, or long, lashing tails reaching out for a nearby vessel. You won't find them on navigational maps from the time, but they were a common feature of the decorative maps created for aristocratic homes. Those maps were, above all, entertainment.

But there were enough stories told by reputable people to give these decorative maps a bit of credibility. One example would be the map drawn around 1530 by Olaus Magnus. He was the Catholic archbishop of Sweden, along with being a well-respected historian in his day. So when his map of Norway showed the waters off the coast to be packed with sea monsters, people believed him.

In fact, when Conrad Gessner published the fourth volume of his *Historia Animalium* in 1558—sort of a collection of all known sea creatures—he included a number of sketches from Magnus's map. To him, and to a lot of other people, they were real.

It's not entirely their fault, though. Humans have been telling stories of the mysterious creatures of the ocean for a very long time. Almost twenty-four centuries ago, Aristotle wrote about a creature he called the *teuthos,* a gigantic, monstrous squid. Centuries later, right in Magnus's backyard, the Norwegians who lived near and traveled through the waters around Norway and Greenland spoke of the kraken. It's a name based on the Norwegian word krake, which refers to an unhealthy animal or a creature that's unnaturally twisted. It's a meaning that fits perfectly with the notion of mysterious sea monsters. And so for a long while, if it was mysterious and dangerous and beneath the waves, it was a kraken.

A lot of these old stories can be explained away with an understanding of just how little people really knew about the ocean in the fourteenth century. When a sailor landed on an island and found the decomposing corpse of a giant oarfish on the sand, he didn't say, "Hey, it's an oarfish." No, he framed the unusual sight through the lens of folklore. It was big and serpent-like, so, naturally, it was a sea serpent. Or a hydra. Or a kraken. You get the idea.

Of course, modern science has given us a better understanding of the ocean. We know more than Olaus Magnus ever did. We know that the giant squid is a very real, very large creature, although it's taken us a very long time to prove that. In fact, it wasn't photographed live in the water until 2004, and it took another two years before it was ever filmed.

The kraken isn't the only ancient sea creature to be debunked by science. On January 9, 1493, Columbus reported sighting something remarkable in the waters off the coast of Hispaniola: three mermaids. "They are not," he wrote, "as beautiful as they are painted, since in some ways they have a face like a man."

Folklore had always portrayed mermaids as part woman, part fish. For thousands of years, humans have been obsessed with the idea of human-fish hybrid creatures. The Babylonians, the Assyrians, and the ancient Greeks all told stories about them, as did cultures from Africa, China, India, and Europe. History, if you'll pardon the pun, is swimming with mermaids. Sailors, who were notoriously superstitious, tried to avoid them. They were viewed by some as bad omens, signs that tragedy was about to strike.

But the mermaids that Christopher Columbus sighted in 1493 were likely nothing more than a group of manatees, a large aquatic mammal that's fairly common near the coastlines around the Caribbean Sea and the Gulf of Mexico. They have fish-like tails, arm-like flippers, and—being mammals—pectoral mammary glands. From a distance, and viewed through a few feet of water, they tick all the boxes.

But not everything can be explained away so easily. Sometimes the stories are simply too numerous, too detailed, and too documented to be brushed aside. Some stories hold on tight long after others have caved in under scientific scrutiny. And no tale from the sea, at least in America, has held on longer than the one that began in New England nearly four hundred years ago.

If it's true, it's more than intriguing; it's downright chilling.

A Cold Wind

In the early days of British settlement of the New World, colonies were often approached as investment opportunities. Financial supporters in England would front the money to hire colonists, buy supplies, and launch the mission. You might think of it on the same level as a privately funded human mission to Mars. Except, for the early colonists, there was profit to be made.

In 1623, a private company was formed in Dorchester, England, with the goal of establishing a profitable colony in North America. Later that year, the expedition landed on the area north of Boston known as Cape Ann, and the colonists got to work. But life in this new land was tough, and within two years their funding was pulled.

Five years later, in 1628, new money and new settlers arrived. Things were looking up. Within two years, progress there was successful enough to warrant sending more colonists. In the decade between 1630 and 1640, more than ten thousand brave souls weathered the Atlantic crossing to start a new life on the northern coast of modern-day Massachusetts.

And more people means more observers. More eyes on this strange new land, full of indigenous people, strange animals, and unknown threats. Fear is a spark that's fanned by large crowds,

and in the right setting it can engulf a culture. And that's just what happened in Gloucester.

The first spark was recorded by John Josselyn, a traveler from England. Josselyn was a keen observer of the natural world and would later go on to publish his adventures in two separate books in the late 1600s. A few days after his ship entered port in the summer of 1648, one of the colonists told him a most extraordinary tale. A sea serpent, the man told him, had been seen on the rocks at the northern tip of Cape Ann. This gentleman described the serpent as an enormous snake, and claimed that it would slither up out of the waters of the Atlantic to coil up there on the rocks.

Other colonists had witnessed it as well. Once, he said, a boat was sailing near that area with four men aboard, two English settlers and two Native Americans. When the Englishmen saw the serpent moving through the water, one of them raised his musket to fire at it. But one of the Native Americans placed his hand on the barrel and gently told him to stop. It was too risky, he said. If the shot didn't instantly kill it, they would *all* be in danger.

In 1641, another man, Obadiah Turner, sighted the serpent in the vicinity of Gloucester. He described it as more than ninety feet long, with black eyes set into a horse-shaped head, and said that his report could be backed up by a number of other settlers. And he wasn't the last, either. For decades, rumors blew across the cold, harsh coastline like a stiff ocean wind.

That's how a lot of folklore works. There are a handful of experiences, and they give birth to a wider story. Story, as we all know, spreads like water. It flows and seeps and has a way of reaching through barriers. Given enough time, story—like water—will leave its mark and transform a place. And Gloucester was certainly being transformed.

One and a half centuries later, on August 6, 1817, two women were walking near the inner harbor of Gloucester when they saw something moving through the water, as if following the tide inland from the sea. They stopped to watch it for a moment before realizing exactly what it was they were looking at. It was a serpent. A monstrously *large* serpent, too large to be anything they might typically see in the waters there. Naturally, they were frightened, and they shared their story with others.

Four days later, on August 10, others had a similar experience. Susan Stover was walking with her father when both of them saw a creature in the water. They described the body as long and serpent-like and said that its head was long, like that of a dog or a horse.

That very same day, Lydia Wonson had her own sighting, except when she saw the serpent, it was coiled up at the water's edge. When it uncoiled itself, Wonson claims it was nearly seventy feet long.

More sightings followed. Local man Amos Story claimed to have watched the serpent for at least half an hour. He saw only portions of it as it moved through the waves, but his reaction was awe and fear. Henry Row, along with his sons, had multiple sightings that week. On August 12, Solomon Allen claimed that the monster actually circled his boat a few times. He described it in roughly the same terms—eighty feet long, head like a horse, black eyes. But he watched it for hours and never felt threatened. In fact, Allen described the creature as almost playful, something he never expected from such an otherworldly monster.

The summer of 1817 was filled with sightings of the Gloucester sea serpent. Every time the tide came in, it seemed, there was something new following it—more whispers, more fear, more first- and secondhand reports. For many tales, that would be enough. Whatever it was, it was already guaranteed a place in local lore.

But not this creature. The sea serpent of Gloucester, you see, was far from finished.

UP CLOSE AND PERSONAL

In the coming days, the culture in Gloucester would shift. For almost two hundred years, the people of the region had whispered about the creature. They warned their children to beware of the coast, to keep a watchful eye on the dark Atlantic waters just beyond their door.

But as the sightings piled up at an alarming rate, people were beginning to wonder if something else should be done besides just talk and worry. Maybe they needed to take action. Perhaps, some suggested, they should hunt it down.

It's a very human reaction. When we fail to understand something, we tend to attack it. If it's an unknown, it could be a threat—at least, that's our gut reaction to those moments. I'm not saying it's a *good* reaction, just the natural one. So the people of Gloucester can't be blamed for deciding to act. They were, after all, afraid for their safety.

The tipping point seems to have been on August 14. It holds the record for the largest number of sightings in a single day—not just in Gloucester, but in all of history. Seventeen, in fact. Seventeen sightings. Seventeen individual descriptions from independent reports. And when that many people have that many frightful experiences . . . well, it has a tendency to push a society over the edge.

On August 14, 1817, Matthew Gaffney decided to take matters into his own hands. He was the carpenter for a local fishing vessel, but that day he didn't go out with his crewmates. Instead, he stayed behind and took his own boat into the waters just south of Gloucester Harbor. He was joined by his brother and one of their friends.

It wasn't long before the three men found what they were looking for. Off in the distance they could see the dark, undulating shape of the sea monster, slipping in and out of the water. So they guided their boat closer for a better look—and, of course, a better shot.

As they approached, they could see the creature in more detail. Same horse-like head. Same dark eyes. It was apparently a dark green color mottled with brown, but white on the underbelly. Here it was, the beast that had been frightening the village. The monster that shouldn't exist. Here was the thing they had come to hunt. So Gaffney reached for his rifle and took aim.

He fired, and all three of them swore he hit the target—right in the head, in fact. But nothing happened. They saw no blood. The serpent didn't even flinch. Instead, it dove under the dark waves. And that's when they noticed that it was headed straight toward their boat.

Maybe that Native American had been right all along: if someone was to shoot it but not kill it, the creature would become an angry, deadly threat. Gaffney and the others braced themselves for an attack. But the attack never happened.

The serpent resurfaced on the other side of their boat and began to coil and uncoil in the water, moving erratically and stirring the ocean into a cauldron of foam. But it never approached them. In the end, Gaffney sailed home empty-handed.

What he didn't know was just how easy it could be to get close to the creature. In fact, two months later, two young boys would accomplish what Gaffney never could: they stood over the serpent's dead body.

Well, sort of. You see, in the late 1700s, there was a Swedish botanist named Carl Linnaeus. He's the person responsible for developing the scientific system for classifying living organisms, the same system we still use today. In the 1790s, Linnaean Societies were formed all across Europe and America with the goal of discovering and classifying new plants and animals.

So when two boys stumbled upon the dead body of a sea serpent on the rocky beach near Gloucester Harbor in October 1817, their parents called on the Linnaean Society of New England to help study it. What they found was a three-foot-long snake-like creature.

It was much smaller than the sightings had reported, but the reason was obvious to the Linnaean Society members standing over it: it was a baby. The full-grown serpent had entered Gloucester Harbor to lay its eggs, and this was one of the young that didn't survive. So the society members declared it a new, undiscovered species of snake and called it *Scoliophis atlanticus*—the Atlantic humped snake . . . for a while. A few days later, another naturalist, Alexandre Lesueur, studied the corpse and said it was nothing more than a common blacksnake. With no specimen left to study today, it's difficult to say who was correct.

And then things sort of slowed down in Gloucester. There were only twelve sightings in 1839, and that decreased to nine in 1875. It's not that the town itself was shrinking—to the contrary, Gloucester has grown a lot since then. But the sightings just sort of faded away.

In the first five decades of the twentieth century, the frequency of serpent sightings dropped to roughly one per year—a far cry from the golden days of the early 1800s. Whether or not that has been a disappointment to the people of Gloucester is unclear, but there's no more fear, no more worry, and no more cautious glances cast at the dark waters of the harbor.

If the Gloucester sea serpent was in fact a real, undiscovered sea creature, we will most likely never know. Whatever it was, it seems to have slithered out of reach, existing now only in the dark pages of history.

And, perhaps, the depths of the Gloucester Harbor.

DEEP FEARS

The ocean is deep and dark and full of mystery. That's the sort of space that invites fear and stories and superstition. For centuries, sailors have been considered some of the most superstitious people in the world. Their culture is full of bad omens, good omens, mythical creatures, and unique rituals.

It's most likely a side effect of their risky profession. On the open seas, your life hangs in the balance every moment of every day. An unexpected storm, a hidden reef, a concealing fog—anything can sneak up on a vessel and pull it down into the depths of those cold, black waters.

So it's no wonder that sailors have feared something darker, something more deadly than just the waves. Whether it's been the tentacles of the kraken, the call of the siren, or the coils of the sea serpent, the ocean's mythology is home to a dangerous aquatic menagerie.

Thankfully, science has pulled the veil back on a number of these tales. Sometimes, as in the case of mermaids, there really is nothing to fear. Other times, the tentacles are just as long as we might have imagined—but far less deadly. But there's so much about the ocean we still don't know. In many ways, it's the final undiscovered country.

Beneath the waters off the coast of Gloucester, there's a shelf in the ocean floor. It's like a plateau that skirts the mainland, where the water is shallower, maybe two hundred or so feet deep. Farther out to sea, the water depth is more than three thousand feet, which makes the waters of the shelf sort of a world of their own.

That shelf extends all the way up the east coast of North America. And it was on that shelf, in the waters of Fortune Bay on the southern side of Newfoundland, that something odd happened in May 1997.

Two fishermen from Little Bay East were in their boat when they saw something large in the water. At first they assumed it was a collection of garbage bags, floating free after having fallen off another ship, so they guided their own boat over to retrieve them.

When they got there, they quickly realized that the shapes weren't garbage bags. They were the humps of a long-necked creature. The skin color was lighter than the Gloucester serpent, sort of a medium gray, but the rest of the description sounds eerily familiar: forty or so feet long, large dark eyes, and a head that both men described as horse-like.

As they approached, the creature lifted its head above the water and looked at them. For a moment, no one moved, no one made a sound—neither the men nor the creature. And then, without warning, it quietly slipped back into the water, disappearing beneath the waves.

Our fear of the sea always seems to float just beneath the surface. And if the stories are true, it's not alone.

Lost Sheep

WEBSTER COUNTY, WEST Virginia, is down in the southeastern corner of the state, right near the Virginia state line. It's beautiful country, right by Shenandoah National Park and the northern tip of a patch of national forest that spans three states. I've driven through it, and I can tell you categorically that it's breathtaking.

But a century or more ago, I can also imagine it was harsh. Especially in the winter. It always is on the frontier, isn't it? One of those frontier towns was, and still is, Bergoo. It sits on the Elk River, one of countless little rivers that cut through the valleys between the countless little mountains that fill up the county.

Today there are just ninety-four people in town, and maybe half a dozen roads, but it's still there, holding on tight. Because it's a tough town, and it's been through a lot. Take the story of Daniel Junkins.

I don't know when he and his family moved onto the mountain by the river, but there was a whole little community there by the 1890s. Maybe he started his family there. He might have even died there decades later. That mountain was their world, their home, and just about all they ever knew.

The winter of 1894–95 was harsh. Again, this was more than a century ago. There were no snowblowers or plows. When it snowed, life sort of came to a standstill. And when it snowed hard for days in late January 1895, Daniel Junkins started to worry about his elderly neighbor, Mrs. Warnick.

On the first of February, Daniel sent his ten-year-old daughter, Landy, out into the snow to check in on Mrs. Warnick. It was a two-mile walk. Now, I'm not going to pick apart his parenting decisions or ponder why he didn't go himself. Two miles is a long walk for a ten-year-old, and in the snow it's even worse. But I think kids were made of tougher stuff back then. At any rate, he sent her.

But Landy never arrived. Of course, her family and neighbors went out looking for her, hoping to find her and bring her home. But all they managed to find was a solitary line of footprints in a smooth field of white. So they followed them.

The tracks went on for some distance, and then, in the middle of an open field, they simply stopped. There was no girl waiting at the end of the tracks, no body or any other clue about where she might have gone. They just . . . stopped.

The search continued, and they worked fast. Winter nights in West Virginia, especially in February, were bitter and deadly. They watched the sun set like a ticking clock and knew when they hadn't found her that their hope had vanished with the light.

They searched again the next day, and then another. But Landy Junkins was never seen again. Her tracks told a bizarre story: she was there one moment, walking and moving in the right direction. And then . . . gone. Vanished without a trace.

ONE OF THE FLOCK

A day or two later, Hanse Hardrick wrapped up his day by guiding his sheep into a small shed he had built to protect them from the cold winter winds. He made sure they had everything they needed, and then latched the door. That door, which faced the house, was the only way in or out.

The next morning, Hardrick went to check on the sheep. He unlocked the door, stepped inside, and then stopped. One of his animals was missing. The remaining sheep had all huddled into one of the corners, as if they were afraid of a predator.

Glancing around, Hardrick noticed that small pieces of wood and bark were scattered all around on the floor. Looking up, he discovered why. There was a large hole in the ceiling. Large enough, in fact, for a sheep to fit through.

The people of Webster County, West Virginia, did the math. They remembered poor little Landy and her mysterious disappearance. They pondered the lost sheep and the hole in the ceiling. Pretty soon they were convinced that something was hunting them from the sky. Little Landy and Mr. Hardrick's sheep were both proof of that.

So their village went on the defensive. Children were kept indoors to protect them. Farmers watched over their livestock with added vigilance. The whole community was in lockdown, with one eye on what was most valuable to them and the other on the sky.

Then, a few days after the sheep was stolen through the roof of the barn, the county sheriff and his grown son were making their way out of the forest after an unsuccessful hunt when they stepped into a clearing. Out there in the open, they saw two deer—a doe and her fawn—trying to fight off something enormous. The men couldn't see it clearly, but from where they stood, it looked like a giant bird, or at least something with huge wings.

Before they could rush toward the animals and try to help, the creature grabbed hold of the fawn and rose into the air with it. They watched as it flew higher and higher, heading straight toward the mountains east of town.

Most historians who have heard these tales have walked away with cold, logical answers. It was an eagle, and nothing more. But what eagle can pick up a ten-year-old child? Or a sheep? Or a fawn?

I get it. It's easy to say it was an eagle. They're predatory birds, and they're big. But these events suggest something else. And the fact that they happened less than a hundred miles from the Ohio River Valley, where there have been sightings of a winged creature that some people called Mothman and others compared to a giant owl . . . well, it makes you wonder.

Oh, and the mountain the Junkins family and their friends lived on? It had a name. For as long as anyone could remember, it had always been called Owls Head.

One Word

THERE'S A SCHOOL in Jefferson, Wisconsin, with a name that sounds like it was pulled right out of the pages of a comic book or dark urban fantasy novel: the St. Coletta School for Exceptional Children. It has a nice ring to it, right?

But St. Coletta wasn't home to a group of crime-fighting superheroes, or even a gathering of exceptional but peculiar students. It wasn't even a school, really. Its original name might hint at the true nature of the place: the St. Coletta Institute for Backward Youth.

It was, for all intents and purposes, a home for mentally disabled individuals. It opened its doors in 1904, and altered its name in 1931 to include the more poetic "Exceptional Children." Along the way, it played host to people from all walks of life. The most famous resident would probably be Rose Kennedy, sister of former president John F. Kennedy. She spent most of her life at St. Coletta after an unsuccessful lobotomy at the hands of Dr. Walter Freeman left her permanently disabled.

While there, she had a private house on the school grounds. St. Coletta had a lot of land—nearly 175 acres, in fact—and that allowed the school to spread out and meet the growing need for housing. But there were other things on the campus as well, things that the school did not build: Native American burial mounds.

Among the night guards in the mid-1930s was a man named

Mark Schackelman. Part of his job was to walk the campus, flashlight in hand, looking for signs of trouble. It was a quiet, peaceful job, most likely, although those Wisconsin winters must have been brutal.

One night in 1936, Mark was walking his usual patrol route through the property, which took him past a number of burial mounds. The beam of his flashlight bounced across the dark grass as he walked. Suddenly he stopped. Someone was kneeling on the ground at the base of one of the mounds.

And the person was digging.

He assumed it was a local, maybe out looking for trouble, or maybe seeing if the mound held anything of value. But when he focused the light directly on the person, he realized it wasn't a person at all. It was a *thing*.

Schackelman said it was roughly human-sized, but it was covered from head to toe in dark fur. And the way it was kneeling didn't seem human, either. But he didn't have a lot of time to study it, because when it noticed the light, it stood up and bolted into the night.

Mark didn't stick around to inspect the area. He raced back to the main campus building and clocked out for the night. But the next day, with the sun shining brightly overhead, he returned and gave the burial mound a second look. There were signs that the earth had been dug up. Huge gouges had been made in the lawn and soil. And in the dug-out areas, Mark could see something that resembled claw marks.

Now, Mark was a lot braver than I would have been in his shoes. He clocked back in that day, and when it came time to patrol the campus in the dark by himself, he did it. Crazy, isn't it?

I don't know if he expected it or hoped not to encounter it again, but when he reached the same spot he had the previous night, he found the creature back on its knees, digging in the ground. But rather than run away, it stood up and stared him down.

Mark got a better look this time. It was about as tall as he was, but the creature's chest was large and muscular. The arms had hands that looked like they had been crossed with the claws of an animal. Tall ears, fur all over, and oddly shaped legs. But the most surprising thing that happened that night was that this . . . *thing* . . . actually spoke to him.

It said only one word, and to be honest, I'm not sure Mark understood that it *was* a word for a very long time. But according to his notes and sworn testimony, it did indeed say something to him: "Gadara."

Mark spent the rest of his life keeping the events of that night a secret. Only his wife ever knew, and that doesn't sound like the behavior of someone who is making up stories to get attention or fame.

In 1958, when he thought he was dying from a terminal illness, Mark finally broke his silence and told his son about it. His son, it just so happens, was a reporter for a local newspaper, and he hoped that by sharing the story locally, others who had had similar experiences might come forward and share theirs.

As far as I can tell, no one did. Mark's experience seems to have occurred in isolation. But sharing the tale did have one added benefit: it gave a lot more people the chance to figure out just what that one little word might have meant, and why the creature Mark encountered might have felt the need to utter it: "Gadara."

Interestingly, people for centuries have viewed werewolves as demonic creatures, human beings possessed by evil spirits and then driven into a beast-like state. They were burned alongside accused witches all throughout the sixteenth and seventeenth centuries. Demons, after all, deserved to be destroyed, they believed.

There's a famous story of demon possession in the Christian Bible. The book of Mark tells of a man who told Jesus he was possessed by a demon called Legion. "Legion," he said, "because we are many."

The city where that happened isn't there anymore. It was the capital of a Roman province for a long time, and then it was destroyed in an earthquake in 747. I bring it up because that city's name has huge significance in the history of folklore surrounding demonic possession.

Its name?

Gadara.

 OUR OTHER HALVES

Unboxed

I F WE'VE LEARNED anything from centuries of exploration, it is that this world we live in is full of life. From the depths of the ocean to the rocky cliffs of our tallest mountains, living creatures have a way of adapting and thriving. In a lot of ways, we can't help but think of this planet as anything other than crowded.

At the same time, though, humans suffer from a disadvantage. We alone have evolved to become walking, talking builders of complex social structures. Only humans go to war, or devote themselves to religious faith, or build elaborate governments to contain our madness and free spirits. Humans are special.

It's this specialness, though, that leaves us isolated and alone. There's nothing else like us on the planet. No other creature can send rockets into space or genetically modify the plants they eat. This world may be overflowing with life, but humans are singular in our place upon it.

Which is why, I think, we tell so many stories of beings that are *almost* human, but not quite. Significant objects, mysterious beings, even otherworldly animals . . . it seems that the more they resemble us, the more frightening they become. The most terrifying stories, it seems, are the ones that suggest that we're not as alone as we assumed.

It's known as anthropomorphism. We give human characteristics to things that are far from human. One of the best places to see this practice in action is in the presence of children. The toys they cherish—the ones that follow them from room to room, or rest in their laps on long car rides, or get pulled under the covers with them at bedtime—take on a personality of their own.

Oftentimes it's just a game. Other times it's a coping mechanism for loss or fear. But sometimes, on very rare occasions, these objects seem to set the rules themselves. *They* pick their own personality. *They* guide the child's decisions. As if someone—or some*thing*—were controlling them.

Playthings

In 1982, a backhoe operator was preparing a building site for development in Titusville, Florida. While working on one of the ponds, he noticed what he thought were rocks visible in the mud. But something didn't sit right with him, and so he climbed out to take a closer look.

What he had thought to be stones actually turned out to be bones. Specifically, human bones. The county medical examiner was brought in, but it became clear almost immediately that the bones belonged to someone who had died a very long time ago. When Florida State University became involved, its researchers uncovered, so to speak, the truth.

The bones belonged to a three-year-old girl who had died more than seven thousand years before Florida became a state. It was clear that she had been buried by her parents, though. They had wrapped her in cloth made from local plant fibers and then placed her in a shallow grave. And she wasn't alone. With her in the ground, placed near her arms in case she wanted them, were toys.

It seems that children have had toys—objects that they loved and played with—for thousands of years. Perhaps tens of thousands. But for a very long time toys were still rare. In a world where everyone had to contribute to the well-being of the community, even the children were expected to grow up fast and do their part.

When they *did* have toys, they were often basic in shape, such as marbles or tops. They would also play with objects meant to represent the things most important to their village or clan: toy animals, soldiers, and religious icons are objects commonly found by archaeologists in ancient graves of children.

Interestingly, the ancient Greeks expected children to give up their toys when they came of age. On the night before their wedding young women would actually take their toys to the local temple, where they would offer them as a sacrifice to the gods.

In European societies, the notion of childhood began to shift after the advent of the Enlightenment in the mid-1600s. Societies became more affluent, and children weren't expected to work as early or as often as they had previously. In addition, their toys became more complex and useful. Jigsaw puzzles were born in 1767 as a way of teaching geography, and board games from the same period were meant to entertain. Toys had evolved.

But throughout all of history, it seems—across cultural boundaries and spanning thousands of years of art and technology— there has been one constant in the world of toys. From the tombs of the pharaohs in Egypt to the shelves of Target down the street, one toy has maintained a universal and timeless appeal: the doll.

Dolls are little representations of us, after all. They personify the people we love and provide comfort to the lonely in a way that no other toy can. And because of that, people get attached. Children refuse to put them down, and even in adulthood, dolls have a tendency to be kept around.

Sometimes, though, the roles are reversed. As unhealthy as it sounds, there have been more than a few stories of dolls—not children—who refuse to let go. They seem to take control, set the tone, and dominate the lives of the people who own them.

And sometimes the consequences have been frightening.

THE GIFT

Thomas and Minnie Otto were a well-off and well-traveled couple who had a deep love of the arts. They were natives of Key West, Florida, and in 1898 they built a brand-new home there on

Eaton Street. Two years after moving in, the couple welcomed their third child to the family, a son they named Robert Eugene, whom they called Gene.

The family quickly settled into the leisurely lifestyle of the Keys. They had more than enough money, and they spent it on convenience, which included a staff of caretakers around the house. Cooks and maids were always at the ready, including a woman from Jamaica who worked as little Gene's nurse.

History doesn't remember her name. If you were a woman in 1904, that was pretty common, unfortunately. If your skin color wasn't pale and your name wasn't European, those chances dropped even more. So we don't know her name. But we *do* know that she loved Gene. She spent hours with him every day. She traveled with the Ottos on their journeys around the country, caring for him like a turn-of-the-century version of an uptown Manhattan nanny. She was close to him.

That's probably why she gave him the doll. It was big—about the size of a four-year-old boy, in fact. It was filled with straw, hand-sewn, and dressed in a white sailor's uniform. And Gene *loved* it. He took it everywhere with him, on travels abroad and on day trips into town with his mother. It was said that Gene even sometimes wore a similar outfit, and the two seemed like siblings.

Gene called the doll Robert, using his own first name, and their relationship got off to a storybook start. The doll had its own chair near the dining room table, and Gene would sneak little pieces of food to it as the family ate. During bath times, the doll would be placed on a dry towel near the tub while Gene played in the water with toy boats and corks and all the usual things that little kids love to bring into the bathtub. And at the end of the night, Gene would bring Robert to bed with him, and the two of them would be tucked in together.

Everything about this is normal. My own children do similar things, naming their dolls and bringing them along for car rides. But for Gene, that's where the normality stopped, because not long after settling into a routine with his new toy, things got weird. According to most reports, it all started with the talking.

Gene's parents would often hear their son's voice coming from his bedroom as he played. Even though he was in there alone, it would always sound like he was deep in conversation with someone else. First they would hear his voice, sweet and tiny, and then another voice would reply, different and rougher than his own. Oftentimes the second voice would sound insistent, while Gene's would sound almost unnerved and flustered. Of course, Gene's parents assumed it was a game and that he was simply playing make-believe. But over time, they began to second-guess that presumption.

During a few of these apparent conversations, Gene's mother would quietly approach the boy's room and then, without warning, burst into the room. Inside she would find her son cowering in a corner of the room, arms wrapped around his knees, while Robert the doll sat on the bed or on a chair. She couldn't be sure, but it seemed to her like the doll was glaring at the boy.

Things escalated from there. The Ottos awoke on a number of occasions to the sound of Gene screaming in his bedroom. They would rush to his room only to find him sitting up in bed, furniture in the room overturned and belongings strewn about. According to Gene, Robert was to blame. Robert, the doll, would be glaring at him from the foot of the bed.

"Robert did it" became a common phrase around the Otto house after that. They didn't believe their son, of course, but the boy blamed the doll for most of the unusual activity. When his parents found toys that appeared to have been mutilated and broken, Gene said that Robert had done it.

Sometimes the Ottos could hear giggling from somewhere in the house. On occasion this happened at night, when Gene was supposed to be in bed. Dishes and silverware were often found thrown about the dining room. Clothing would be found on the floor, appearing to have been shredded by some unknown person. Sometimes servants would enter unused guest rooms, only to find that the bedding had been disturbed and pushed to the floor.

The staff would even find themselves locked out of the house when making their nightly rounds. If Gene was clearly not at fault, sometimes the servants themselves were blamed for the disturbances. As a result, turnover at the house was high, with a constant rotation of servants coming and going.

The one constant through all of this was Robert, the strange doll in the white suit. And some reports say that he did more than create a mess. He may have killed.

A Box of Trouble

Hearing giggles from distant parts of the house was one thing. Sure, it would unnerve most of us. I know it would freak me out. But the Ottos soldiered on, putting up with the repeated excuses. They were strict parents, maybe even a little overbearing by today's standards, and were always quick to punish Gene for the mischief. It was one thing to make a mess. But staff were hard to train, and having them frightened away all the time wasn't congruent with their life of convenience. And so they punished Gene.

To the boy's credit, he appeared to have been a true believer in his own stories. He would put up a short fight, blame the events on the doll, and then take the consequences like a responsible child.

But there were other reports about the doll, and these were things that could in no way be blamed on the boy. Visitors to the house reported that the doll would blink. Some of them claimed to have heard the laughter themselves, and at times when the Otto family wasn't home.

Neighbors said they would sometimes see the doll at the upstairs windows, moving from one to another, glancing out through the curtains toward the street. Servants would find Robert in a completely different part of the house from where he had been left moments before. Sometimes the sounds of little feet could be heard moving from room to room.

All of this became too much, and extended family stepped in to find a solution. One of Gene's great-aunts visited the family and pleaded her case. The doll was cursed, she said. Some evil spirit lived inside it, and if they wanted to be free of the chaos and random episodes of disturbance, they needed to get rid of it once and for all.

On her recommendation, Robert was taken away from Gene and placed inside a box. The box was then moved up to the attic of the large house, out of sight and—at least in theory—unable to cast his shadow of fear over the house anymore.

The next night, the aunt was found dead in her bedroom. She was an older woman, and so the official story—that she had died of a stroke—was passed around and believed by many. But the Ottos didn't buy it. Out of fear for their own safety, Robert was brought out of storage and returned to their son's side.

And that's how things remained. As all kids do, though, Gene grew up. He trained as a painter, traveled throughout Europe, and eventually married an accomplished pianist. But after his parents passed away, Gene and his wife moved back to Florida and took up residence in his old childhood home on Eaton Street.

Gene spent his days painting, and his wife, Anne, settled into domestic life. And somehow, in the middle of it all, was Robert. Rumors in town spoke of how the doll still had a place at the dining room table, that there was a chair beside their bed for him to sit on during the night, and that Gene had a habit of taking the doll with him as he moved about the house.

There were whispers that his wife, Anne, hated the doll. That she was unnerved by the presence of the doll so close to their marriage bed and stopped allowing Gene to bring it into the room. For a while he complied, and Robert was locked back in the attic. But according to reports, that didn't help.

Robert would sometimes be found sitting in a rocking chair downstairs, even though he was supposed to have been locked up. The couple would hear footsteps in the attic at night and the soft, distant sound of laughter. Local legend claims that all of this drove Gene's wife insane, eventually ending her life.

MATTERS OF POSSESSION

The study of folklore often encounters the same patterns throughout the world and across the centuries. One of the common themes that we can see is the dehumanization of people of minority status. The witch trials stand as a somber example of this, where the accused—often women, often poor, and often social outcasts already—were stripped of their humanity and treated like animals and monsters.

Robert the doll, though, stands on the opposite side. Rather than being one more tale of someone having their humanity stolen from them, Robert—a cloth-and-straw doll without a soul—appears to have had humanity bestowed upon him.

Why? It's hard to say. Perhaps it's because Gene Otto's parents needed an excuse for their son's atypical behavior. Maybe it was a culture of superstition brought into the house by servants with a different ethnic background. Somehow a living, breathing Robert was an easier story to swallow than the alternative.

We'll never know for sure whether Gene Otto invented it all. He passed away in 1974—with Robert at his side, some say.

For a while, the house remained uninhabited, unless you count Robert as a resident. But eventually a new family moved in and made the house on Eaton Street their own. They restored a lot of the original charm of the house, and in the process they found the doll. Maybe they were compelled to, or maybe they had heard about it from locals, but whatever their reason, the new family packed up the doll and moved it to the attic.

The family later donated Robert to a local museum, but it wasn't charity that motivated them; it was fear. You see, not long after moving in, they began to experience odd things. Things that Gene Otto would have known all too well: soft giggling, light footsteps in the attic, and random, unexplainable messes.

The family's ten-year-old daughter reported that the doll would appear in different parts of the house on its own, and that on a handful of occasions it even tried to attack her—a claim that she makes even now, as an adult.

But the final straw came later, when the girl's parents were awakened in the middle of the night. In the darkness of their room they could hear laughter and the sounds of movement. Alarmed, one of them flicked on a bedside lamp, only to feel their hearts stop.

There, at the foot of their bed, was Robert the doll, a kitchen knife in his hand.

Do Not Open

I N 1970, DONNA was twenty-eight and going to school to become a nurse. She lived in an apartment with her roommate and friend, Angie, and the pair did all the normal things that two college-age women would do: played host to friends, went out, and studied.

For her birthday that year, Donna's mother gave her something she'd found at the local thrift store. It was an oversized Raggedy Ann doll, perhaps two feet tall. It was certainly an odd gift for a mother to give to her adult daughter, but I've heard of worse. Regardless, Donna seemed to appreciate the thought.

Her roommate, Angie, had different feelings, though. Shortly after the doll moved in, Angie began to notice odd behavior. On several occasions, Angie stated, she would leave the room, only to return and find that the doll had shifted position. Sometimes its legs would be crossed, sometimes its arms. Sometimes both.

These instances increased in frequency over time. Soon both women were finding that the doll—which they had named Annabelle—had actually moved around the apartment. Donna would place the doll on the couch before going to work, and when Angie came home later, Annabelle would be on Donna's bed, with the bedroom door shut.

Let's be clear: this is the point where I would have purchased a bottle of lighter fluid and a metal trash can. I can't think of a birthday gift I *wouldn't* burn if it started doing things like this. But the women seemed to have put up with it. Maybe it was the sentiment; the doll was a gift, after all. Whatever their motivation, they kept it around, something they would later regret.

COMMUNICATIONS

That's when the messages started to appear. Donna and Angie would enter a room and find Annabelle sitting on the couch or a bed, and a scrap of old parchment would be nearby. Two things were odd about this: first, the women owned no parchment, so it was unclear where it had come from to begin with. And second, these scraps of paper had words written on them.

Not just words; these were notes. Usually written in red, in a faltering, almost childlike handwriting, these messages included the phrases "Help me" and "Help us."

The women brought in a spiritual medium, someone to help them communicate with what they assumed was a spirit inside the doll. Let's give Donna the benefit of the doubt. She was training to be a nurse, so she clearly felt a sense of duty to help people in need. Maybe, just maybe, these notes—these cries for help— somehow tugged at her heartstrings.

The medium told them a story that seemed to make sense. Annabelle was possessed by the spirit of a young girl who had died long before their apartment building had been built, and she was buried there beneath their feet. This spirit, according to the medium, liked the women, and she wanted to stay with them. Donna and Angie agreed.

Again, suspend your disbelief. Yes, most of us would have taken a blowtorch to the doll long before, but we were never in Donna's shoes. We can play armchair exorcist all we want, but we can't change their decisions.

The young women's permission might have opened the door for bigger problems. Hindsight is always 20/20, after all. They began to notice a thick red substance seeping from Annabelle's hands. But it was Angie's fiancé, Lou, who felt the true power of the spirit inhabiting the doll.

THE NIGHTMARE

The Old English word for demons and incubi is *mare,* which is where we get the modern term *nightmare.* A thousand years ago, a nightmare was what happened when a demon paralyzed you in your sleep, in order to haunt or torment you. Today, we call the condition sleep paralysis, but centuries ago it was believed that demons were the cause.

I mention this because, according to Lou, he had a nightmare. I don't want you to picture a grown man having a bad dream. I want you to picture him having an ancient, fear-filled, paralyzing nightmare. Literally, the stuff of legends.

When Lou awoke, he couldn't move. Naturally, he panicked, and he looked around the room for the cause of his inability to move. Nothing seemed out of the ordinary—not until he glanced toward his feet, that is.

According to Lou, there at his feet was Annabelle the doll. And as he watched, it slowly began to move up his legs, over his abdomen, and onto his chest. He claims the doll began to strangle him, but after a moment or two, he blacked out. When he awoke the next morning, his torso was covered in scratches.

MOVED

At the end of their collective rope, the women contacted Ed and Lorraine Warren, well-known paranormal researchers from the area. The Warrens arrived with a priest, and an exorcism was performed on the doll before removing it from the apartment.

The goal was to move Annabelle to the museum that the Warrens had started, a place where artifacts and tangible proof from their research could be seen by others. But even getting Annabelle there proved to be a challenge.

According to Ed Warren, the couple avoided the highway, anticipating a "rough ride," and at one point they had to stop and sprinkle the doll with holy water. They claim that their power steering and brakes failed to work for a portion of the trip as well.

In the end, Annabelle was placed in a special case in the Warrens' museum. The case has a number of locks on it to discourage visitors from trying to touch or hold the doll, and each of the locks has been soaked in holy water and blessed by a priest.

You can still visit and see Annabelle for yourself, if that's how you roll. Just be careful. The sign on the glass case holds a simple yet powerful message: "Warning: Do Not Open."

A Devil on the Roof

IN MARCH 2014, a hiker in Lithuania stumbled upon a warm
spring that was melting the ice on a frozen pond. It's not unusual to find things like this, but he was curious. I would be,
too: the pond was frozen over, but there was a nice window into
the still waters beneath. I have to think any one of us would have
leaned in for a closer look.

When he did, though, he witnessed something that his mind
had trouble processing. It appeared to be a living creature, but it
was unlike anything he had ever seen. Thankfully, we live in a
very connected, very digital age, and he used his phone to take a
short video.

I have no idea what the creature was, or if it even was a living
thing. And I'm not going to discuss it today, or tell you more stories about similar sightings, because there aren't any. It was a one-
off, a random occurrence that had never happened before and
probably would never happen again.

Some stories are like that. Sometimes we bump into something
new, with no history or record of events to lend it pedigree or
validity. Those stories frustrate me.

Other stories, though, go *deep*. Some legends have been told for
centuries. Some creatures have been sighted by hundreds of people over the years, and each new sighting lends credence to the
story. Even if it's all made up or just one big misunderstanding,

these layers upon layers of story seem to somehow give life to the creatures they describe.

When we find these deep wells of folklore, our minds are presented with a challenge: do the centuries of firsthand accounts serve as proof, or do they highlight our incredible, cross-cultural, nearly *genetic* predisposition to gullibility?

Few places challenge us to such a degree as the Pine Barrens of southern New Jersey. Inside that wooded expanse, mystery runs far and wide. Mystery and, some say, the Devil.

THE PINES

When we think of the East Coast of the United States, we think of urban sprawl, of endless strings of bedroom communities looping around massive metropolitan centers. New York City, Boston, Philadelphia, Washington, D.C.—all of these places are symbols of humanity's inability to leave an undeveloped area alone.

What most people don't know, however, is that there's a huge expanse of forested land cutting through the southern part of New Jersey that simply boggles the mind. It's called the Pine Barrens, and it's the largest undeveloped area of land in the Mid-Atlantic seaboard. Seriously, this place is massive: there are 1.1 million acres of forest, and beneath it all are underground aquifers that are estimated to contain more than seventeen trillion gallons of the purest drinking water in the country.

As you might imagine, such a massive area of untouched land comes with its own treasure chest of mythical creatures and frightening folklore. The local Lenape tribe of Native Americans tell stories about the *manetutetak,* or wood dwarves, who live in the forest—a local version of the global "little people" legend.

There are other creatures rumored to exist in the Pines, including Big Red Eye, the Hoboken Monkey-Man, undocumented species of large cats, the Cape May Sea Serpent, the Lizardman of Great Meadows, and even something called a Kim Kardashian.

New Jersey, you see, is full of monsters.

But hovering over them all, like a patriarch perched at the top of an ornate family tree, is something that has haunted the Pines for nearly three hundred years.

The original story goes something like this. in 1735, one Mrs. Shroud of Leeds Point, New Jersey, became pregnant with her thirteenth child. According to the legend, Mrs. Shroud secretly wished that this child would be a devil or demon child. Sure enough, when the child was born, it was misshapen and malformed.

Mrs. Shroud kept the deformed child in her home, sheltered from the curious eyes of the community. But on a dark and stormy night—because bad things only ever happen on dark and stormy nights, of course—the child's arms turned to wings, and it escaped, flying up and out through the chimney. Mrs. Shroud never saw her devil child again.

That's the story. Or one version of it, at least. A more prominent legend identifies the mother as Mrs. Leeds (not a Mrs. Shroud from Leeds Point), who was from Burlington, New Jersey. Mrs. Leeds, according to the legend, had dabbled in witchcraft despite her Quaker beliefs, and this hobby of hers made the old women attending her birth more than a little uneasy.

To their relief, though, a handsome baby boy was born that stormy night, and he was quickly delivered to Mrs. Leeds's arms. That was when he transformed: his human features vanished, his body elongated, and even his skin changed. The baby's head became horse-like, and hooves replaced his feet. Bat-like wings sprouted from his shoulders, and he grew to the size of a man.

Other origin stories have persisted through the centuries. One claimed that the monster was the result of a treasonous relationship between a colonial Leeds Point girl and a British soldier, while another story tells of a Gypsy curse. There seems to have been no town or county in the Pines area without its own version of the story, and many of them vary wildly. One thing unites them all, however: the descriptions of the creature.

In all the stories, it was some sort of hybrid or mutation of a normal animal. Most of the tales describe it in the same terms: head like a horse, wings like a bat, clawed hands, long serpent tail, and legs like a deer. In some accounts, the creature is almost dragon-like.

Coincidentally, the Lenape tribes refer to the Pines area as Popuessing, a word that means "the place of the dragon." Dutch explorers named the area Drakekill, *kill* being the Dutch word for "river," and *drake* meaning "dragon."

Whatever the truth is behind the origins of this legend, and whatever its core features really are, the people of the Pines were united in what they called it: the Jersey Devil. And this was more than just a story that was passed from person to person. Over the centuries that followed, countless eyewitness reports surfaced that pointed toward one overwhelming conclusion: the Jersey Devil was real.

GLIMPSES

What makes the Jersey Devil so special is the quality of many of the sightings. Individuals with no need to make up stories for political or professional reasons all seem to have found the courage to report incidents that would normally be laughable.

Stephen Decatur was a United States naval officer who was known for his many naval victories in the early 1800s. Decatur was, and still is today, a very well-respected figure in American history. There have been five warships named after him. He's had his own stamp through the U.S. Postal Service, and in the late 1800s it was *his* face that graced the $20 bill, rather than Andrew Jackson's.

According to the legend, Decatur visited the Hanover Iron Works in Burlington, New Jersey, in the early 1800s. The facility there manufactured cannonballs, something Decatur was very familiar with, and he had arrived to test some of the product.

On this occasion, Decatur was said to have been on the firing range operating a cannon. While there, he witnessed a strange creature flying overhead. It was unlike anything he had ever seen before, and like a true American, he aimed a cannon at it. He fired, and the shot was said to be true, striking the creature in midair. Mysteriously, though, nothing happened. The creature continued on uninterrupted.

Another early famous resident of New Jersey was Joseph Bonaparte, the brother of none other than Napoleon Bonaparte. Napoleon had appointed his brother king of Spain in 1808, but Joseph abdicated just five years later before moving to the United States. He took up residence in a large estate called Breeze Point near the Pine Barrens, and lived there for nearly two decades.

One of his favorite pastimes was to go hunting in the Pines. On one of those hunting trips, the former king of Spain was in the woods near his home when he discovered some strange tracks in the snow. They looked like the tracks of a donkey, but there were only two feet present, not four. Bonaparte commented that one of the feet appeared slightly larger than the other, as if deformed in some way. He followed the tracks into a clearing, but stopped when the prints vanished. It was as if the animal had simply taken flight.

As he was turning to leave, Bonaparte heard a strange hissing sound. He glanced back, only to find himself standing face-to-face with a large creature. He described it as having bat-like wings and the head of a horse, and it stood on thin hind legs. Before he could remember to use his rifle, the creature hissed one last time, flapped its wings, and flew off into the sky.

He later described the events to a local friend, who simply smiled and congratulated the man. "You've just seen the famous Jersey Devil," he told him.

The following decades were filled with more and more sightings and reports. In the early 1840s, a handful of farmers began to report the death of livestock on their land. In most cases, tracks were found, but they could not be identified. Others claimed to have heard high-pitched screams in the Pines, a sound that would forever after be connected with the Jersey Devil.

By 1900, belief in the Jersey Devil was widespread and stronger than ever. Nearly everyone in the area believed that something otherworldly lived inside the Pines, and anytime disaster or death entered their lives, they cast blame on this creature. But some had also begun to do the math: if this monster really *was* the child of Mrs. Shroud and was born in 1735, then it was very, very old. Folklorist Charles B. Skinner commented on this in a 1903 publication:

It is said that its life has nearly run its course, and with the advent of the new century many worshipful commoners of Jersey have dismissed, for good and all, the fear of the monster from their mind.

Skinner, you see, thought that it was gone, that the Jersey Devil was too old to carry on terrorizing the people of the Pines. But when the events of 1909 unfolded just six years later, one thing became very clear: Skinner couldn't have been more wrong.

1909

January 1909 was a busy month for the Jersey Devil. In the early-morning hours of January 16, a man named Thack Cozzens was out for a walk under the stars in Woodbury, New Jersey. A sound caught his attention and he glanced up, only to see a large dark shape fly past. Cozzens recalled noticing that the creature's eyes glowed bright red.

That same morning in the town of Bristol, Pennsylvania, twenty-six miles away, a number of people reported seeing a similar creature before dawn. One witness, a police officer named James Sackville, actually fired his handgun at it, without effect. E. W. Minster, the town postmaster, also saw the flying thing, and according to him, it unleashed a high-pitched scream.

When the sun rose that morning, several people reported finding strange hoofprints in the snow. No one could identify the kind of creature that would leave such tracks.

One day later, on the seventeenth, distinctive hoofprints were found in the snow outside the home of the Lowdens in Burlington, New Jersey. The tracks surrounded their trash can, which had been knocked over and rummaged through.

Other people found tracks on their rooftops. Trails were followed into the street, where the tracks would simply vanish. The Burlington police tried tracking the creature with the help of hunting dogs, but the dogs refused to follow the trails.

At two-thirty in the morning on Tuesday, January 19, a Mr. and Mrs. Evans were asleep in bed in Gloucester, New Jersey, when a scream awoke them. They both climbed out of bed and approached their window, then stopped, paralyzed by fear. There, on the roof of their shed, stood a creature unlike anything they had ever laid eyes on. According to Mr. Evans, it was roughly three feet tall and had the head of a horse. It walked on two legs and held smaller, claw-like hands against its chest. It had leathery wings and a long, serpentine tail.

The couple managed to frighten the creature away after watching it for nearly ten minutes. Later that day, professional hunters were called in to attempt to track the creature, but they had no success.

The following day brought more of the same. A Burlington police officer was the first to see the creature, followed by a local minister. A hunting party that was formed to track the beast claimed they watched it fly off toward Moorestown. In Moorestown, it was seen at the Mount Carmel Cemetery. From there it was seen to fly toward Riverside, and there, hoofprints were found in a cluster around a dead puppy.

A day later, an entire trolley full of passengers in Clementon watched a winged creature circle above them. The Black Hawk Social Club reported their own sighting, and when a Collingswood fireman saw one up close, he turned his hose on the creature, chasing it off.

Later that night, a woman named Mrs. Sorbinski in Camden heard a noise outside in the dark. She grabbed her broom and stepped outside, only to find the mysterious beast trying to catch her dog. Mrs. Sorbinski beat at the creature with her broom until it released the dog and flew away.

When a crowd gathered as a result of her screaming, they all claimed to see the creature off in the distance. The mob charged toward the thing, and a police officer even fired shots, but whatever it was managed to escape into the sky.

The creature made a few more random appearances across New Jersey during late January of that year, but it was one final sighting in February that leaves many questions to be answered.

An employee of a local electric railroad was out working on the tracks when he saw what he described later as the Jersey Devil flying overhead. He claimed to have watched the creature fly into one of the overhead electrical wires, generating an explosion large enough to melt the metal tracks directly underneath.

A search was made, but no body was found.

ALONE AND AFRAID

Maybe the stories of the Jersey Devil are really about fear. Fear of the unknown, fear of the dark, fear of what might be lurking out there in the trees. Humanity has feared those things for millennia. But perhaps the people of the Pines feared something more basic, more fundamental than whatever might be waiting for them in the darkness. Perhaps they simply feared being alone.

There is nothing worse than experiencing a loss you can't explain, or noises you can't identify, especially if you are in a new and strange place. The sources might very well be real and normal, but in the setting and culture of their day, the unexplainable served only to highlight the loneliness of the early settlers of New Jersey.

The Barrens had a way of giving permission to fear the unknown. They still do to this day. When settlers discovered rare or different-looking plants and animals inside those woods, it became easy to take it one step further: demon children, creatures dancing on rooftops, livestock and pets being attacked. We explain our existence with fantasy because sometimes that's the only thing that can help us cope.

In 1957, some employees from the New Jersey Department of Conservation found a partial animal corpse in the Pines. It was a mangled collection of feathers, mammal bones, and long hind legs that appeared to have been burned or scorched.

It might be logical to assume that the creature that flew into the electrical wires in 1909 had literally crashed and burned, only to be discovered decades later. It might, in fact, sound like the creature was gone for good.

But in 1987, an unidentified woman in Vineland, New Jersey, reported that her German shepherd had been killed during the night. The dog had been torn to pieces and dragged more than twenty-five feet from the end of its chain.

The only evidence the authorities could find around the body were hoofprints.

Over the Top

THE STREETS OF London were a place of fear in 1790. There had been dozens of attacks, all reported by women. A man, it seems, had been stepping out of the shadows or from around corners and pricking them with a pin.

Sometimes he was covert about it. There are reports that he fitted a bouquet of flowers with a sharp object and would ask women if they'd like to smell the blossoms. Who could resist? Others say he attached small blades to his knees and then used them to stab women in the back of the legs. And as the stories spread, so too did the panic. They called him the London Monster, and within weeks the entire city was on alert.

In the autumn of 1803, the people of London were obsessed with a new story. It seemed that a ghost had been seen in the Hammersmith area of the city. There were whispers that he was the victim of a suicide, doomed to haunt our world forever. And many people claimed to have seen him.

After months of hysteria and rumor, a police officer actually witnessed the ghost while on patrol. Francis Smith pulled his gun, called for the fiend to stop, and fired. His shot was true, and the ghost fell limp to the ground. It fell because it was, after all, just a man. Thomas Millwood had been a plasterer by trade, and because of this, he wore all-white clothing. Officer Smith was tried for murder and found guilty.

Few things can unite a city like fear. Hysteria spreads, in much the same way the plague moved across Europe in the seventeenth century. But that's not the unusual part. What's truly odd is the depths to which people will go to believe these fears. How easily they fall in with the public outcry and believe whatever it is they're told.

For as horrible as the London Monster and the Hammersmith Ghost stories sound, a new fear swept the city decades later. This fear permeated so deep, and spread so fast, that it left a mark still visible today. Fear, even when it's built on lies, can spread like fire.

But sometimes, on rare occasions, there's a very good reason to be afraid.

FROM THE SHADOWS

On a cool September night in 1837, Polly Adams was on her way home from the Green Man, a public house in the Blackheath area of London. She was with friends, and they talked and laughed as they walked toward Shooter's Hill. Nearly home, the group was startled when a figure seemed to jump out of the darkness of an alley.

Before anyone could react, the figure grabbed at Polly. According to her later deposition with the police, the stranger was clad in a black cloak, but his eyes seemed to burn with light. Oddly, she remembered that the man smelled of sulfur, and then she added—as if it were a normal thing to notice about a midnight attacker—that he also spat blue fire from his mouth.

Rather than help, Polly's three companions ran quickly away into the night, afraid for their lives. And rightly so. The attacker ripped through Polly's blouse with hands that seemed more like claws than anything else, but after tearing at the flesh of her stomach, the figure stopped. Pushing her to the ground, it turned and bounded away into the night.

One month after Polly Adams was attacked while walking home from the Green Man, Mary Stevens was making her way back to work after a short visit with her parents in nearby Battersea. Mary worked as a servant in a home on Lavender Hill, just south of the Thames, and decided to cut through Clapham Common. Maybe not the smartest decision, no matter what century you live in.

Yet Mary did just that, and set off on a quick walk through the dark trees and bushes toward her place of employment. Near the edge of the park, a figure jumped out of the shadows. The man grabbed her and pushed her to the ground, where he began to kiss her. Mary struggled, but the man's grip was beyond tight.

According to Mary, the stranger then ripped at her clothing with clawed hands that felt as "cold and clammy as those of a corpse." Afraid for her life, she screamed, forcing the attacker to release her and flee the scene. The screams brought several nearby residents to her aid, and a search was organized to locate the stranger, but no trace of him could be found.

The following evening, in the very same neighborhood where Mary Stevens lived, another dark figure was spotted. This time, rather than an assault, a mysterious person stepped out into the path of an oncoming carriage. The coachman, surprised by the appearance of the dark figure, lost control of the carriage before crashing into a building. The coachman was severely injured, and the mysterious man cried out with a ringing, high-pitched laugh that chilled witnesses to the core.

Then, as if his work were done, the man jumped over a nearby wall and escaped. The wall, mind you, was more than nine feet tall.

Three months later, the Lord Mayor of London, a man named Sir John Cowan, spoke up at a public session at the Mansion House about a complaint he had received in the form of a letter. This letter was anonymous, but the writer claimed to be a resident of Peckham, close to Battersea and the 1837 attacks. The letter described how the attacks had all been a prank put on by an unnamed aristocrat as part of a dare. Researchers have speculated for over a century as to who the nobleman might have been, but no theories have ever panned out.

Later, in January 1838, the mayor showed off a pile of letters he had received from people in and around London, all claiming to have witnessed, or been the victim of, attacks similar to what Polly Adams and Mary Stevens suffered.

Though the claims can't be proven, some letters reported that people actually died of fright, while others were permanently traumatized by their encounters with this mysterious figure. And many of the reports contained eerily similar pieces of information. This stranger was said to be able to leap over very tall fences and walls. He was always described as having red eyes and clawed hands. And he always got away.

Like a fever, the hysteria spread throughout London and the surrounding countryside. It didn't matter that the Lord Mayor was skeptical of the whole thing; people everywhere seemed to be catching glimpses of dark shapes leaping tall buildings and terrorizing their neighbors and servants.

Like any movement or public experience, the people of London went looking for a name. What would they call the creature— human or not—who was the center of all these stories? By late winter of 1838, they found it, a name that would forever become part of Victorian folklore.

They called him Spring-Heeled Jack.

CLOSE ENCOUNTERS

To this point, sightings of Spring-Heeled Jack had consisted of secondhand accounts and attacks on women with little power to demand attention. But in the winter of 1838, all of that changed.

On the night of February 28, Lucy and Margaret Scales set off from the home of their brother, who worked as a butcher on Narrow Street in the Limehouse district. History hasn't remembered their destination; all we know is that at about eight-thirty that night, the two young women walked off into the shadows, naively confident of their safety.

Minutes later, their brother the butcher heard screams off in the distance, in the direction of a street known as Green Dragon Alley. When he realized that the voice was that of his sister Margaret, he dashed off to find her. I like to imagine he still had on his bloody apron, and most likely picked up a meat cleaver before making the run.

When he found his sisters, Margaret was on her knees in the dark alley, Lucy's body cradled in her arms. The young woman wasn't dead, but she was unconscious, and Margaret was hysterical. As their brother helped the two women home, Margaret told him the story of what had happened.

They had stepped a few paces into the alley, when a dark figure stepped out of the shadows and approached them quickly. Lucy had been standing in front of her sister, just a few paces separating the two women. Because of this, it was Lucy who took the full brunt of the assault.

The figure, Margaret said, was that of a man. She described him as very tall and thin, dressed in the manner of a gentleman, and wrapped in a large dark cloak. He held a lantern known then as a bullseye, the small round type typically carried by officers of the law. And maybe that was why the women let him approach without becoming apprehensive.

That's when things took a turn for the worse. According to Margaret's report, which she later filed with the office of the police in Lambeth, the cloaked man stepped close to Lucy and spat blue flames at her face. The flames, she claimed, erupted from the man's mouth, and the sight of them blinded and shocked Lucy, who collapsed on the spot.

Margaret worried that she was next, but she had also been concerned for Lucy, who lay on the cobblestones, writhing in the throes of some kind of seizure. And then, as if his mission had been accomplished, the dark figure leapt over Margaret and onto the roof of a nearby house before vanishing into the London darkness.

Sometime during the same week, the shadowy figure of Spring-Heeled Jack made another appearance. Jane Alsop was reading a book around nine o'clock at night. She lived in one of the nicer neighborhoods in the East End of London, along with her father and two sisters. On the night in question, it was she who was closest to the front door, which is probably why she was the one who heard the shouting.

From across the small yard, a voice cried out in the darkness. There was a gate there that allowed access to the property and served as a small measure of security. But the voice belonged to someone professing to be a police officer. An officer, in fact, who claimed to have captured none other than Spring-Heeled Jack.

The man had called out for a light, and Jane—being a dutiful citizen—grabbed a lit candle and exited her home to deliver it to the officer. As she handed it to him, the man tossed off his cloak, exposing his true appearance by the light of the flickering flame. This was no police officer; what Jane saw took her breath away.

The figure was clothed in what appeared to be a tight-fitting one-piece suit of white fabric, along with a metal helmet. According to Jane, the man's eyes glowed red and were set within a face more hideous and frightening than any she had seen before. And then, without warning, the figure spat blue flames from his mouth.

This time, though, Jack wasn't content to stop there. With Jane partially blinded by the flash of bright flames, he reached out and grasped her with his arms. In the report that her family filed later that night at the same Lambeth police office where Lucy Scales had told her story, Jane recounted that the man, if that's what he really was, tore into her dress with fingers that felt to her like metal claws. He ripped through the fabric and then cut her skin, tearing deep, painful gashes in her abdomen. Jane screamed, perhaps from the pain, or maybe from her primal fear. And then she ran.

Her front door was just a few yards away and open, and so she bolted quickly for that sliver of light. She was mere steps from the doorway, a heartbeat from safety, when Jack caught up. His clawed hands grabbed at her neck and shoulder. Sharp, metallic fingers tore at Jane's young flesh. Patches of hair were pulled free from her scalp. Blood was everywhere.

Her family had heard her screams, though, and just as her attacker was slashing at her face, her father reached toward her from within the house. Two sets of arms, outstretched to touch the same target—one set to harm, the other to save.

Thankfully, it was Jane's father who won. Grabbing her by the arm, he pulled hard and brought her back inside, slamming the door shut behind her.

Near and Far

Many of the details surrounding Spring-Heeled Jack—details that were so out of the ordinary—seemed to be echoed in each new eyewitness account. The red eyes. The white bodysuit. The sharp claws. But something set Jane Alsop's story apart from all the others.

She was well-off. Not part of the elite, but high enough up the social ladder that her story caught the attention of the local newspapers as well as the police. And when upper-class people feel threatened, they take action.

When word spread that Jack was hunting women throughout London, the police began to arrest suspects, although none was ever brought to trial. Groups of vigilantes banded together and patrolled the city streets at night, both to assist the police in protecting the people of London and with the hope of capturing the mysterious attacker.

Upon reading about the attacks that had begun to plague the good people of London, one seventy-year-old retired military veteran actually dusted off his guns, pulled on his boots, and rode off in search of the monster responsible. Though he was never successful in capturing—or even setting eyes on—the mysterious Spring-Heeled Jack, the gesture did much to calm the nerves of the locals.

How could it not? He was, after all, the Duke of Wellington, the man who had fought Napoleon and won.

Needless to say, the stories began to spread. Several penny dreadfuls were written about the mysterious Jack, whose exploits were perfect for the cheap serialized fiction that the genre was built on. In theaters around London, several plays appeared that featured the subject. Even the Punch and Judy puppet shows across London found a way to incorporate this shadowy public menace. In shows that once had featured the Devil, performers changed his name to Spring-Heeled Jack.

There were a handful of additional sightings over the years to come. But while some of them were in the southwestern area of London, where the original attacks had occurred, and Surrey county beyond that, others popped up in some more distant locations.

One report, in Northamptonshire, described an encounter with a creature that was "the very image of the Devil himself, with horns and eyes of flame." In Devon, an investigation was mounted to find the man assaulting women in the area, and the suspect's description had some similarities to Spring-Heeled Jack.

Lincolnshire, on the eastern coast of England, was the location of another documented sighting in the 1870s. One witness described a caped figure who was seen leaping over cottages in a small village. When the locals grabbed their guns and tried to shoot the figure, they claimed they could hear their bullets strike him, but the only result was a metallic ringing sound. Jack got away.

One of the last encounters of note occurred in Aldershot, on the very edge of Surrey County. It was geographically closer to London than most of the 1870s sightings, and some researchers believe that this proximity to the original reports lend this story more validity.

On a night in August 1877, Private John Reagan was standing guard in a small booth near a military munitions depot. While inside, he claimed to hear something metallic being scraped along the wood of the booth. He stepped outside, rifle in hand, and patrolled the area to find the source.

When he was satisfied that nothing was there, he headed back to his station inside the booth. And that's when something touched him. Looking up, he saw the figure of a tall man, wrapped in a cloak and wearing a metal helmet. Then the figure leapt into the air and landed behind him.

Reagan pointed his weapon at the figure and called out for a name, but he claims the visitor, whoever it was, simply laughed.

The soldier fired, to no effect, and the figure advanced. Then, without warning, blue flames erupted from his mouth.

That's when Reagan did what any good soldier would do under the circumstances: he ran for his life.

Spring-Heeled Jack never left the public mind. But as the legend slowly settled into popular culture, reports of actual appearances became less and less frequent. And then, just as Jack had seemed to cross the threshold into mythic territory, he did what every eyewitness claimed he was gifted at: he disappeared.

A Leap of Faith

There's a lesson deep inside the story of Spring-Heeled Jack. Like all of the most powerful and devastating diseases of the last thousand years, ideas have a tendency to spread like fire. Today we use the term "viral," and in many ways, that's close to the truth. Fear, panic, and hysteria are all communicable diseases. And when a culture is infected, sometimes there's no way to stop it.

But unlike the plague or some new strain of the bird flu, it stands to reason that we could, at the very least, calm our fears and put out the fires of hysteria. So why is it so hard to do so? Spring-Heeled Jack is just one of countless examples that have been repeated all around the world throughout history. You would think we would have figured it out by now.

Maybe we actually like mass hysteria. Not the hysteria itself, mind you. What I mean is, what if there's something about being part of a larger story that resonates with people? It binds us together. It unites us in a global conversation. It builds community.

The big fears never really go away. Although Spring-Heeled Jack disappeared from the public eye in the last decade of the nineteenth century, some think he's still around. In 1995, a school in a small West Surrey village was closed by the town. The students and teachers wanted to mark the occasion, and so they put on a disco-themed celebration to say goodbye to one another and the school they loved.

That night, as the party was winding down, a handful of students ran back into the school, screaming about something they had seen outside. When asked by the teachers about it, these students all told the same story. They had all left the party earlier and had been hanging out near the playground. While there, a shadowy figure had approached them in the darkness. As the shape moved closer, they saw more details. The man wore black boots and a dark hooded cloak. But it was what they saw beneath the cloak that frightened them the most.

A one-piece suit of white cloth, and glowing red eyes.

Missing the Point

IN SEPTEMBER 1952, something bright flashed across the dark West Virginia sky and came to rest on a nearby farm. A trio of local boys saw it happen with their own eyes and ran home to report it. The mother of one of the boys agreed that it was worth looking into, so she gathered a group of older boys, and together they all walked over to find whatever it was that had fallen to earth.

When they arrived, they found what they described as a ball of fire, and the air was thick with a mist that burned their eyes and noses. When one of the boys noticed a pair of red lights in the shadows nearby, he turned his flashlight on it. There, they say, stood a dark figure with bright eyes and a pointed head. They couldn't see arms, but when it saw the light, it glided toward them and hissed. Naturally, they all ran away.

They claimed it was an extraterrestrial, protecting the ship it had just crash-landed. Keep in mind that this was 1952. The Roswell, New Mexico, incident had taken place just five years before, and many people were expecting it to happen again: a real-life UFO crash.

Later reports suggest something much less fantastical, though. On that very same night, a meteor had been sighted crossing the sky over Maryland, Pennsylvania, and—you guessed it—West Virginia. And that mysterious, armless, pointy-headed creature that flew toward them? Nothing more than a local owl.

Our world is full of things that are hard to explain—things that frighten us and cause us to doubt our safety. It might happen less and less often in this connected, modern culture of ours, but it's still part of our legacy. People have always seen things that are hard to believe.

Sometimes, though, people see what they *want* to see, rather than reality. The challenge lies in distinguishing between the two. Fact or fiction? Truth or lie? Figment of the imagination or something more? But when dozens of people manage to see the same strange thing, our clarity has a way of falling apart.

It's a Bird, It's a Plane

For as long as we've been looking up, humans have been seeing things they can't explain. And every time it's happened, those experiences get framed within whatever worldview or experience people had at the time. One of those common interpretations, for a very long time, was sky serpents.

The English county of Devon has played host to at least two sightings of a mysterious event that was recorded as a "twisting serpent" in the sky. In both 1388 and 1762, something long and glowing appeared in the English skies, remaining visible to multiple witnesses for more than six minutes.

In 1857, the crew of a steamboat on the Missouri River in Nebraska saw something similar. Witnesses later described it as resembling "a great undulating serpent, in and out of the lowering clouds, breathing fire." Sixteen years later, a number of farmers in the Texas town of Bonham saw something in the sky that defied all explanation. They said it was twisting and writhing like a snake, but enormous and yellow.

Witnesses seemed to come from all walks of life. In 1897, a Michigan paperboy named John Rosa stopped to chat with a local police officer while he was out at four in the morning on his delivery route. Both Rosa and the officer looked up and saw an enormous silvery serpent fly across the sky. Similar events have been recorded in Brazil, South Carolina, Maryland, and northern Europe, and those accounts span centuries. Clearly, something was going on.

But most of those sightings are easy to explain away with a bit of knowledge about how meteorological events work, and with a bit of an open mind. Comets, meteors, northern lights . . . all of these natural, regularly occurring events could explain the odd sightings people have claimed to be fiery snakes in the sky. As is so often the case, when we see what we want to, it prevents us from seeing everything else.

But other sightings are harder to explain. When they get closer to the earth and even stand on solid ground, our ability to filter the truth from the fantasy starts to break down. The mysterious creature witnessed multiple times in Cornwall, England, is a prime example of this, and to this day, it hasn't been easily explained away.

In April 1976, the Melling family from Lancaster was vacationing in Cornwall. On the twelfth of that month, Don Melling's two daughters—twelve-year-old June and nine-year-old Vicky—were exploring the woods near a church in Mawnan. While they were there, they reported seeing a strange, bird-like man in the air above the church. It frightened them so much that they convinced their parents to pack up and end their vacation early.

Nearly three months later, in early July of that year, more sightings were reported near Mawnan church. Again, two girls—this time Sally Chapman and Barbara Perry—heard a hissing sound in the night sky and looked up to see something unexplainable. They described it as a "big owl with pointed ears, as big as a man." They also added a new detail: red, glowing eyes. It was sighted again the following day by three other travelers, and it's been seen off and on for years ever since.

Back in the United States, similar creatures have been witnessed. In December 1975, two police officers in Texas saw something they would never be able to forget. One morning they were patroling the city of Harlingen when something flew over their car. According to their report, that something was a giant bird with a wingspan that measured more than ten feet across.

A few days later, a similar creature was sighted by two local teens. When they reported it to their parents, everyone headed out to have a look. All they found were a set of enormous tracks in the dirt—tracks made by large, three-toed feet. They made the evening news for that discovery, and then the community erupted in hysteria. Half a dozen more sightings were reported over the following month.

The officers in Harlingen later admitted that whatever it was they'd seen could have been a pelican. Maybe. They weren't sure, really. But others absolutely insisted it was an enormous bird of mysterious origins. Heck, one man claimed he was even attacked by it. That many sightings . . . well, it makes you wonder what was really going on.

And that's the trouble with all of these stories, isn't it? There are always loose ends. Bits and pieces that can't be explained away, no matter how expertly we apply logic to them. Which, of course, is why they're still told to this day.

It seems that these stories always have two sides: the passionate eyewitness and the cold voice of reason. And that's pretty much par for the course for humans. We often refuse to believe the things that others claim to have seen just because those stories drift outside the realm of accepted reality. Most of the details, along with the mystery itself, can be explained away with reasonable logic.

But sometimes there's more than one event, more than a handful of sightings, more detail or evidence than logic can explain away. Sometimes the reports are so strong that they become hard to ignore.

When the unexplainable becomes the believable, that's when things truly become horrifying.

SHADOWS AND LIGHT

When World War II ended in 1945, a number of military-related factories around the United States were closed up and either abandoned or converted into something more practical. The Gopher

Ordnance Works in Rosemount, Minnesota, for example, is now a concrete skeleton of what it once was. The Dodge Chicago plant was first transitioned into a shopping mall, and now a portion of it is used to manufacture candy.

About six miles north of the West Virginia town of Point Pleasant, a TNT plant and storage facility was built, but it shut its doors after the war ended. It was constructed on property that had originally been a game preserve. But rather than transition it back when they were done, the manufacturing facilities were simply left to rot, including the dozens of concrete igloos that had been used for storage.

Today it's used as a wildlife preserve, and homes have even been built nearby. Still, it's probably safe to say that after the war ended, the old TNT factory property didn't see much action. Not until the mid-1960s, at least, when something unusual began to take place.

On the night of November 15, 1966, a car entered the abandoned property. Inside were two young couples: Steve and Mary Malette, and Roger and Linda Scarberry. They were just out looking for some innocent fun, and that search had led them onto one of the dirt roads that cut through the old factory grounds.

The car was full of laughter, conversation, and the beat of the radio, but all of that came to an end when the very edge of their headlight beams illuminated something odd. Linda Scarberry later described it as an unnaturally large man-shaped figure. Most frightening, though, were the eyes, which glowed in the darkness with a red light.

Whatever they'd seen, the thing didn't appear to see them. At least, it didn't react to their presence. I have a hard time understanding how the bright headlights of a car could fail to catch the attention of anything close to sentient in the middle of a dark wildlife preserve, but according to all four of the witnesses, it just sort of waddled off away from the road at a slow, rambling pace.

The two couples didn't spend any time debating what they'd all seen. They didn't stop and get out to investigate. They were too afraid to do anything other than turn the car around and head back toward the exit of the preserve as quickly as they could. All they wanted to do was get away. But that wasn't going to be as easy as they thought.

A minute or two later, as they were winding their way back through the dirt roads that led to the exit, they saw it again. This time the four witnesses were able to get a better look at it. They described the same tall, human-like shape and red eyes, but said this time they were able to see something else: wings that stuck out from the center of the creature's back, they said, "like an angel." They weren't able to see any arms, and the head was sort of indistinguishable from the body, but all of that could have been a trick of shadows and light.

It was something that seemed like a cross between a giant bird and an enormous man. Which was, of course, impossible. But that didn't mean it wasn't frightening. And when the creature spread its wings and flew after them, they were downright horrified. So they sped up.

Roger Scarberry later told the police that he managed to coax his old Chevy up to a hundred miles an hour, but when they glanced behind the car, the flying thing was still there, still chasing them. And over the roar of the engine they could all hear a sound. A sort of high-pitched squeaking noise. All of it—the sight of the creature, the eerie noise, and the fast pursuit—gave them the incentive they needed to head back to town as quickly as they could.

It was only after the car had entered the city limits of Point Pleasant and was bathed in bright electric light that the bird or creature—*whatever* it had really been—finally gave up and turned around. It quickly vanished into the night.

The two young couples were understandably terrified by what they'd seen. But they were also unanimous on the details. Something large, something that could fly and scream at them, had chased them all the way from the wildlife preserve into town. So they decided to tell the police.

Roger turned the car toward the Mason County courthouse, and before long they were reporting the events to an officer inside. The deputy sheriff agreed to send a handful of officers out to the preserve immediately, and the young couples bravely went with them. Unfortunately, they found nothing definitive that proved the couples' story, though there were some tense moments. While searching the general area of the sighting, sounds could be heard in the darkness outside the glow of their flashlights. One of the officers even claimed he saw movement and a cloud of dust that could have been made by someone walking down a path, but whatever caused it remained hidden from view.

Most chilling of all, though, was when one of the officers saw what he described as a shadow in the night sky overhead. It seemed to be circling above one of the abandoned buildings, slow and deliberate, like a large bird.

Everyone got back in their cars, and they left as fast as they could.

FLEETING VISIONS

Oddly enough, the events of November 15 weren't the first of their kind in the area. They were just the first to be given anything close to a reasonable amount of attention by the authorities and the press. Sightings of something large and extraordinary had actually been occurring in the area for years.

According to historian and professor James Gay Jones, the first local sighting might have occurred in the early 1900s. In that tale, multiple families in the area witnessed a creature that they described as man-sized, with a wingspan of more than twelve feet. They claimed that this man-bird had no discernible head, something that sounds oddly similar to the thing the two young couples witnessed in 1966.

In 1961, two people from Point Pleasant were driving south of town along the Ohio River when they saw something step out into the road in front of them. They described it as a large man, but covered in gray fur, or maybe feathers, with wings protruding from its back. A moment later it launched itself into the air and flew away.

On November 1, 1966, just two weeks before the frightening car chase and the police investigation, a number of National Guardsmen were outside at the armory, a military facility east of town, when they saw something in the trees nearby. It was perched on the branch of a tree in the distance, but all of the men agreed it was too large to be a bird. It was man-sized, they said. Maybe larger. This time, though, it was brown.

Then, just three days before the two young couples had their experience in Point Pleasant, five men saw something in Clendenin, a town about eighty miles to the southeast. Ken Duncan and his co-workers were digging a grave in the local cemetery, getting it ready for a burial later that day, when a large bird took off from one of the trees at the edge of the property. As it flew closer, though, all of the men became convinced it wasn't a bird at all. It was as large as a man, but with wings.

After the events of November 15, all of those disconnected, unreported sightings started to get pulled into the larger story. The local newspaper, the *Point Pleasant Register,* ran a headline the next day that declared "Couples See Man-Sized Bird . . . Creature . . . Something." It was an odd story, for sure. The paper just didn't know what to do with it. And I don't blame them.

The following evening, Raymond Wamsley drove north toward the wildlife preserve on his way to see a friend who lived in one of the homes built near the property there. With him in the car were his wife and another friend, Marcella Bennett. When they arrived at their friend's house, they parked in a shadowy dirt lot across the road, then got out and approached the front porch.

Unfortunately, their friend wasn't home, so they turned around and returned to their car. It was on their way back that they spotted a sight none of them would forget. Just a few feet from the car, farther back from the road in the darkness, something large seemed to rise up from the ground. It happened suddenly, and the sight of it horrified them. Bennett later described it as an enormous figure, roughly the shape of a human, but with glowing red eyes. They stood beside their car, paralyzed with fear, while they watched a pair of wings unfold from the creature's back. And then it was gone.

They weren't the last in town to see something that fit such an almost unbelievable description. On the morning of November 25,

Tom Ury was driving to work just a couple of miles north of the wildlife preserve when he saw something on the side of the road. Maybe he thought it was a hitchhiker or a local out for a walk. Whatever he might have assumed, the closer he got to it, the less it made sense.

It was an enormous man-shaped figure, and as he passed it, the creature spread huge wings and took flight. Tom sped away, horrified by what he'd seen, but the thing—whatever it was—followed him. Tom reached seventy-five miles per hour, but it kept up, even circling his car. When it finally disappeared, Tom went home. He said he was just too frightened to work after that.

There were others. Connie Jo Carpenter saw something large on the twenty-seventh that flew toward her car. On the twenty-eighth, Richard West called the police in a panic. There was something on his neighbor's roof, he told them. It was a man. With wings. Later an elderly man from Point Pleasant claimed he looked out his window and saw a winged man with gray fur and bright red eyes just standing there in his yard.

The sightings continued for months, sometimes in the area of Point Pleasant and sometimes farther away. The Ohio River valley seemed to be the focal point of many reported encounters with the creature, but the descriptions varied just enough to make that assumption far from definitive. And then, of course, there were the dreams.

A year after the 1966 sightings, multiple people claimed they were having nightmares about death, and they blamed them on the mysterious creature. One woman said her dreams involved Christmas presents and people drowning. Another woman dreamed of people dying in the nearby Ohio River. Each of them believed that the bird-man creature's appearance had something to do with it. But, of course, these were just dreams, and as we all know, dreams don't come true.

Or do they? On the evening of December 15, 1967, the nearby Silver Bridge, which connected Point Pleasant with Ohio to the west, collapsed into the river. When it did, it took forty-six lives with it. People driving home from work. Families returning from after-school programs. Folks coming back from their holiday shopping. And floating in the water, they said, among the wreckage of cars and metal support beams, were tiny pops of color.

Christmas presents.

PRECURSORS

There's a lot to be said for seeing what we want to see. And when a whole community gets caught up in something as sensational as a man-sized bird-thing . . . well, it's easy to see how things can get out of control, and fast. In the years since, there've even been stories in Point Pleasant of UFOs, of government cover-ups, and aliens. And the creature has been given a sensational, mysterious name: the Mothman.

Others, though, take a more logical approach, claiming that what people saw in every instance was just a large bird. Nothing more than shadows and hysteria convinced people that they were seeing something otherworldly. Biologists have suggested it was a sandhill crane. Or, much as with the events from 1952, it was just an owl, enlarged by the viewers' adrenaline and an overactive imagination.

We see what we want to, whether we're a skeptic or a believer. We wear our own pair of colored lenses, and they tint the world we see. Sometimes that causes us to dismiss things we should give more attention to. Other times it convinces us that the unexplainable is undeniable.

None of this, of course, sheds light on the odd connection between the sightings of these creatures and the tragedies that followed them. The first recorded appearance of the Point Pleasant creature, way back in the early 1900s, was said to have occurred just prior to "a tragic event." And the collapse of the Silver Bridge in 1967 certainly deepened that possible connection. Unlike the creature itself, though, those are harder to explain away with simple wildlife biology.

Meanwhile, large man-bird creatures are still occasionally sighted, and oftentimes very far from Point Pleasant. Creatures matching the Mothman description have been spotted in Singapore, Argentina, England, Mexico, and Brazil, among other places. Most witnesses describe the same glowing red eyes, human-like body, and enormous wings.

In April 1986, there were similar sightings in a small Russian town located in a river valley just north of a wildlife preserve. Witnesses claimed to see a large creature they described as a tall, headless man with enormous wings and eyes that glowed with a bright red light. All of those details, from the location to the physical description, sound eerily like the Point Pleasant incident.

These sightings in the Russian town went on for over two weeks, and locals began to refer to it by name. They called it the "black bird." And just as odd as the sightings themselves are the reports of eyewitnesses having nightmares later. What those dreams entailed, no one really knows.

We don't know because there's no one left in town to ask about those dreams, or the sightings of the "black bird" creature. You see, all fourteen thousand residents were relocated about thirty years ago, shortly after a reactor at their nuclear power plant tragically failed.

The city, you see, was *Chernobyl*.

 BEYOND THE VEIL

Passing Notes

WE LIVE IN a crowded world. As of this episode, the U.S. Census Bureau puts the number of human lives on our pale blue dot of a planet at about 7.3 billion. I'm not sure I need to unpack that for you; that's simply a lot of people.

And because of that, there are very few places where we can go to be truly alone. Our cities are congested. Our highways and parking lots seem to be overflowing. It boggles the mind thinking about just how many people are around us on a daily basis. Which is why our homes offer a bit of peace and escape. At home, we feel as if we're in control. It's a personal space where strangers aren't allowed in without invitation, where we can let down our guard and feel safe.

Our dwelling places have been a refuge for us ever since humans gave up the nomadic, hunter-gatherer life and settled in one location. Still, multiple religions throughout history have taught us to believe that, while we might think we are alone, there is another world behind the thin veil of reality.

Heaven, the otherworld, the afterlife . . . we can call it whatever we want, but humans—for the most part, at least—have always believed it's there, waiting for us. It was in the mid-nineteenth century, though, that some people in the United States and Europe began to propose new ideas about it.

They claimed that, rather than being passive, this otherworld was active and thriving. And if we understood how, we could even interact with it. We could even *communicate* with it. Some people took hope in this. Some fought against it. Regardless, this new belief spread.

Few people, though, expected the darker side of this new vision. They celebrated the hope that came from discovering a new door and relished their chance to open it and walk through. But just because we *can* doesn't mean we *should*.

Some doors, you see, are closed for a reason.

OUTSIDE FORCES

In 1848, something odd was going on at the home of John and Margaret Fox, who lived in Hydesville, New York. They were a poor family, but their fortunes changed when their two youngest daughters, Kate and Margaret, started to communicate with an unseen entity in their home through a series of clicks and knocks.

When word got out about what they could do, the girls—twelve and fifteen years old at the time—were asked to bring their abilities to the stage in Rochester, New York. And that was the moment that launched their career. Kate and Margaret toured the country performing group séances in front of sellout crowds. They inspired a whole slew of imitators, and the girls made a good living at it for close to forty years.

The Fox sisters came on the scene at a time when there was a growing interest in forces outside of our own existence. While spiritualism itself is said to have blossomed in upstate New York, some people think we can thank Franz Mesmer for getting it started.

Mesmer was a German physician who started out investigating the healing power of magnets but moved on to believe that inside and outside forces influenced our human experience. He focused on the healing powers of his theory but never found success in the medical field. Later researchers transitioned his work into a field they called "neuro-hypnosis" or "nervous sleep," which eventually simply became known as "hypnosis."

Today, when we think of mesmerism or of being mesmerized, we think of hypnosis. But it was the spiritualist movement that found the most hope in this idea. It took their beliefs in something that sounded insane—communicating with the dead and learning from them—and put it in the realm of science. At least, that's what they thought.

In 1888, forty years after their careers began, the Fox sisters confessed to their trickery. Both of them, it seems, could rotate their ankles and bend their toes in a way that produced audible clicks. Each séance they performed had been an act, nothing more. But the world of spiritualism that they brought to the forefront of popular culture didn't just go away. It had already taken root, and despite their confession, it showed no sign of stopping.

Spiritualism received a mixed reception. In some ways, these were teachings in contradiction to the accepted theology of a very large portion of Christianity, and some spoke out about that. In other ways, though, spiritualism seemed to confirm what most churches already taught: that even after death, we maintain our personalities and live on in another manner. For those who had lost loved ones or who had a deep curiosity about the afterlife, séances offered a chance to say goodbye, to say hello, or just to learn.

Popular figures lined up on both sides of the fence. In the 1920s, magician and performer Harry Houdini was a vocal opponent and actively sought to disprove anyone who claimed to be in communication with the world beyond the veil. John Nevil Maskelyne, another stage magician and the inventor of the pay toilet, actually sat in on séances and pointed out the trickery as it happened.

But not everyone saw it as a farce. Sir Arthur Conan Doyle, creator and author of the Sherlock Holmes novels, was an avid supporter of spiritualism. He even belonged to a London organization known as the Ghost Club, rooted in a deep belief in the supernatural and the otherworldly. Other members included Charles Dickens, W. B. Yeats, and Charles Babbage, one of the fathers of the programmable computer.

There were others, though, who took things too far. Thomas Bradford was one of those people. In 1920, he placed an ad in a Detroit newspaper seeking others who were as curious about the afterlife as he was. He was looking for a partner, someone to converse with, to support each other and to further each other's knowledge of life after death.

When Ruth Doran replied, the two struck up a partnership and friendship. Their goal was to become of one mind, they said, to be attuned to each other in a way that death could not break. And then, in February 1921, Bradford and Doran took their research to the next level.

Bradford locked his apartment door, turned on his heater, blew out the pilot light, and then waited patiently for the room to fill with gas. He died of asphyxiation shortly after, with the plan to reach out to his partner from beyond the grave and confirm their beliefs. So Ruth waited.

She never heard from him again.

THE GUESTS

When his wife passed away, Presbyterian minister Eliakim Phelps found himself alone at the age of fifty-nine. His children had all grown up and moved out, and so he looked for a change in his life that would bring him some semblance of happiness. He found that change in a younger woman, and soon the two were married.

His new bride was in her mid-forties and came into the marriage with three children under the age of sixteen. Shortly after, though, Mr. and Mrs. Phelps welcomed another son into their lives, and then in November 1847, the family purchased a home in Stratford, Connecticut. It was a unique and sprawling mansion built just twenty-two years prior by a retired sea captain, but it had sat unoccupied in the years since his death in 1845.

It was a *large* house, too. Those who visited there said that the layout had more than a passing resemblance to a ship, something one might expect from a home built for a sailor. The main hallway was an unbelievable seventy feet long, and there were five bedrooms on the second floor, with two more on the third. It provided all the space a family of six might need, and then some.

They moved into the mansion in February 1848, and for the

first two years, life there was uneventful. But on March 10, 1850, all of that changed. They'd gone to church that morning, as you might expect from a minister and his family. Upon leaving, Eliakim Phelps locked the doors because no one would be home. Even the maid was off for the day.

When they returned home later that morning, the front door of the house was standing wide open. Phelps stepped inside carefully and noticed that more doors had been opened inside the home. Furniture had been toppled, dishes lay broken on the floor, and everyday objects like books and decorations were scattered about. They'd clearly been robbed.

The nursery was found in chaos as well, with furniture tossed on the bed. In a panic, Phelps checked the downstairs closet where they kept the valuable family silver and discovered it was still there, untouched. Even his gold pocket watch was right where he had left it. Which brought up a question: if they *had* been robbed, what valuables had actually been taken?

Concerned, Phelps suggested that the entire family travel upstairs together to continue their inspection. They looked inside each room, one by one, searching for signs of the same chaos and vandalism, but every room they checked seemed to be untouched. If someone *had* broken in, perhaps they had been frightened off before having a chance to come upstairs.

The last room they checked was that of Mr. and Mrs. Phelps. The space was clean and tidy and the bed was still neatly made, but in the center of it was Mrs. Phelps's nightgown. It had been laid out in the shape of a person, with sleeves crossed over its front the way a corpse's arms are crossed over its chest. Even a pair of stockings had been added to the arrangement, giving it the appearance of feet. And there, on the nearby wall, was a series of indecipherable scribbles, something that looked and felt evil to the core.

As hard as it is to believe, though, the family brushed these events off as a simple prank, some random act of vandalism and nothing more. Even harder to believe, when it came time to return to church that day for the afternoon schedule, the entire family willingly did so. Everyone, that is, except Mr. Phelps.

He stayed behind, relocked the doors and windows, and then took a seat in one of the upstairs rooms with his pistol in hand to wait for the vandals to return. But when nothing unusual happened for over an hour, Phelps quietly slipped out of the room to inspect the rest of the house.

Downstairs, he slowly pushed open the door to the dining room, and then froze. Nearly a dozen figures stood in the room. Some stood tall, holding Bibles. Others were bowed low to the floor. All of them, though, seemed focused on the shape of a small, otherworldly creature above their heads. Phelps stared at it for a moment before realizing it was a small statue hanging from the ceiling by a string.

It was a lot to take in, I suppose. That might explain why it took Phelps so long to notice the other oddities in the room. The women who were gathered around the figure weren't moving. They weren't even real. Each one, it turned out, was nothing more than clothing taken from a room upstairs.

They were life-sized rag dolls. Someone—or some*thing*—had gathered the clothes, pinned them together into human shapes, and then stuffed each of them with rags.

All without Phelps hearing a thing.

THE HARD-KNOCK LIFE

Eliakim Phelps took the blame for the figures. No, he hadn't created them. And no, he didn't tell people that he had. He fully admitted that they were peculiar—otherworldly, even. He didn't know how to explain their appearance, but he believed that he had unintentionally played a part in it all.

He blamed the events of the week before. On March 4, a friend had visited the Phelps home. It had been a typical visit. After dinner with the family, both men retired to the study for drinks and deeper conversation. And, with this being 1850, the spiritualist movement was fresh on this visitor's mind. It's hard to say what they talked about. Maybe the Fox sisters came up. Maybe they discussed stories of reported hauntings or unusual activity written about in newspapers. What we do know, though, is that the conversation eventually turned to séances.

The word "séance" is French, and it simply means "session" or "sitting." In the spiritualist movement, though, a séance was something more: it was an attempt to communicate with the spirit world, to reach out through the thin curtain between life and death and feel in the dark for something tangible, something real. A séance was, and is, an act of hope.

For Phelps and his visitor, though, it was a curiosity, and they decided right then and there to try one. Maybe it was the scotch they'd been sharing, or the late hour. It's hard to say for sure what drives people to do things that are out of character for them, but it happens nonetheless.

The two men were said to have conducted their own short, amateur séance right there in the study, and according to Phelps's own admission, it appeared to have been successful, albeit underwhelming. After calling out for a response from the spirit world, the men reportedly heard a distant knocking. (Back then they called it "rapping," but, please, don't confuse that with the work of Jay-Z.)

It's most likely the men forgot about that evening altogether. But after the March 10 incident with the life-sized dolls, things in the Phelps household only became more outlandish. Things were escalating, it seems, and it was happening in the presence of multiple witnesses. Phelps himself was a skeptic, and so to help him document these experiences, he often brought in equally skeptical colleagues.

Later reports detail how the activity in the house grew more and more unnatural. Objects would appear from thin air and move slowly across a room. Some of these objects would even land softly, as if being set down by a guiding hand. Food would appear during meals, sometimes dropping right onto the table.

Even heavy objects such as the fireplace tools were said to have moved around the room on their own. At one point, Phelps called on another minister, the Reverend John Mitchell, to help him investigate further. The two men locked themselves in the parlor and waited, knowing it would be impossible for someone—one of the children, they assumed—to sneak in and toss objects through the air.

While inside the room that night, it's reported that the men witnessed dozens of items appear in the air and then fall to the floor. Many of those items turned out to be clothing from upstairs, as if they had been falling through a hole in the ceiling. Clothing, mind you, like those used to create the life-sized figures that Phelps had seen weeks before.

The stories caught the attention of other members of the Phelps family. Once Eliakim was paid a visit by his adult son Austin—a theology professor—and Phelps's own brother Abner, one of the most prominent medical doctors in Boston at the time. While there, the two men heard knocking at the front door. When they opened it, no one was there. Of course they assumed it was a prank. In a house full of children, that was the logical explanation.

So they then systematically inspected all of the rooms in the house, looking for the person responsible for the noise. Doors were checked, children were isolated and watched. In the end, their search came to a frustrating conclusion that evening when both men heard the knocking once more, this time while they were standing on either side of the door.

Granted, flying skirts and invisible knocking were things most families might be able to work around. There didn't seem to be anything malicious or dangerous about the activity, so throughout all of this, Phelps acted without urgency. In many ways, it seems that he was more of a curious observer than a concerned homeowner.

But that was all about to change.

Eviction Notice

The physical attacks began as pinches and slaps sometime during April 1850. One reporter, who had come to the Phelps home to discuss their experiences, actually witnessed some of those attacks. No one, from what they could tell, had faked it.

It became more life-threatening when Mrs. Phelps awoke in the middle of the night to find a pillow being pressed over her face and something wrapped around her throat. She survived, but it became clear that day that the spirit, if that's what it really was, was far from benign. And then it turned its sights on their young son, Henry.

Henry was just eleven at the time, and although no one is sure why, he became the primary focus for the attacks doled out by the unseen force in the house. Rocks were thrown at him on multiple occasions. He was sometimes seen to be levitated up toward the ceiling, and a newspaper reporter once witnessed the child being picked up and thrown across a room. All by an unseen force.

Henry occasionally went missing, too, much to the concern of his parents. The first time it happened, he was found up in a tree outside, bound with rope and unaware of how he got there. Another time he was found inside one of the home's closets, resting on a shelf too high for the boy to have climbed himself. There was a noose around his neck.

Henry suffered more than anyone else in the Phelps household that year. He was pushed into a cistern of water, the clothing he had on was torn apart, and on one occasion a fire was ignited beneath his bed, threatening to burn him alive. Thankfully, he managed to escape most of these attacks unharmed, but the danger was very real.

As the attacks on Henry continued, Phelps grew more and more frustrated. He began to shout out to whoever was responsible, speaking to empty rooms and demanding that the activity stop. It never did, though, and on more than one occasion, mysterious notes would appear—rough handwriting on scraps of paper—with messages for the homeowner. The notes themselves are now lost, but Phelps reported that their contents were beyond disturbing.

As a final attempt to free his home from whatever force was inhabiting it, Phelps gathered witnesses for a second séance. His hope was that he might learn something about the spirit, something that would help him get rid of it or at least appease it. Phelps had lost hope, and now his rational mind was leaning into unknown territory out of desperation.

The séance revealed very little new information, but according to reports from Phelps and other witnesses, the spirit *did* identify itself. It claimed to be a deceased male clerk who once had worked with Mrs. Phelps on a financial matter. The name was investigated and certain details matched up with public records, but it was still unclear what the spirit wanted and how they might finally be rid of it.

The notes continued to appear as well. Once, a paper drifted onto the table during a tea party hosted by Mrs. Phelps. Phelps himself received dozens, many of which referenced common names for the Devil from that era. Bynames including Beelzebub, Sam Slick, and Sir Sambo all found their way onto these notes.

Finally, in September of that year, a note appeared on the desk while Phelps was there working. Deciphering the message as best he could, he realized that it was a question, presumably from the spirit who haunted the house.

"When are you planning to leave?" it asked.

It was a clear and powerful message. Phelps and his family weren't welcome there anymore. Perhaps it was a threat. Perhaps the attacks would increase, or more dramatic events might follow. If a small fire could be lit beneath Henry's bed, it didn't seem like a stretch to imagine the entire house being at risk of burning down.

Phelps took a moment to process the question, then reached for the paper. Taking his pencil, he wrote his answer below the messy handwriting: "October 1."

There was no reply that day, but Phelps stuck to the agreement. On October 1, 1850, the family returned to Pennsylvania, and he followed shortly after. Weeks later, though, they all returned. I'm not really sure why, to be honest. Maybe they wanted to give it another try. It was their home, after all.

But the activity continued. There was more knocking, more writing on the wall, and more objects that moved through the air as if they were dangling from invisible strings.

One final note appeared in the house in May 1851, and after that, the family moved out for good.

Alive and Well Today

Most of us know someone with a story to tell about unexplainable things: objects that seem to move without our involvement, sounds we can't explain, the feeling of being watched when there's no one else in the room or even the house. It's easy to understand why some people have a desire to search for the truth. But what if the act of reaching out for answers has real-world consequences? Certainly the events in the Phelps mansion confirm something of that kind. Maybe those events were the result of a family with a very open mind, doing their best to interpret admittedly unusual experiences.

Or perhaps there really *is* something beyond the veil, and it reaches through from time to time in order to affect the lives of the living. It's a difficult question to answer. Even impossible, perhaps. Which is why we keep asking it.

Remnants of spiritualism have stuck around, embedded in our popular culture. Classic horror novels such as *The Haunting of Hill House* by Shirley Jackson and Richard Matheson's *Hell House* both drew heavily on that world, featuring séances, automatic writing, and otherworldly activity.

Even today, with movies such as *The Exorcist* and *What Lies Beneath,* the notion of reaching out to communicate with the world beyond our own is alive and well. And maybe there's a good reason for that.

Another family bought the mansion after the Phelps family moved back to Pennsylvania, and over the years the home changed hands often. By the 1940s it had been converted into a facility for the care of the elderly. And when a Mr. and Mrs. Caserta—both of whom were registered nurses—moved there in 1947, there were already more stories filling the hallways: of doors that wouldn't stay shut, knocking, whispers, and random noises that seemed to have no explanation.

But it was their infant son, Gary, who encountered the most trouble. One night, the couple was pulled from sleep by one of the patient buzzers. Mr. Caserta quickly stepped out of their room and descended to the second floor to see what was wrong. As he did, he caught the scent of smoke.

He quickly ran from room to room, checking in with each patient, but all of them were asleep. Finally, at a loss for answers, he dashed back up to the third floor and into Gary's room. Inside, he found smoke billowing from the direction of the crib. Rushing over, he saw that the blanket at Gary's feet was burning, small flames slowly spreading to the sheets.

One other night of sleep was interrupted by the same buzzer system, and this time both of Gary's parents exited their room just in time to find the boy crawling toward the top of the staircase. How the boy got out of his crib and into the hallway was a mystery.

In each instance, the alert system saved Gary's life. Needless to say, the Casertas were very thankful for the person or people responsible for telling them that Gary needed help. It was ironic, really; the buzzer system was designed to allow them to help the patients, but twice, it seemed, the patients had helped *them*. So they asked each of them, one by one. None of the patients claimed responsibility, though.

Now, clearly the Casertas didn't know the Phelpses. And while the locals had always whispered of the old hauntings, they most likely didn't know the full extent of the stories. They certainly didn't know about the contents of those otherworldly notes that would appear to the Phelpses from time to time.

Given the chance to read them, though, they would have been surprised by what that final note said a century before, in May 1851: "The evil one has gone, and a better one has come."

The Bloody Pit

MOST PEOPLE ARE afraid of the dark. And while this is something that we expect from our children, adults hold on to that fear just as tightly. We simply don't talk about it anymore. But it's there, lurking in the back of our minds.

Science calls it nyctophobia: the fear of the dark. Since the dawn of humanity, our ancestors have stared into the blackness of caves, tunnels, and basements with a feeling of rot and panic in our bellies. H. P. Lovecraft, the patriarch of the horror genre, published an essay in 1927 titled "Supernatural Horror in Literature," and it opens with this profoundly simple statement: "The oldest and strongest emotion of mankind is fear, and the oldest and strongest kind of fear is fear of the unknown."

People fear the unknown, the "what if," and the things they cannot see. We're afraid that our frailness and weakness might become laid bare in the presence of whatever it is that lurks in the shadows. We're afraid of opening up places that should remain closed.

And sometimes that's for good reason.

ACCIDENTS HAPPEN

The Berkshire Mountains, which extend north to south across the western sides of Massachusetts and Connecticut, are not the Rockies by any stretch of the imagination, but in 1851 those hills were in someone's way.

The Troy and Greenfield Railroad Company wanted to lay some track that would cut through the mountains in the northwest corner of Massachusetts, and so they began work on a tunnel. On the western end sat the town of Florida, with North Adams holding up the eastern end. Between those towns was about five miles of solid rock.

This building project was no small undertaking, no matter how unimpressive the mountains might be. It ultimately took the work crew twenty-four years to wrap things up and had a total cost of $21.2 million. That's $406.5 million in today's dollars, by the way. See, it was a big deal.

Monetary costs aside, however, construction of the tunnel came with an even heavier price tag: at least two hundred men lost their lives cutting that hole through the bones of the earth.

One of the first major tragedies occurred on March 20, 1865. A team of explosive "experts" (I use that term loosely, because nitroglycerin was incredibly new to just about everyone in America at the time) entered the tunnel to plant a charge. The three men—Brinkman, Nash, and Kelley (Kelley's first name was Ringo, which I think is just awesome)—did their work and then ran back down the tunnel to their safety bunker. Only Kelley made it to safety, however. It turns out that he set off the explosion a bit too early, burying the other two men alive. Naturally, Kelley felt horrible about it, but no one expected him to go missing, which he did just a short while later. Poor Ringo.

The accidents didn't end there, though.

THE SHAFT

Building a railway tunnel through a mountain is complex, and one of the features most tunnels have is a vent shaft. Constant coal-powered train traffic could result in a lot of smoke and fumes, so engineers thought it would be a good idea to have a ventilation shaft that would extend to the surface above and allow fumes and groundwater to be pumped out. This shaft would be roughly thirty feet in diameter and would eventually stretch more than a thousand feet down and connect with the train tunnel below. By October 1867, however, it was only five hundred feet deep. Essentially, it was a really, really deep hole in the ground.

To dig this hole, they constructed a small building at the top, which was used to house a hoist that would get the debris out, as well as a pump system to remove groundwater. Then they lowered a dozen or more Cornish miners into the hole and set them to work.

You see where this is going, right? Please tell me you see where this is going.

On October 17, a leaky lantern filled the hoist house with naphtha, an explosive natural gas, and the place blew sky-high. As a result, things started to fall down the shaft.

What things? Well, for starters, three hundred freshly sharpened drill bits. Then the hoist mechanism itself. Finally the burning wreckage of the building. All of it fell five stories down the tunnel and onto the thirteen men working at the bottom. And because the water pump was destroyed in the explosion, the shaft also began to flood.

The workers on the surface tried to reach the men at the bottom but failed. One man was lowered into the shaft in a basket, but he was pulled back up when the fumes became unbearable. He managed to gasp the words "No hope" to the workers around him before slipping into unconsciousness.

In the end they gave up, called it a loss, and covered the shaft. But in the weeks that followed, the workers frequently reported hearing the anguished voices of men crying out in pain. They said they saw the lost Cornish miners carrying picks and shovels, only to watch them vanish moments later. Even the people in the village nearby told tales of odd shapes and muffled cries near the covered pit. Highly educated people, upon visiting the construction site, recorded similar experiences.

Glenn Drohan, a correspondent for the local newspaper, wrote, "The ghostly apparitions would appear briefly, then vanish, leaving no footprints in the snow, giving no answers to the miners' calls." Voices, lights, visions, and odd shapes in the darkness—all the sorts of experiences we fear might happen to us when we step into a dark bedroom or basement.

A full year after the accident, they reopened the shaft and drained out the several hundred feet of water that had accumulated. They wanted to get back to work. But when they did, they discovered something horrific: bodies . . . and a raft. Apparently some of the men had survived the falling drill bits and other debris long enough to manage to build a raft. No one knows how long they stayed alive, but it's clear that they died because they had been abandoned in a flooding hole in the ground. After that, the workers began to call the shaft by another name: the Bloody Pit.

Catchy, eh?

A STORIED PAST

About four years after the gas explosion, two men visited the tunnel. One was James McKinstrey, the drilling operations superintendent, and the other was Dr. Clifford Owens. While in the tunnel, the two men—both educated and respected among their peers—had an encounter that was beyond unusual. Owens wrote:

> On the night of June 25, 1872, James McKinstrey and I entered the great excavation at precisely 11:30 p.m. We had traveled about two full miles into the shaft when we finally halted to rest. Except for the dim smoky light cast by our lamps, the place was as cold and dark as a tomb.
>
> James and I stood there talking for a minute or two and were just about to turn back when suddenly I heard a strange mournful sound. It was just as if someone or something was suffering great pain. The next thing I saw was a dim light coming along the tunnel from a westerly direction. At first, I believed it was probably a workman with a lantern. Yet, as the light grew closer, it took on a strange blue color and appeared to change shape almost into the form of a human being without a head. The

light seemed to be floating along about a foot or two above the tunnel floor. In the next instant, it felt as if the temperature had suddenly dropped and a cold, icy chill ran up and down my spine. The headless form came so close that I could have reached out and touched it but I was too terrified to move.

For what seemed like an eternity, McKinstrey and I just stood there gaping at the headless thing like two wooden Indians. The blue light remained motionless for a few seconds as if it were actually looking us over, then floated off toward the east end of the shaft and vanished into thin air.

I am above all a realist, nor am I prone to repeating gossip and wild tales that defy a reasonable explanation. However, in all truth, I can not deny what James McKinstrey and I witnessed with our own eyes.

The Hoosac Tunnel played host to countless other spooky stories in the years that followed. In 1874, a local hunter named Frank Webster vanished. When a search party found him stumbling up the banks of the Deerfield River three days later, he was without his rifle and appeared to have been beaten bloody. He claimed he'd been ordered into the tunnel by voices and lights, and once he was inside, he saw ghostly figures that floated and wandered about in the dark. His experience ended when something unseen reached out, took his rifle from him, and clubbed him with it. He had no memory of walking out of the tunnel.

In 1936, a railroad employee named Joe Impoco claimed that he was warned of danger in the tunnel by a mysterious voice. Not once, but twice. I'm thinking it was Ringo, trying to make up for being an idiot.

In 1973, for some unknown and godawful reason, a man decided to walk through the full length of the tunnel. This brilliant man, Bernard Hastaba, was never seen again. One man who walked through and *did* make it out, though, claims that while he was in the tunnel he saw the figure of a man dressed in the old clothing of a nineteenth-century miner.

He left in a hurry, from what I've read.

Stories about the tunnel persist to this day. It's common for teams of paranormal investigators to walk the length of the tunnel, although it's still active, with a dozen or so freight trains passing through each day.

There are rumors of a secret room, or many rooms, deep inside the tunnel. There's an old monitoring station built into the rock about halfway in, though few have been brave enough to venture all the way there and see it. Those who have report more of the same: unexplained sounds and lights.

Oh, and remember Ringo Kelley, the sloppy demolition expert who got his two co-workers killed in 1865? Well, he showed up again in March 1866, a full year after the explosion. His body was found two miles inside the tunnel, in the *exact* same spot where Brinkman and Nash had died.

He had been strangled to death.

Dinner at the Afterglow

THE SAN JUAN Islands are a cluster of small, wooded islands off the coast of Washington State, just across the water from Vancouver Island. The westernmost of those small plots of land is San Juan Island itself. With a population of less than seven thousand, it has the welcoming feeling of a small, quiet town.

Seriously, this place is quiet. The most exciting thing most people can think of about their home there is that one of the residents is Lisa Moretti, a retired female WWF wrestler. But on the northern tip of the island, just beyond Roche Harbor and the resort there, is a road that leads into the woods. What is hidden in those trees, away from the prying eyes of tourists and residents alike, is something so unusual—so out of the ordinary and bizarre—that it practically *begs* for a visit.

Traveling down the long dirt road that runs into the heart of the forest like a withered artery will bring you to an iron archway mounted on stone pillars. The words "Afterglow Vista" are woven into the metalwork. Beyond that, deeper into the woods, is a series of stone stairs that lead up a small hill. It is the thing on top of that hill that immediately catches the eye of every visitor, without question.

It's an open-air rotunda, a ring of tall stone pillars standing on a flat circular limestone base. They're connected at the top by thick Maltese archways, but nothing covers the rotunda; its interior is completely exposed and visible.

What's inside it? A large, round stone table, surrounded by six stone chairs. Odd, but not creepy—until you realize the purpose this monument serves.

It's a tomb. Resting inside each of the chairs are the cremated remains of a human being.

A History in Lime

In the late nineteenth century, San Juan Island became known for lime deposits. Then, as now, lime was an essential ingredient in important products such as steel, fertilizer, and cement, and the lime industry of San Juan Island provided much of the community's jobs and revenue.

In 1886, a man named John S. McMillin purchased a controlling interest in the major lime deposits, and he eventually developed the industry there into the largest supplier of lime on the West Coast. In the process, he built the twenty-room Hotel de Haro at Roche Harbor, and the company town that surrounded it. In addition to the lime factory itself, he built the barrel works, warehouse, docks, ships, offices, church, general store, and barns. He even built houses for the workers, with single men living in large bunkhouses and families being given small cottages that had been built into neat rows. All the structures belonged to McMillin, but his army of employees—more than eight hundred of them at the peak of the business—gave them life. The town was self-sufficient, with its own water, power, and telephone systems, and he paid his workers in company scrip—company currency that was good only at the local company store. Of course, workers could still draw their salary in U.S. currency whenever they wished, but the scrip was used in the store all the way up to 1956.

That wasn't all McMillin would build, though. He was far from done.

John S. McMillin was an uncommon man. He was born in 1855

and attended DePauw University in Indiana back when it was called Asbury University. There he joined the Sigma Chi fraternity and helped guide the young organization to form a Grand Council and Executive Committee at the national level. As a result, he was elected the very first Sigma Chi Grand Consul. In addition to his fraternity connections, McMillin was a Freemason, reaching the thirty-second degree (out of thirty-three). He was prominent in business and politics, and even counted as a friend Teddy Roosevelt, who frequently visited and stayed in the hotel.

McMillin had four children, and nearly the entire family considered themselves devout Methodists. Only one child, they say, left the family faith, and in doing so he might very well have locked himself out of the McMillin story forever.

You see, all of those worlds of interest, as different from one another as they were, coexisted inside the mind of John McMillin. So when the time came to plan an eternal resting place for him and his family, each element had influence on those designs. The result, as you might have guessed, was the eerie stone edifice located deep in the forest.

THE MAUSOLEUM

The structure really is a thing to behold. Once you've read about it, you'll want to visit some websites to see the true beauty of what McMillin built.

When it was first constructed, the forest around it was far less thickly wooded, and visitors could see Afterglow Beach off to the northwest, perhaps giving the structure its name. It was designed to be a *tholos,* a circular Mycenaean temple, and was crafted from local limestone and cement.

But what's really fascinating is the large number of secret messages and hidden meanings that were built into the structure, some relating to the Knights Templar, and others reflecting McMillin's values as a Methodist and a Mason. For example, approaching the mausoleum requires traveling up three separate sets of stairs, and

each set has its own meaning. There are three steps in the first flight of stairs, and they are said to represent the three ages of man. The second set contains five steps, representing the five senses. And the third set contains seven steps, which stand for the seven liberal arts and sciences.

Around the table are seven pillars that hold up the arches above. Oddly, one of the seven pillars is broken—the westernmost one—but it was intentional. Only a small portion can be seen on the base and protruding from the archway above. This break is said to be a reminder that death never lets us finish our work.

There's room around the table for seven chairs, but the spot that should hold the seventh—closest to the broken pillar, in fact—is missing. Some say it was never there to begin with, and that it's meant to represent the son who walked away from McMillin's Methodist faith.

Depending on who you are, if eternity is a gathering at the table, not finding a seat with your family would be a ruthless punishment indeed.

HAUNTINGS

These are all fantastic architectural details, but what can't be documented in any photograph of the mausoleum is the long list of reported sightings, all of which started sometime in the mid-1950s.

The mausoleum was built with no dome on top, although the plan had originally been to construct one. The dome would have been expensive, amounting to about 40 percent of the total budget, and so it was scrapped near the end to save cash. Even still, visitors on rainy days have frequently reported that they feel no rain on them while inside the ring of stone pillars. Some people have spoken of cold spots near the table, while others have heard voices, even when no one else was around.

Those daring enough to actually sit on one of the chairs—keeping in mind that they are tiny little tombs containing the remains of the McMillin family—say that they felt very uneasy doing so, and more than one person has reported the sensation of hands pushing them off.

A frequent account is of seeing strange lights at night, including blue lights that seem to hover above the chairs. Some visitors have also reported seeing the members of the McMillin family themselves on nights with a full moon, seated around the table laughing and talking.

The mausoleum isn't the only place with uncanny activity, though.

Originally John McMillin built the family home right beside the Hotel de Haro, and his longtime secretary, Ada Beane, had a cottage on the other side of the hotel. Later, the Roche Hotel was built around the old hotel, and the other buildings were combined into the structure. Beane's cottage, for example, became the current dining room and hotel gift shop.

That hotel restaurant has been the focus of quite a bit of the odd activity. The resort's restaurant manager has reported that on more than one occasion he has closed up shop, turned off the lights, and headed for the door, only to look back over his shoulder and see that a candle on one of the tables had reignited. When he walked back in and blew it out, all of the kitchen hood fans turned on at once.

Other appliances have been known to turn on as well. Employees over the years have reported stoves, blenders, and toasters switching themselves on and off. The storeroom door has been known to open and close by itself. Furniture in the back room has even been found rearranged in the morning with no explanation.

The gift shop, located in another part of the old cottage, has also been home to spooky activity. One former employee once watched as several glass shelves cracked and shattered one by one, all without anyone touching them.

In the hotel itself, there are rumors of ghosts. The second floor is reported to be haunted by what has been described as a middle-aged woman wearing a long dress. Employees have told the owners that they frequently hear the sound of rustling clothing in rooms where no one else should be.

Is it the ghost woman's dress they hear?

LEFTOVERS

It's funny how the people who live around us have a way of making an impression on us. We feel them when they're here, like the gravitational pull of another planet, but sometimes we even feel them when they're gone. After their death they leave behind memories, treasured gifts or belongings, or perhaps a worn spot on a favorite piece of furniture.

Ghosts are a concept almost as old as time. The people we love are here for a while, and then they're gone, and humans have always struggled to understand what happens to them after death. Maybe ghost stories are a way for us to grapple with our own loneliness and loss. Perhaps they're our way of bolstering ourselves against our own impending death. We must go *somewhere*, right? Are we ready? Will we be forgotten?

John McMillin believed with all his heart that his life needed to be remembered, and that his body and those of his family deserved a resting place equal to their position in life. The Afterglow Vista stands as proof of one man's faith in something beyond the veil.

And that light over the limestone seats that some people report having seen since the 1950s? Well, it turns out there just might be an explanation, depending on what you're willing to believe.

Remember how the building that houses the hotel's gift shop and dining room used to be the home of Ada Beane, McMillin's longtime secretary? Along with being a key figure in the day-to-day business of the company, she also helped as a governess to the McMillin children. She was practically part of the family.

So when Beane died before McMillin, it was obviously an emotional loss. Rumors persist to this day that her death was suicide, but official records list nothing more than natural causes. Regardless, the family lost someone dear when she passed away.

After her death, her body was cremated and the ashes placed in a mason jar, and that jar somehow made it onto the mantel in the office of Paul McMillin, John's youngest son. It wasn't until the mid-1950s that the resort manager learned from Paul—still alive and working for the company—that she was there. And that's when they moved her.

Where did they take her remains? Why, to join the others. Her ashes were added to the copper urn in one of the seats around the stone table in the mausoleum, putting her back where she belongs, among friends as dear to her as family.

But Beane might not have been too pleased about that decision. Perhaps, after looking over the family and estate for all those years, being moved to the cold, dark tomb didn't settle well with her. It was only after the move that people began to see lights and hear voices there. At the same time, the pranks and unusual activity started up inside the hotel.

Coincidence? Or the actions of an upset woman who would rather spend her eternity away from the tourists and cold rain of the Afterglow Vista?

Can you blame her?

Homestead

H OME SWEET HOME.

For most of us, those words are about as true as they get. The place we call home can easily become the center of our universe and is often the source of our feelings of security and peace. Most people who tell you stories about their childhood home do so with wide eyes and a wistful smile. Home is, as they say, where the heart is.

Our home is the place where we experience life. We fill each room with our laughter. We chase our passions. We make plans for the future. You might remember holidays in the living room, or breakfast conversations, or exploring the attic on a winter day. These homes—in one sense nothing more than buildings that we dwell in—somehow become a part of us.

But life isn't always roses and laughter. Sometimes the things we experience are difficult, or painful, or both. Sometimes people do things that leave a lasting mark, like an echo that carries on through the years. And on occasion these dark moments are even experienced within our home.

From *Macbeth* to *American Horror Story,* from the work of Shirley Jackson to that of Stephen King, it has been made abundantly clear just how much power a home can have over our lives. Maybe it's the tragedy or the memories. Maybe it's the dark acts committed in the shadows. Or maybe it's the secrets, both metaphorical and literal, buried beneath the foundation. Whatever the reason, it doesn't take a popular novelist or even a historian to point out the simple truth: there's no place like home.

And considering what's been known to happen there, that might be a *good* thing.

ABOVE AND BELOW

When Christopher and Elizabeth Crawley built their home in the New South Wales town of Junee, in southeastern Australia, they envisioned a normal, happy future for themselves. Christopher had caught wind of the impending construction of the Great Southern Railway Line through Junee, and so he'd erected the Railway Hotel across from the station. And it paid off.

In 1884, they finished construction on their home, which they called the Monte Cristo. It wasn't a mansion by any stretch of the imagination, but it did have nine rooms, a stable for his prized racehorse, a dairy barn, and a separate ballroom—although that eventually became the servants' quarters.

But life wasn't idyllic for the Crawley family. While carrying one of the little Crawley girls, their nanny dropped her down the stairs, and she died from the injuries she sustained. The nanny claimed that an unseen force had reached out and knocked the child from her arms. Whatever the cause, the Crawleys had to go through the ordeal of burying a child—something no parent should have to endure.

In 1910, Mr. Crawley's starched shirt collars began to rub the skin on his neck raw. The abscess became gangrenous, and in December of that year he died as a result of a heart attack, brought on, they say, by the wound.

After her husband's death, Elizabeth—already known to be a harsh, disciplined woman—went into a state of mourning that lasted the rest of her life. She converted one of the upstairs rooms into a chapel and spent much of her time there. According to local lore, she left the house on only two occasions before her death in 1933.

Other tragedies found their way into Monte Cristo. A pregnant maid committed suicide by jumping from the top story of the house. She bled to death on the front steps. Morris, the stable boy, burned to death in a fire. And in 1961, the caretaker of the house was shot and killed by a local who had been inspired by the recent Hitchcock film *Psycho*.

Today, many young children feel anxious near the stairs. A dark stain has been seen on the front steps of the house, but it seems to fade in and out of view over time. The figure of a young woman in a white gown has been witnessed passing before the windows of the front balcony, and some believe it's the spirit of the pregnant maid, repeating her final moments over and over. Others claim to have seen a young boy wandering around near the site of the coach house.

A few visitors to the house have encountered the figure of an older man in the upstairs hallway, and most have assumed it to be Mr. Crawley. But it's his wife, Elizabeth, who is most commonly seen, almost as if she hasn't fully let go of her home yet. She has been reported to appear in the dining room, where she has ordered people to leave the room. Others have seen her ghostly figure in the chapel upstairs, dressed in black as if in mourning for a lost loved one.

Across the world in the state of Kentucky, another home became the scene of tragedy and pain. The names have slipped from history, but in Allen County, one of the families living there in the early 1860s owned a number of slaves. According to the local stories, most of the slaves lived in their own quarters on the property, but the husband kept chains in the basement of the family home for times when he wanted to discipline one or two.

When the Civil War broke out, word began to spread among the slaves of the South that it would be better to escape and run north, and so plans were made in the slave quarters over many weeks. Finally the night came, and the entire group of slaves left the homestead and headed north. All of them, that is, except for the two still chained up in the basement of their owner's home.

Whether because he heard the noise of their escape or because he was out on his usual evening rounds, the man soon discovered that his slaves were gone. The stories describe how he spent hours that night on horseback with his gun, riding north and looking for his runaway slaves. But they were never discovered.

Instead, the man returned home empty-handed and full of rage. Fueled by his anger, he descended into the basement, where he shot and killed both captive men, and later he buried the bodies there in the cellar. Months later, the man was called into service with the Confederate Army, and he died in battle.

His widow never opened the cellar door again. In fact, even though it was in the middle of the house, she had it boarded up. There's a lot of symbolism in that single action, if you're looking for that sort of thing. I think she just wanted to make sure no one ever found the bodies her husband had buried beneath the dirt floor down there.

Years later, when she fell ill and passed away, the house was sold to distant relatives. When the new family began to move in, they opened the cellar and discovered that it reeked with a power-ful odor. They vented the space and cleaned it as best they could, but the smell never went away.

It wasn't long before their children began to tell them about hearing sounds at night that seemed to come from the cellar. The parents dismissed it as childhood fantasies, but the stories continued.

One night, many months later, the husband and wife were both pulled from sleep by strange sounds. She stayed in bed, while he went down to investigate. From their room she heard a loud cry and then a crash. She leapt out of bed and ran to the cellar door. Opening it, she found her husband lying dead on the dirt floor at the bottom of the cellar stairs, his neck broken and twisted.

There are many stories like these, but they all teach the same bitter lesson: sometimes our homes attract tragedy. Sometimes we create it ourselves.

FAMILY TIES

When Daniel Benton built his small red cape-style home in Tolland, Connecticut, I doubt he imagined it would still be standing today. It's not enormous like some of the plantation homes one might find in the South, but for a house built in 1720, it was comfortable. And in complete contrast to our modern, mobile life in the twenty-first century, it stayed in the Benton family until 1932. That's more than 210 years, for those of you who are counting, and that's a very long time.

The family grew, and by the 1770s, Daniel Benton had three grown grandsons who lived in the house with him. One of them, Elisha, had taken an interest in a young woman in town named Jemima Barrows. She was the daughter of a cabinetmaker, and in a social station below that of the Bentons, and so Elisha's family looked down on the romance. They did everything they could to discourage them, but Elisha and Jemima were stubborn.

In 1775, an alarm was raised in Lexington, Massachusetts, that was heard across the countryside thanks to riders like Paul Revere. Colonists from all across New England came to join the fight, and among them were the three Benton grandchildren. While Daniel Benton was sad to see his grandchildren go off to war, he felt some relief, too, knowing that the separation just might be the thing Elisha needed to take his mind off the young woman. It is thought by historians that Daniel hoped the war might bring an end to their relationship forever. He was only partly right.

A year later, in 1776, all three of the Benton brothers were captured by British forces and taken to Long Island, where they were imprisoned on ships in Wallabout Bay, now home to the Brooklyn Navy Yard. These prison ships were notorious for their unsanitary conditions and the diseases that ran wild among the inmates. It was even thought that the British soldiers working the ships actually handed out food and bedding that was contaminated with smallpox.

Soon, Daniel Benton received word that his two older grandsons had died while onboard the prison ship, but no word came of the whereabouts of Elisha. He sent for word and waited impatiently, but before he could learn the truth, Daniel Benton passed away.

It was weeks later when the answer finally came: Elisha was

free and being brought home, but he was sick with smallpox. This was bittersweet news for the Benton family. On one hand, Elisha was coming home. That was a good thing for everyone. But on the other, smallpox was deadly. Nearly half of everyone who contracted the disease eventually died, and those were not the kind of odds that gave people hope.

When his fellow soldiers brought Elisha into the house, he was guided straight to a room near the kitchen known as a "dying and borning room," where those giving birth or sick with illness could be kept away from the rest of the house and cared for. It was a colonial America version of quarantine and intensive care.

But word spread of Elisha's return. Not every soldier and sailor returned from war, which is something that even homes today still deal with. And one of those who caught wind of the young Benton's arrival was Jemima Barrows. She had waited and stayed true to her beloved, and there was nothing she had hoped for more. Elisha had come home.

I imagine she ran rather quickly to the doorstep of the Benton home. I would imagine that she knocked—being from a lower social status, after all—but it must have been hard for her to not kick the door in and race to find her beloved. Jemima knew her place, though, and she waited for someone to come to the door.

She was told that Elisha was sick and that she needed to go back home, but Jemima turned out to be a very stubborn young woman. Even when they told her that he was dying from a highly contagious and deadly disease, she wouldn't relent. And in the end, she won: Jemima was allowed into the house, where she set herself up as his sole caretaker and nurse.

After a time, Jemima's parents became worried. Their daughter hadn't come home all day. So they made their way to the Benton home and asked if they had seen her. When they discovered that she was, in fact, in the room caring for a smallpox patient, it is said, they wept. Jemima's mother said that they would go back home and get clothing for their daughter, and then quickly left the Benton house.

They never came back.

THE GREAT DIVIDE

Elisha Benton died on January 21, 1777, after weeks of battling the smallpox that ravaged his body. Jemima stayed by his side the entire time, caring for him through it all. But her sacrifice did not come without a price. In the final days of Elisha's life, she too began to show signs of the illness. Within weeks, she also was dead.

The couple was buried on the Benton family property, alongside the stone walls that line the road to the house. But due to burial customs of the time, they were not allowed to share the same plot. Instead, they were separated by about forty feet, one grave on either side of the road.

It sounds like the end of a tragic story, and in some ways it is. Elisha and Jemima were never able to marry, and their young lives were cut short. But in other ways they live on. According to some, it's their separation outside that has led to the reports of their restless spirits within the home.

The Benton home was sold in 1932, and then again in 1969 to the Tolland Historical Society. It was converted into a museum shortly after, but the influx of visitors served only to draw out reports of mysterious occurrences.

One member of the staff claimed that her dog would not enter the dining room. When she picked the animal up and moved it to the sitting room, it refused to go anywhere else after that. Others have felt an overwhelming sense of foreboding and unwelcome. One woman, after cheerfully asking to visit the second floor, climbed the narrow staircase, only to return moments later, telling the staff, "I never want to go there again."

Noises have been heard throughout the house that are difficult to explain. Knocking, footsteps, and what sounds like the snapping of branches have all been reported by visitors. Some have even heard distant voices, and sometimes the movement of furniture. Others have heard what they describe as a weeping woman, someone who is mourning a deep loss. Those familiar with the homestead's past have assumed the woman is Jemima, crying for her lost love. A few have even seen the figure of a young woman in a white dress in various places in the house, searching for something no one else can see.

At times the home has been used by overnight guests. One couple actually lived there for a few weeks while their own house was being renovated, and on one occasion entertained a guest of their own. They claimed that on the night of their friend's visit, the conversation in front of the fireplace was interrupted by the sound of footsteps thumping down the hallway from the eastern door of the home. The sounds moved closer and closer to the living room, and then just stopped. The couple's guest was packed and gone within fifteen minutes.

Another couple who stayed overnight in the Benton homestead reported a very odd experience during their stay. Their hosts had retired to sleep upstairs, and they themselves had settled in down in the living room, which was serving double duty as a guest room. The wife claimed that she was awakened in the middle of the night. It was nearly completely dark in the room, but she felt as if someone—or some*thing*—was in the room with her. And then, as if materializing out of the darkness, a pair of legs appeared near the head of the bed. A man, she assumed, was standing there, close to her.

Her first assumption was that her host had come down to play a joke on her. Maybe that's the kind of guy he was, but the middle of the night is probably the worst time to play a joke, no matter who you are. Either way, she decided to call his bluff and wait to see what he would do.

Nothing could have prepared her for what happened next, though. A hand came out of the darkness and quickly covered her mouth. She flinched but held her ground. If he was going to try to frighten her, she decided, he was in for a surprise. She pretended not to care, but after a few moments it became hard to breathe, and in the end panic took over. Pushing the hand away, she sat up and whispered harshly at the figure, "What are you up to?" Almost instantly, everything vanished: the legs, the hand, all of it. Just . . . gone.

The following morning she brought up her experience at

breakfast and asked the hosting couple why they'd decided to pull that sort of prank. The husband and wife looked at each other with confused expressions on their faces.

They each made the same claim: no one had come downstairs during the night.

Pieces of Us

The places where we live can take on a certain life of their own. We fill them with our personality, our celebration, and sometimes even our tragedy. And although we can move on—whether by packing up and moving out or by leaving this earthly life—we often leave pieces of ourselves behind.

Like a forgotten cardboard box in the back corner of the attic, some of our echoes stay behind where others can discover them. Some call them ghosts. Others think of them as bad vibrations. I don't think any of us would be wrong, no matter what language we use. In the end, something stays behind, and it's not always easy to see.

Sometimes it is, though. A few years ago, an architectural photographer visited the Benton homestead with his sister in order to get some pictures for a project they were collaborating on. They wandered the property outside looking for the best view of the house. It's gorgeous, really, if you have a thing for antique homes, and the deep red paint on the wood clapboards is very classy and elegant.

Their project involved using Polaroid cameras, the kind that immediately kicks out a small, white-framed photograph that slowly develops into clarity. When they found the perfect place to shoot the house—very near the graves of Elisha and Jemima, incidentally—the photographer took a picture.

Something was wrong with the photo, so he took another. That one, too, was off. He showed it to his sister, and they tried a third. Then a fourth. Then a fifth and a sixth. Finally they switched to a backup camera, one that had just come back from being repaired at a camera shop, but the photographs that came out of the new camera were the same. It wasn't the camera, they realized eventually. It was the house.

All of the defective photos had the same flaw, as clear and easy to spot as the house itself. There, in each image, the second-story window was glowing, as if something bright and hazy was just behind the glass.

Adrift

I HAVE A CONFESSION to make. Keep in mind, I write about frightening things for a living. I haven't read a horror novel yet that's managed to freak me out. And yet . . . I'm deathly afraid of open water.

There, I said it. Even though I live near the coast and I've been out on the water before, I hate being on boats. I'm not even sure why, to be honest. I just am.

Perhaps it's the idea that thousands of feet of cold darkness wait right beneath my feet. Maybe it's the mystery of it all, of what creatures—known and unknown—might be waiting for me just beyond the reach of what little sunlight passes through the surface of the waves. But I'm pretty sure that what really makes my skin crawl is the thought that, at any moment, the ship could sink.

Maybe we can blame movies like *Titanic* or *The Poseidon Adventure* for showing us how horrific a shipwreck can be. But there's a far greater number of true stories of tragedy at sea than fictional ones. And it's in these real-life experiences—these maritime disasters that dot the map of history like an ocean full of macabre buoys—that we come face-to-face with the real dangers that await us in open water.

The ocean takes much from us. But in rare moments, scattered across the pages of history, we've heard darker stories. Stories of ships that come back, of sailors returned from the dead, and of loved ones who never stop searching for land.

Sometimes our greatest fears refuse to stay beneath the waves.

DEEP HAUNTINGS

Shipwrecks aren't a modern notion. As far back as we can go, there are records of ships lost at sea. In the *Odyssey* by Homer, one of the oldest and most widely read stories, we meet Odysseus shortly before he experiences a shipwreck at the hands of Poseidon, the god of the sea. Even farther back in time, we have the Egyptian *Tale of the Shipwrecked Sailor*, dating to at least the eighteenth century BCE.

The truth is, for as long as humans have been building seafaring vessels and setting sail into unknown waters, there have been shipwrecks. It's a universal motif in the literatures of the world, and that's most likely because of the raw, basic risk that a shipwreck poses to the sailors on the ships.

But it's not just the personal risk. Shipwrecks have been a threat to culture itself for thousands of years. The loss of a sailing vessel could mean the end to an expedition to discover new territory, or it could turn the tide in a naval battle. Imagine the results if Admiral Nelson had failed in his mission off the coast of Spain in 1805. Or how differently Russia's history might have played out had Tsar Nicholas II's fleet actually defeated the Japanese in the Battle of Tsushima. The advancement of cultures has hinged for thousands of years, in part, on whether or not their ships could return to port safely. But in those instances when ancient cultures have faded into the background of history, it is often through their shipwrecks that we get information about who they were.

In 2014, an ancient Phoenician shipwreck was discovered in the Mediterranean Sea near the island of Malta. It's thought to be at least twenty-seven hundred years old, and it contains some of the oldest Phoenician artifacts ever uncovered. For archaeologists and historians who study this ancient people, the shipwreck has offered new information and ideas.

The ocean takes much from us, and on occasion it also gives back. Sometimes, though, what it gives us is something less inspiring. Sometimes it literally gives us back our dead.

One such example comes from 1775. The legend speaks of a whaling vessel discovered off the western coast of Greenland in October of that year. Now, this is a story with tricky provenance, so the details will vary depending on where you read about it. The ship's name might have been the *Octavius,* or possibly the *Gloriana.* And from what I can tell, the earliest telling of the tale can be traced back to a newspaper article from 1828.

The story tells of how one Captain Warren discovered the whaler drifting through a narrow passage in the ice. After hailing the vessel and receiving no reply, Warren brought his own ship near and the crew boarded the mysterious vessel. Inside, they discovered a horrible sight.

Throughout the ship, the entire crew was found frozen to death where they sat. When they explored further and found the captain's quarters, the scene was even more eerie. There in the cabin were more bodies. A frozen woman, holding a dead infant in her arms. A sailor holding a tinderbox, as if trying to manufacture some source of warmth. And there, at the desk, sat the ship's captain.

One account tells of how his face and eyes were covered in a green, wet mold. In one hand the man held a fountain pen, and the ship's log book was open in front of him. Captain Warren leaned over and read the final entry, dated November 11, 1762— thirteen *years* prior to the ship's discovery:

> *We have been enclosed in the ice seventy days. The fire went out yesterday, and our master has been trying ever since to kindle it again but without success. His wife died this morning. There is no relief.*

Captain Warren and his crew were so frightened by the encounter that they grabbed the ship's log and retreated as fast as they could back to their own ship.

The *Octavius,* if indeed that was the ship's name, was never seen again.

The mid-1800s saw the rise of the steel industry in America. It was the beginning of an empire that would rule the economy for over a century, and like all empires, there were capitals. St. Louis, Baltimore, Buffalo, Philadelphia—all of these cities played host to some of the largest steelworks in the country.

And for those that were close to the ocean, this created the opportunity for the perfect partnership: the shipyard. Steel could be manufactured and delivered locally, and then used to construct the oceangoing steamers that were the lifeblood of late nineteenth-century life. The flood of immigration through Ellis Island, for example, wouldn't have been possible without the steamers. My own family made that journey.

One such steamer to roll out of Philadelphia in 1882 was the SS *Valencia*. She was 252 feet long and weighed in at nearly sixteen hundred tons. The *Valencia* was built before complex bulkheads and hull compartments, and she wasn't the fastest ship on the water, but she was dependable.

She spent the first decade and a half running passengers between New York City and Caracas, Venezuela. In 1897, while in the waters near Guantánamo Bay in Cuba, the *Valencia* was attacked by a Spanish cruiser. The next year, she was sold and moved to the West Coast, where she served in the Spanish-American War as a troopship making the voyage between the United States and the Philippines.

After the war, the *Valencia* was sold to a company that used the ship to sail between California and Alaska, but in 1906 she filled in for another ship that was under repair, and her new route became San Francisco to Seattle. They gave the ship a checkup in January of that year, and everything checked out good. For a twenty-four-year-old vessel, the *Valencia* was in perfect working order.

She set sail on the twentieth of January 1906, leaving sunny California and heading north. The ship was crewed by 9 officers and 56 crewmembers, and played host to 108 passengers. Somewhere near Cape Mendocino, off the coast of northern California, the weather turned sour. Visibility dropped and the winds kicked up.

When you're on a ship at night, even a slow one, losing the ability to see is a very bad thing. At night the crew typically rely on the stars in the same way sailors did centuries ago. But even that option was off the table for Captain Oscar Johnson, and so he used the only tool he had left: dead reckoning.

The name alone should hint at the efficacy of the method. Using last known navigational points as a reference, Captain Johnson essentially guessed at the *Valencia*'s current location. But guessing can be deadly, and so instead of pointing the ship at the Strait of Juan de Fuca, between Vancouver Island and the mainland, he unknowingly aimed it at the island itself.

Blinded by the weather and set on the wrong course by faulty guesswork, the *Valencia* struck a reef just fifty feet from shore near Pachena Point, on the southwest side of Vancouver Island. They say the sound of the metal ripping apart on the rocks was like the screams of dozens of people. It came without warning, and the crew reacted by immediately reversing the engines and backing off the rocks.

Damage control reported the hull had been torn wide open. Water was pouring in at a rapid pace, and there was no hope of repairing the ship. The *Valencia* lacked the hull compartments that later ships would include to guard against sinking in just such circumstances, and the captain knew that all hope was lost. So he reversed the engines again and drove the ship back onto the rocks. He was trying not to destroy the *Valencia* completely but to ground her, hoping that would keep her from sinking quite so quickly.

That's when all hell broke loose. Before Captain Johnson could organize an evacuation, six of the seven lifeboats were lowered over the side. Three of those flipped over on the way down, dumping out the people inside. Two more capsized after hitting the water, and the sixth boat simply vanished. In the end, only one boat made it safely away.

Frank Lehn was one of the few survivors of the shipwreck. He later described the scene in all its horrific detail:

> *Screams of women and children mingled in an awful chorus with the shrieking of the wind, the dash of rain, and the roar of the breakers. As the passengers rushed on deck they were carried away in bunches by the huge waves that seemed as high as the ship's mastheads. The ship began to break up almost at once and the women and children were lashed to the rigging above the reach of the sea. It was a pitiful sight to see frail women, wearing only night dresses, with bare feet on the freezing ratlines, trying to shield children in their arms from the icy wind and rain.*

About that same time, the last lifeboat made it safely away under the control of the ship's boatswain, Timothy McCarthy. According to him, the last thing he saw after leaving the ship was "the brave faces looking at us over the broken rail of a wreck, and of the echo of a great hymn sung by the women through the fog and mist and flying spray."

The situation was desperate. Attempts were made by the ship's remaining crew to fire a rescue line from the Lyle line-throwing gun into the trees at the top of the nearby cliff. If someone could simply reach the line and anchor it, the rest of the passengers would be saved. The first line they fired became tangled and snapped, but the second successfully reached the cliff above.

A small group of men even managed to make it to shore. There were nine of them, led by a schoolteacher named Frank Bunker. But when they reached the top of the cliff, they discovered the path forked to the left and right. Bunker picked the left.

Had he instead turned right, then men would have come across the second rescue line within minutes, and possibly saved all remaining passengers. Instead, he led the men along a telegraph line path for over two hours before finally managing to get a message out to authorities about the accident, making a desperate plea for help.

Help was sent, but even though three separate ships raced to the site of the wreck to offer assistance, the rough weather and choppy sea prevented them from getting close enough to do any good. Still, the sight of the ships nearby gave a false sense of hope to those remaining on the foundering vessel, and so when the few survivors onshore offered help, they declined.

There were no more lifeboats. No more lifelines to throw. And no ships brave enough to get closer. The women and children stranded on the ship clung to the rigging and rails against the cold Pacific waters, but when a large wave washed the wounded ship off the rocks and into deep water, everyone was lost.

All told, 137 of the 173 people aboard the ship died that cold early January morning. If that area of coastline had yet to earn its modern nickname of "Graveyard of the Pacific," this was the moment that cemented it.

The wreck of the *Valencia* was clearly the result of a series of unfortunate accidents, but officials still went looking for someone to blame. In the aftermath of the tragedy, the Canadian government took steps to ensure lifesaving measures along the coast that could help with future shipwrecks. A lighthouse was constructed near Pachena Point, and a coastal trail was laid out that would eventually become known as the West Coast Trail.

But the story of the *Valencia* was far from over. Keep in mind that there have been scores of shipwrecks, tragedies that span centuries, in that same region of water. And like most areas with a concentrated number of tragic deaths, unusual activity has been reported by those who visit.

Just five months after the *Valencia* sank, a local fisherman reported an amazing discovery. While exploring seaside caves on the southwestern coast of Vancouver Island, he described how he stumbled upon one of the lifeboats within the cave. In the boat, he claimed, were eight human skeletons. The cave was said to be blocked by a large rock, and the interior was at least two hundred feet deep. Experts found it hard to explain how the boat could have made it from the waters outside into the space within, but theories speculated that an unusually high tide could have lifted the boat up and over. A search party was sent out to investigate the alleged finding, but it was found that the boat was unrecoverable due to the depth of the cave and the rocks blocking the entrance.

In 1910, the *Seattle Times* ran a story with reports of unusual sightings in the area of the wreck. According to a number of sailors, a ship resembling the *Valencia* had been observed off the coast. The mystery ship could have been any local steamer except for one small detail: this ship was already floundering on the rocks, half submerged.

Clinging to the wreckage, they say, were human figures, holding on against the wind and waves.

HOPE FLOATS

Humans have had a love affair with the ocean for thousands of years. Across those dark and mysterious waters lay all manner of possibility: new lands, new riches, new peoples to meet and trade with. Setting sail has always been something akin to the start of an adventure, whether the destination was the Northwest Passage or just up the coast.

But an adventure at sea comes with great risk. We understand this in our core. It makes us cautious. It turns our stomachs. It fills us with equal parts dread and hope. Because there, on the waves of the ocean, everything can go according to plan—or it can fail tragically.

Maybe this is why the ocean is so often used as a metaphor for the fleeting, temporary nature of life. Time, like waves, eventually wears us all down. But our lives can also be washed away in an instant, no matter how strong or high we build them. Time takes much from us, just like the ocean.

The waters off the coast of Vancouver Island are a perfect example of that cruelty and risk. They can be harsh, even brutal, toward vessels that pass through them. The cold winters and sharp rocks can threaten the survival of a ship. And with over seventy shipwrecks to date, the Graveyard of the Pacific certainly lives up to its reputation.

For years after the tragedy of 1906, fishermen and locals on the island told stories of a ghostly ship that patrolled the waters just off the coast. They said it was crewed by skeletons of the *Valencia* sailors who lost their lives there. It would float into view and then disappear like a spirit again before anyone could try to reach it.

In 1933, in the waters just north of the twenty-seven-year-old wreck of the *Valencia,* a shape floated out of the fog. When a local approached it, the shape became recognizable: a lifeboat. It looked as if it had been launched just moments before. Yet there, on the side of the boat, were pale letters that spelled out a single word.

Valencia.

Adrift

Take the Stand

ON JUNE 24, 1408, a French court sentenced a murderer to death by execution. She had entered the home of a neighbor and found a four-month-old child inside, alone and unattended. Although she never disclosed her reason for doing so, she killed the child right there in the house.

After her trial, she was moved to the prison to be held until her execution. The others who were imprisoned there most certainly jeered at her. They called her names. Yes, they were hardened criminals, but to kill a child . . . even *they* were appalled. (The prison, however, treated her the same as those men by charging her family the same rate for her daily meals.)

On July 17, she was guided to the platform and a rope was placed around her neck. A crowd was most likely gathered that day to watch the spectacle. Like the criminals inside the prison, they too must have mocked her and shouted insults. And then, after the trap door snapped open and she plummeted to her death, it was over.

History is full of these stories. A criminal goes to trial, and justice wins the day. What was odd about the trial of 1408, though, was the suspect. She wasn't a local woman, or even a relative of the child she killed. She wasn't even human.

She was a pig. Literally, a farm animal. Tried in a court of law, sentenced to be put to death, and then executed on the gallows three weeks later.

During the long history of criminal trials, spanning cultures and centuries, all manner of oddities have entered the courtroom. As unusual as it might sound to put livestock on trial, humans have been guilty of worse.

And sometimes even the *dead* get to testify.

THE ERRAND BOY

Edward Shue was a stranger when he rolled into the small West Virginia town in the autumn of 1896. He claimed to have come from Pocahontas County to the north, but whether or not he was a mystery to everyone in town, he brought a necessary skill. Edward was a blacksmith, and he quickly found work in a local shop owned by James Crookshanks.

Within days of arriving, one of the local women caught his eye, and so Edward set his sights on winning her affection. Elva was young and beautiful, and the locals couldn't really blame the newcomer for falling head over heels for her. For her part, though, the feeling was mutual, despite the fact that Edward was at least a decade older than she was. Within a matter of weeks, the couple was married.

The first few months of their marriage were mostly uneventful, although it was later said that the young bride had become pregnant shortly after the wedding. The local physician had been treating her for slight complications with her pregnancy since the new year, but most of the people in town had no idea. It seems Elva was good at keeping secrets.

On the afternoon of January 23, 1897, with snow on the ground and a chill in the air, Andy Jones stepped into the warmth of the blacksmith shop. He was just eleven years old, but he worked for the newlyweds as an errand boy and housekeeper when they needed him. It was a common thing to see his small shape darting up and down the road, running messages from husband to wife and back again.

Edward told Andy that he was going to stop by the market before coming home at the end of the day, and so he instructed the boy to go and ask Elva if there was anything else she needed him to purchase. This was before text messaging, before the telephone, before email. So Andy, in his own way, was a premodern SMS service.

The boy ran off, and when he arrived at the couple's house, he let himself in. When he did, he was horrified to find Elva lying facedown on the floor at the foot of the stairs. One hand was pinned beneath her chest, while the other arm was stretched out. The house was deathly quiet.

At first he thought she was sleeping. He called out to her as he approached, but stopped when he noticed the odd bend in her neck. Even to his young, immature mind, something seemed wrong. Rather than moving closer, he backed slowly away, then turned and bolted home. Once there, he told his mother about everything he had seen.

Moms always have a way of knowing what to do, it seems. She quickly headed out the door to call on the town doctor, George Knapp, and took Andy with her. It took them nearly an hour to track him down and bring him to the blacksmith's home, but when they arrived, there was no body on the floor of the hall.

It might have been easy to write it off as a prank. Certainly in our own day and age, with tales of the boy who cried wolf, there's always a small suspicion that unbelievable stories might actually just be lies. Thankfully, though, they heard the sound of sobbing from the second floor of the home. Andy and his mom politely let themselves out, but Dr. Knapp headed upstairs.

He entered a main bedroom to find Elva's lifeless body laid out on the bed, with Edward seated beside her. He had apparently come home after Andy left and discovered his dead wife on the floor. After carrying her up to their room, he had changed her into a dark, formal dress with a high collar and long sleeves, and then arranged her for burial.

He was in tears, cradling her head and sobbing. When Dr. Knapp entered the room, Edward didn't look up. Attempting to be as respectful as he could of the man's loss, the doctor quietly inspected Elva's body for anything that might hint at the cause of her death. Having recently helped her with some other medical issues, he was familiar with her current state of health. At first glance, he felt that nothing seemed out of the ordinary, but he wanted to be thorough.

It was only when he reached for her head and neck that Edward stirred. He pushed the doctor's hands away and continued to gently run his fingers through her hair, sobbing deeply the entire time. It was clear to Dr. Knapp that the man simply needed to mourn. Picking up his things, he let himself out and exited the house.

While Edward grieved the loss of his young bride, Dr. Knapp went back to his office and recorded what little information he'd been able to ascertain. He listed her cause of death as "everlasting faint" before amending it to add the phrase "complications from pregnancy."

Life was hard in rural West Virginia at the end of the nineteenth century, that much was certain. What Dr. Knapp didn't know, however, was how much harder it had been for Elva Shue.

THINGS BURIED

The burial didn't go as planned. It began with Edward's rather unorthodox appearance at the undertaker's hours before the graveside service. He insisted on helping the undertaker position his wife in the coffin, and then placed one of her favorite scarves around her neck. He added two other items of clothing, pressing them in on either side of her head. He said it was so she could rest easier.

At the funeral, he continued to act in odd ways. He paced beside the casket the entire time. He stooped low every now and then to adjust her clothing, to make things perfect. And he wept continuously as he did this. It was the sort of panicked, nervous fussing you might expect from a distraught spouse.

The man was clearly grieved. He and Elva *had* been newly-weds, after all. This loss, so close to the emotional high of their wedding . . . well, it must have been crippling. And everyone seemed to understand that. Everyone, that is, except for Mary Heaster, Elva's mother.

Mary didn't trust Edward. And maybe that distrust was simply fueled by her dislike of the man. After all, he had rolled into town—a total stranger, an older man, a mysterious past—and taken her daughter from her. Maybe she just had issues of her own to deal with. Or maybe a mother's intuition *is* always right. No one knew for sure; they just knew she hated the guy.

Mary Heaster wrestled with this uneasy feeling for weeks. She had trouble sleeping, and understandably, she found it difficult to move on, to take a much-needed deep breath and press forward through life. And according to her testimony, she also prayed. It was a source of solace for her, and probably one of the ways she was grieving the loss of her daughter. Every day and every night, she prayed for the truth. But mostly she prayed for one specific thing: she wanted her daughter to return and tell her side of the story. Sure, all of us long for the ones we've lost. We'd love one more cup of coffee with them, one more hug, one more conversation. I know firsthand just how hard it is to let go. But Mary wanted her daughter to literally come back, and she prayed hard for it every day. And then it happened.

Mary told others that it happened over the course of four nights, each night revealing more truth, the experience becoming more visual and real. She said that her daughter, whom she had always called Zona, came into her room and spoke to her, first as a ball of light, and later as a fully formed body.

According to Mary, this was no dream; it was a vision. Her daughter revealed that Edward had killed her after months of physical abuse. There'd been an argument that final day, and Edward had strangled her right there at the foot of the stairs, breaking her neck high up beneath the skull. Once the story was told, Mary said, her daughter vanished once again.

Whatever suspicion she might have had prior to this vision, Mary Heaster quickly became a woman on a mission. She went to the local prosecutor, a man named John Preston, and told him the story. At first there wasn't much he was able to do. The case was closed, and a ghostly vision was far from being a valid reason to open it back up again.

But he wanted to help. Maybe, he told her, if there was something new, some new piece of information that could help call the official cause of death into question, it might justify digging deeper. Mary agreed, and John Preston got to work.

Not being a friend or relative of Elva's, Preston hadn't attended her funeral. When he started to ask around, though, people who had been there started to share interesting observations: Edward's odd behavior around the coffin, the positioning of the clothing around the area of her neck and head, his insistence that he never leave her side. All of it smelled a bit odd to an outside observer.

Preston took his suspicions to Dr. Knapp and asked the man if he'd seen any unusual details when he examined Elva's body the afternoon she was discovered. At first Knapp was defensive and stood by his work, by his medical opinion. We've all been there, I think—those moments when we know we might have made a mistake but we refuse to admit it. Dr. Knapp tried to make one of those prideful stands.

But Preston refused to let the matter rest, and eventually the physician caved in and told him the truth. Yes, he *had* examined her, but Edward had made a complete examination impossible. He was too protective, too territorial. Knapp admitted that he hadn't been able to fully examine her neck, and that omission had haunted him ever since.

In the end, that was the key they'd been looking for. Those details were enough to reopen the case, and with it, Elva Heaster Shue's grave. Dr. Knapp was assisted by two other physicians, who came to town to help with the exhumation, and after the coffin was set up in the local schoolhouse, they opened the lid.

What they found inside changed everything.

Lasting Marks

Elva's neck was badly bruised. It wasn't an oversight by Dr. Knapp, though. Sometimes bruising happens deep beneath the skin, and it's only after death that the marks rise to the surface. Here they were, and these marks were damning: clear finger impressions on both sides of the throat.

The doctors then conducted an autopsy on Elva's body and discovered what the marks hinted at. Her windpipe had been crushed, ligaments had been torn, and the vertebrae at the base of her skull had been completely displaced. Elva's death had been no accident: someone had strangled her, gripping her throat until the physical trauma ended her life.

The first thought on everyone's mind was that Edward had killed her, but that was quickly tempered by more sober thoughts. There was no proof tying Edward to the murder of his wife, no evidence that pointed definitively to him. Yes, there were finger marks, but those fingers could have belonged to anyone, right?

On the other hand, Mary Heaster knew all about the cause of death *before* the exhumation. She claimed that her knowledge had come to her through an otherworldly vision, that her deceased daughter had actually stepped through the veil between life and death and revealed the truth to her. But no one really *believed* that, did they?

Mary, it seemed, was more of a suspect than Edward was, and that didn't sit well with John Preston. He'd hoped that her vision would be dismissed for the insanity that it was, that it was just crazy enough to help her avoid suspicion. To help that along, though, he needed to know more about the other suspect, and so he began to investigate Edward Shue's past. What he found was shocking.

Edward Shue, it turned out, was a new name. His real name was Erasmus Stribbling Shue, though many who knew him prior to his days in West Virginia called him Trout. And Trout, it seems, had quite the past. Most important, Elva hadn't been his first wife, or even his second. She'd been his third.

The first marriage was in 1885 to one Ellie Cutlip. They even had a daughter together, but divorced in 1889 when Edward was sent to prison for stealing a horse. John Preston actually managed to track her down and interview her, and she was quick to tell him about how abusive and violent Edward had been toward her.

After getting out of prison, Edward married a second time, in 1894. Her name was Lucy Tritt, but she died within a year of the wedding. Preston was unable to track down a cause of death, but there were stories. There are *always* stories. And these stories spoke of how Lucy had been killed by Edward, who vanished from town a short while later.

At the time, the rumors had been dismissed. Death, even among the youth, was not uncommon. Tragic, yes, but it happened. Now, though, with a third wife in the grave, it raised all sorts of questions.

It was enough to arrest Edward. His trial began on June 22, 1897. Although the prosecution lacked the physical evidence to connect him to the death of Elva, they built their case on his string of marriages, and specifically on the death of Lucy Tritt Shue. There was a pattern, they told the jury, and that pattern should be proof enough. Edward Shue, they declared, was a cold-blooded killer.

The jury found him guilty, but rather than the death penalty that everyone expected, Edward was sentenced to life in prison. This didn't sit well with some. On July 11, while Shue was sitting in the county jail waiting to be transported to prison, a mob of nearly thirty angry men gathered outside of town. They were armed with guns and a brand-new rope tied into a noose.

Thanks to a tip from a local farmer who saw the men gathering, the sheriff was able to keep Edward safe. He rushed him out of the jail and into a hiding place until the chaos blew over. And then, as promised, Shue was delivered to his new home at the West Virginia State Penitentiary.

He died there three years later when a wave of pneumonia and measles swept through the prison. Mary Heaster died thirteen years after that, at peace with her role in the trial.

OTHERWORLDLY TESTIMONY

I doubt we could ever know for sure if Mary Heaster's ghostly visitor was really her daughter, back from the grave. It might very well have been nothing more than a personification of her suspicion and intuition. Or perhaps it was a projection of her grief and loss and pain. We'll never know for sure, but the effect was real enough.

When Mary Heaster took the stand in court that day in June 1897, John Preston was careful to avoid any mention of her vision. Partly it was because he didn't want her to sound like she had prior knowledge of the cause of her daughter's death, but mostly it was because that story made the woman sound crazy. She believed the ghost of her daughter had appeared in her bedroom and told her the truth. That was probably enough to discredit her as a witness against Edward Shue, and Preston wanted to avoid that at all costs.

The defense attorney noticed the omission, though, and decided to use it against them. While Mary was still on the witness stand, he grilled her about the vision she claimed to have experienced. I've read the court transcripts. I've read his insistence that it had been nothing more than a dream. That she'd been exhausted, obsessed, and overwhelmed with her loss.

But Mary stuck to her guns. It had been a vision, not a dream. She'd been fully awake when it happened, and it had really *had* happened, she said. And the judge allowed the testimony to stand. So when the jury retreated to make their decision, they did so with a ghost story as a piece of the evidence. It took them less than an hour to reach a verdict.

Sometimes folklore creeps into our lives and pushes us in a direction we never thought we'd go. Over the centuries, it's driven people to murder, to steal, to abuse, and to build social rules that oppress certain types of people. In that way, folklore is often an excuse for bad behavior.

But folklore is also like a gem: we can hold it up, turn it, and watch the light play off dozens of facets. The story of Mary Heaster and Edward Shue reveals the hopeful side of folklore, giving us all a glimpse of the power and sway it commands.

As rare as it was, this was a moment when folklore took the stand in a court of law. When belief had weight, and the supernatural world—at least for a few moments—entered public opinion and actually meant something. Yes, folklore can transform people into monsters; occasionally, though, it's empowered us to dig deeper for the truth.

The grave, it seems, can't always stop justice.

The Devil's Beat

IN EARLY 2012, a team of archaeologists discovered something groundbreaking inside a cave in southern Germany. They'd been working in the region for years, chasing a theory that early humans had followed the Danube River north into central Europe about forty-five thousand years ago.

The caves had provided a mountain of evidence, including early human jewelry and cave art representing humans and their growing collection of mythical heroes. But this cave added a new element to our picture of that early culture. There, in the dust and sediment of this dark cavern, researchers found flutes.

They were all made of bone—some mammoth, some bird. But they'd all been crafted in a way that would be completely recognizable to us today, too. Holes were drilled into one side, spaced out at regular intervals. And they are, to date, the oldest instruments uncovered in the world.

Music has been a part of human culture for thousands of years. And if you ask an archaeologist, she would probably tell you that even *older* instruments once existed. They're just impossible to find. Our voices, after all, are the original musical instruments. And shortly after that, scientists believe it was percussion that was invented next.

Music is in our blood. It's in our *soul*. The human experience, whether it was that of a nomadic Paleolithic hunter or a modern college student, would be incomplete without music. It pulls at our emotions. It inspires us. It helps us remember key lessons, and it's the central form of worship for many people around the world. Music is . . . well, it's *life*.

But part of life is death. And pain and sorrow and fear. And while it's not as common, music has been present in those moments as well.

Sometimes it's even caused them.

THE HEARTBEAT OF HUMANITY

One of the earliest physical instruments, according to most archaeologists, was the drum. It was probably a simple stone in the beginning, and the musician would bang another stone against it, or a stick. Which makes it hard to nail down a date for the earliest history of the drum, because every early human dig site seems to be crawling with sticks and stones.

It wasn't until around 6000 BCE that we started to see manmade drums, skins that were stretched tight over pottery or shells. But these early drums weren't unique to one place. We've uncovered them in Egypt, China, and almost every other ancient civilization we know of. Drums are, and always have been, global.

And their uses are as varied as the cultures that have created them. They've served as instruments of worship, as tools of communication, and as the driving force within ceremonial traditions that stretch back hundreds, even thousands, of years. It's like a heartbeat: wherever there is human activity, there's percussion.

One significant use of drums throughout history has been within the military. The ancient Chinese used drums to pass orders over vast distances and to synchronize the marching of foot soldiers. The war drum appears in the military history of the Aztecs, many peoples of West Africa, India, most ancient Near Eastern kingdoms, and so many more. But it wasn't a prominent tool in Europe until the start of the Crusades.

One unique moment in military history, as far as I can tell, happened in the aftermath of the English Civil War. During the nine-year war between the Royalists and Parliamentarians, soldiers on both sides of the conflict fought for the future of their country. And even when it ended in 1651, much of the military was kept active, known then as the New Model Army.

But when Charles II reclaimed his father's crown in 1660, everyone was sent home. Many of these soldiers had been in service for years and had very little to go back to. No jobs, no homes, no fortunes. So one common procedure was to give soldiers permission to become beggars. They were literally given badges and papers that made it legal for them to wander certain areas looking for charity or work. And military drummers were no exception.

So there you go . . . a lot of history in just a few paragraphs. It might not be dark or frightening, but every historical moment needs context. Now, let's shift gears, shall we?

In the year following the restoration of the monarchy to England, Ireland, and Scotland, in a small town about eighty miles west of London one man had an encounter with one of these licensed beggars. John Mompesson was visiting a friend in the town of Ludgershall. And it was while he was there that he heard the sound of a drum from outside the house, in the village.

Now, John was a former officer in the military. Like a lot of men his age, he'd served in the English Civil War. He knew the traditions and the rules, but he also knew how they were being abused. Plus, being a tax official, he had a professional interest in making sure that everyone with a license to beg did so within the boundaries of the law.

So when he heard the drummer, he asked his friend, who was a local bailiff with a bit of authority. This friend told him the beggar was a man named William Drury, and said that Drury had flashed his permit around town, asking for money and drumming for attention. But John wanted to be sure, so he asked to meet the man.

When John approached Drury, he asked to see the man's beggar's badge and paperwork, which would have had the signatures of the military officers who issued the license. Drury cheerfully handed them over. But there was a problem.

You see, John recognized the names on the paperwork. Both Sir

William Cawly and Colonel Ayliffe were men he'd served with. So John was familiar enough with their signatures to recognize these as forgeries. Drury was caught in the act, and John had him arrested and taken into custody.

Drury immediately confessed to the local constable, and in an effort to stop his illegal begging, the man's drum was taken away from him. Drury begged for it to be returned, but instead it was moved to the bailiff's house, where John had been visiting. So when the beggar was finally hauled off to jail, he went without his precious drum.

That was in March 1661. The following month, John traveled to London for business and was gone several days. I doubt he thought much about the events in Ludgershall or the drummer who had tried to cheat a village.

When John arrived back home, he probably hugged each of his three children, gave his wife a kiss, then made his way toward his favorite chair to rest his tired body after a long day of travel. And there, waiting for him, was a mysterious package.

His wife explained that it had arrived while he was away. But she hadn't opened it. That was John's business, after all. Now, maybe it was in a sack, or perhaps it was wrapped in cloth like a present. However it had arrived, John set about opening the package. And then, suddenly, he stopped.

The object inside . . . was a drum.

KNOCK, KNOCK

It wasn't just *any* drum, of course. It was *the* drum. The beggar's drum. But according to John's wife, the drum wasn't the only unusual thing that had arrived while he was gone.

She told him that the night after his friend the bailiff had dropped off the package, a group of thieves had come to the house. It seemed to her as if a dozen or so men had run around the house, pounding on all of the doors for a short while. And then they vanished.

The next night, the men were back. If they were thieves or

bandits, they never tried to break inside. But they pounded. John's wife knew this because she could hear it loudly inside the house. Needless to say, she was glad for John's return.

Three nights after he came back from London, it happened again. In the middle of the night, they were both startled by the sound of someone pounding on the front door. John slipped out of bed and grabbed two pistols, one in each hand, and cautiously approached the door. Then, carefully, he opened it.

There was no one there. Outside, the darkness was still and silent. But before he could close the door, the knocking started up again from a different part of the house. Maybe whoever was outside was just confused about which door to knock on. Maybe they needed help. Or maybe they were playing a game. Filled with an odd mixture of fear and frustration, John locked the front door and ran as fast as he could to the other door.

This door, though, was like the first. No visitor was waiting for him on the other side. No bandit was there, gun in hand. The doorstep was empty. But before he could think what was going on, the knocking sounded for a third time—this time from high up on the second floor of the house. John dashed to the stairs as fast as he could.

He probably could have guessed what he'd find. He likely knew it before he opened the door that led out onto the roof of the second floor. But he did it anyway. And sure enough, just outside the door, there was . . . nothing. No midnight visitor, no bandit, no trickster. Just darkness.

But not silence. Not this time, at least. As John stood there, staring out into the night, he claims he heard something. It was like the sound the wind makes on a stormy night, except it was different, more sinister. He described it as "hollow." It seemed evil and empty. Almost *hungry*.

John closed and locked the door and prayed for the sound to stop, and for a while it did. He climbed back into bed, and he and his wife tried to sleep. But the noises picked up again later. This time, the pounding seemed to come from the very air around their home, as if someone were knocking on thin air.

However much John wished it could have been an isolated

event, it wasn't. For the next month, the pounding continued each night. It was loud and constant. Almost rhythmic. Almost . . . like a *drum*.

And then the noises crept inside. They were just as loud, but now they were emanating from the room where John kept the confiscated drum, the one William Drury had begged to have returned to him. And John couldn't help but wonder: What if Drury had died? What if the drummer was dead because of what John had done, and now the man was back to haunt him?

The events that followed were completely unnerving to John and his family. The furniture would shake along with the drumming sounds. But only at night. Only when they were trying to get some rest. It would start up, wake the household, and then fade away after an hour or two.

To make matters worse, that hollow sound—the sound that John had heard outside after returning from London—was back, but like the drum, it had also moved indoors. Week after week, month after month, the torment continued. It seemed as if it would never end.

Then John's worst fears came to life. You see, if the events so far were indeed caused by the angry spirit of the beggar William Drury, then sounds could hardly be seen as definitive proof. But over time the activity evolved. Objects began to move. John's elderly mother, who lived with the family, even found her Bible in the fireplace, buried in the ashes.

And then things got personal. It started to attack the family.

GETTING PERSONAL

It was the children who seemed to be the focus of the attacks. Some nights their beds would shake violently, as if something invisible were slamming into them. Other times, loud scratching noises could be heard beneath the beds. On a few occasions, the children themselves were even affected. Mysterious, invisible hands lifted them up until they were suspended in midair over their beds.

Fearing for the safety of their children, John and his wife moved them to another room in the house where nothing unusual had taken place so far. But once they were settled there, the invisible forces followed them in, and everything continued. And it wasn't just the children who were encountering the unexplainable.

One of the servants who lived and worked in the household was also named John. According to John Mompesson's own account, early on the morning of November 5, 1662, this servant named John ran to the room where the children were sleeping because the noises had started again. Across the room, the servant could see two boards that had been placed there, leaning against the wall. And one of them was moving.

I'm not sure what inspired the servant to do it, but he spoke and asked for the board to be brought to him. There was silence for a moment, and then one of the boards floated up from the floor and moved toward him, stopping about three feet from where he stood. The servant extended a hand and asked again, and this time the board moved right into his hand.

John, the homeowner, walked in a moment later to find the servant passing the board back and forth with some invisible force. Frightened by what it might mean, John told the servant to stop, which he did. But that was a breaking point for John Mompesson. Something was in his house—something he couldn't see or control—and it was interacting with his family.

In early December 1662, John wrote a desperate letter to a relative named William Creed, who happened to be a professor of divinity at Oxford. If anyone had the wisdom and knowledge to help him, John assumed that this would be the man. Sadly, Creed was just as perplexed as everyone else.

There were more and more new experiences each day. John noticed that an odd odor would fill the house from time to time. They heard the sound of heavy chains being rattled and dragged on the floor. Loud voices came from empty parts of the house. There was even heavy breathing, as if someone large and invisible were standing in the room with them.

All the while, the drumming continued, sometimes so loud that the neighbors could hear it. And all that noise drew public attention. People traveled from far across the area just to hear the drumming and to experience the hauntings for themselves. But with fresh eyes and ears also came fresh news.

You see, up until this point, John Mompesson had assumed the drummer had died or had been killed, and that his spirit was the cause of all their troubles. But word reached him in the summer of 1663 that this wasn't true at all. William Drury was alive and well. After a short stint in a Gloucester jail for stealing some pigs, the man had escaped. Then he'd purchased himself a new drum and gone back to wandering the area again.

But there were other rumors. It was said by some that Drury had bragged to more than a few people about bewitching John's house. And according to the beggar's old military friends, Drury had a reputation for being a sorcerer.

Of course, rumors didn't mean that Drury really was a sorcerer. It could very well have just been a lot of unchecked superstition. But for a man as desperate as John, these notions represented hope. He was looking for a logical explanation for his situation, and these tales of witchcraft did the trick.

So Drury was brought to Salisbury, where he was put on trial for the spiritual equivalent of aiding and abetting a criminal. They accused him of sorcery and presented the evidence against him: the drumming, the invisible forces in the house, the rumors, all of it. In an age when witchcraft was considered real, possible, and punishable, Drury's freedom was suddenly on the line.

Judge Isaac Burgess listened to it all. He weighed the evidence. And, it seems, he brought common sense to the table. Because on August 3, 1663, Drury was acquitted. Not easily, they say. It was a tough choice, but in the end, he wasn't charged with witchcraft. That didn't mean he was off the hook, though. There was still the theft charge, so the very next day he was taken back to a Gloucester jail.

The results of that trial are important to our story, because when he was finally convicted of *that* crime, Drury was placed on a prison ship and sent to live in a penal colony. And then, as if a switch had been flipped, the drummer's hold over the Mompesson household—the drumming, the noises, the invisible hands, all of it—just stopped.

Their nightmare was finally over.

SPHERE OF INFLUENCE

On the surface, this is just one more in a long line of haunted house stories. I get that, trust me. But the drummer of Tedworth is much more than just a spooky poltergeist tale.

It's the story of one family's struggle to understand their unusual experiences in a world that was quick to reach for supernatural explanations. It's a story that had what many other tales always seem to lack—eyes on the ground, contemporary documents that still exist today, and multiple testimonies by outsiders about what they experienced at the house.

Still, it *is* a haunted house story. It's a tale that plays with our ability to suspend disbelief. It presents us with something that, at first blush, seems trivial, almost laughable: a household of normal, rational people held hostage by a drum.

It's easy to wonder: was it a haunting or was it witchcraft? Because those are different things in folklore. It resembles so many different types of supernatural activity that it's a hard story to pin down. But perhaps, in the end, it was something much more mundane.

There's a good chance this story was actually grounded in something less superstitious but no less dark and evil: politics. As I said earlier, William Drury had been a drummer in the English Civil War. And he had served with the Parliamentarians.

John Mompesson, on the other hand, had served as an officer on the side of the Royalists. Which means that he and the drummer were political enemies. It would be like watching a Union officer and a Confederate soldier meeting each other just a year after the end of the American Civil War. You can end a war, sure, but bad blood is a lot more difficult to put a stop to.

After nine weeks of silence and peace in the Mompesson household, it all started happening again: the noises, the breathing, the moving objects . . . and the drumming.

We don't have to take John's word for it, either. There were witnesses to it. One pair, an attorney named Anthony Ettrick and his friend Sir Ralph Bankes, actually spent the night and reported knocking sounds. They claimed to be able to request that the spirit knock in specific numbers, and that it complied willingly.

Naturally, this perplexed John Mompesson. It frustrated him, too. And maybe even frightened him. So he began to ask around. He had connections, after all. And soon enough, he received the news he'd already feared.

William Drury had escaped and was already back on English soil. Back, and in the area again. If the explanation for the mysterious sounds involves the drummer needing to be in close proximity to the house, his return and the resumption of the sounds certainly seem to support it.

Is this proof that a political argument rarely finds a peaceful solution? Or one more clue that hints at a supernatural explanation? Either way, it's proof of the magical nature of music.

If you can hear it, it has power.

Mary, Mary

PLANES AREN'T SUPPOSED to collide with each other. Just taking statistics into account, you're a lot more likely to hear about automobile collisions than those involving airplanes, because of the simple fact that there are a lot more cars on the road today than planes in the air. Still, as unusual as it sounds, it happens.

In the late 1950s, two military planes were flying off the coast of Georgia, above Tybee Roads, the spot where the Savannah River's estuary meets the waters of the Atlantic. Those waters are a busy shipping lane, but on February 5, 1958, the sky above was busy as well.

At two o'clock that morning, a B-47 bomber was running a simulated mission along the coast, heading up from Florida. At the same time, an F-86 fighter plane was patrolling from the north. When they collided, it wasn't disastrous, like you might see in a movie—neither plane exploded—but both were badly damaged. The pilot of the fighter plane had to eject and let the plane drop into the sea. The bomber, though, managed to stay in the air. The aircraft lost a lot of altitude, and it was clear that the crew was going to need to make an emergency landing, and fast. To help with this, they requested and received permission to jettison some extra weight.

They dropped only one thing, though. On board was a bomb that weighed nearly eight thousand pounds. A *nuclear* bomb. And they released it off the coast of Tybee Island, where it plummeted into the sea below. The military tried to recover it later that year, but the mission was a failure. The bomb is still there to this day.

That's the trouble with a world as big as ours. Things—even large things—are easy to hide. It adds a layer of mystery to our experience, an element of unknown risk. But the hidden things of our world aren't limited to objects. Even *people*—the ones who live and breathe and move around us all the time—can act a lot like the cold, dark waters of the sea. At the end of the day, you never know what lies hidden just beneath the surface.

MARY . . .

Mary was born in 1847, and she was just six months old when she had her first seizure. Her muscles twitched uncontrollably, and the pupils of her eyes dilated. Her parents, Asa and Ann Roff, were of course sick with worry. The seizure, which seemed to be epileptic, left Mary unconscious for several days, and for a while they assumed the worst. Still, she recovered, and life moved on, though she continued to suffer seizures.

In an effort to find some relief for their daughter, the family moved from Indiana to Texas when she was about ten. A year later, they followed the newly built Peoria Railroad back north and settled in the brand-new town of South Middleport, Illinois. They built one of the first houses there, started a new life, and hoped for the best. But Mary's seizures didn't cease.

By the time they moved to Illinois, she was having them at least once a day. This was before even the earliest anti-epileptic drugs, such as potassium bromide, and the lack of options left Mary and her parents feeling depressed and hopeless. Add to this the intense drain that regular seizures had on her physical health, and it's easy to see how dark those days must have been for her.

One of the methods they tried for a while was bloodletting. It's a practice that dates back thousands of years, and it's been done with many sorts of implements, from knives and needles to spring-loaded cutting devices. One of the professions that historically delivered bloodletting services was, of all people, the barber. Even today, you can find barber shops that still use the red-and-white striped pole outside. It's a carryover from another era, designed to represent blood and bandages.

Mary's preferred method, though, was actually leeches. And because she complained constantly of headaches, she would place them on her temples, believing they would help. She used them so often that she even began to view them as pets. Like a child with a kitten, time spent with her leeches would often put a smile on Mary's face.

(As an aside: if your kid asks for a dog for Christmas, I can't help but feel like they're missing out on a fun pet option here. Leeches are really cheap to feed, and you don't have to walk them. Just putting it out there.)

Mary went on like this for about three years, with the use of the leeches escalating slowly. All the while, she was a sad young woman, and rightly so. But she was also bright, excelling in her studies and even becoming an accomplished pianist. Her music choices reflected her mood, though, leaning more toward the dark and melancholy.

In 1864, at the age of eighteen, she took the bloodletting to a new level, cutting herself on the arm with a knife. The loss of blood was so heavy that it caused her to pass out. When she did regain consciousness, something seemed off. She spent days screaming and thrashing around on her bed. There were periods of several hours at a time when multiple adults had to hold her down to prevent her from hurting herself.

And then, like a tropical storm that's passed through a city, everything went calm. Instead of uprooted trees and leveled buildings, though, Mary was left awake but unresponsive. It was as if something inside of her had broken. People would walk into the room and speak to her, but she didn't seem to notice them. No eye contact. No reply. If she could see and hear them, she certainly wasn't acknowledging them.

Mary was still able to carry out many routine daily activities, such as dressing herself or putting her hair up with pins. But her parents started to notice something odd about it all. When Mary did those things, her eyes were open, but she didn't seem to be using them. She was completing tasks that required sight, but her eyes never moved, never shifted or focused on the task at hand. It was as if she wasn't really seeing anything at all.

So they decided to test it out. They put a blindfold on her and then asked her to repeat the same tasks. Mary complied, and successfully, too. Even with a dark blindfold on, she could dress herself completely, even picking up pins off the dressing table and using them to do her hair. Of course, all of that could have been muscle memory, but there were other, less explainable things she could do. For example, still blindfolded, she had an encyclopedia placed in front of her. Even though she couldn't see the pages, she opened the book up to the word "blood"—and then proceeded to read the entry word for word.

This made a lot of people in town curious. She was doing something that no one should be able to do, and they wanted answers. So they began to come to the house to test her. One person suggested that she might have memorized the encyclopedia entry— she'd been obsessed with blood for years, of course—so they asked for a more difficult test. They took a few of Mary's personal letters, written in her own hand, and then shuffled them into a larger stack of papers. Still blindfolded, Mary was able to pull out her own and then read them aloud to the people in the room.

A local newspaper editor even stopped by to do his own experiment, and his was the most astounding of them all. He arrived with an envelope in his coat pocket. It was still sealed, and inside it, he told everyone, was a letter from a friend who lived far away.

He handed the envelope to a blindfolded Mary, who turned it over and over but never opened it. And then, without hesitation, she announced the name of the person whose signature was on the letter. The editor opened it up and checked; Mary was correct.

But it wasn't all magic shows and wonder. No, Mary was continuing to have seizures on a daily basis, and as a result, her depression was deepening. And that led to more cutting. It's tragic, really—in the middle of the nineteenth century, mental health care still was practically medieval, and that meant that Mary was left to suffer largely without help beyond her own family.

On July 5, 1865, Mary's parents left her home alone while they took a short trip. Mary got up that day, made herself breakfast, and then went back up to her bedroom. It was there that she had a powerful seizure and died as a result.

She was only nineteen years old.

. . . MARY . . .

A year before the tragic death of Mary Roff, Thomas and Lucinda Vennum welcomed a daughter into their family. Mary Vennum was born in Illinois in April 1864, and almost immediately the family took to calling her by her middle name, Lurancy.

In 1871, when Lurancy was just seven, her family moved up from Milford to South Middleport, but in the years between Mary Roff's death and the Vennums' move, the town had become the county seat of the newly formed Iroquois County. In honor of a well-known Native American woman who'd been born in the area, the town changed its name to Watseka.

For a while, Lurancy's childhood was healthy, happy, and un-remarkable. But in early July 1877, at the age of thirteen, Lurancy started to complain that she'd been hearing voices in her bedroom. She claimed they were calling out to her, saying her name over and over. Her parents, chalking it up to the overactive imagina-tion of a child, largely ignored her.

Then, on the night of July 5, Lurancy had a small seizure that left her in an odd state. She was still conscious, but she stayed mysteriously rigid for nearly five hours. When she finally snapped out of whatever trance she seemed to have been in, she told her parents that she felt rather strange. Of course she did, they said. She'd had a seizure, after all.

The following day, Lurancy had a second seizure and entered into that awake-yet-stiff state once more. This time, though, she spoke. Her parents sat beside her bed and listened as she told them what she could see. But even though her eyes were open, she didn't describe the bedroom to them. She described Heaven.

Specifically, she described seeing her two siblings, her sister

Laura and brother Bertie, both of whom had passed away young. In fact, Lurancy had been only three when her brother died, and the family rarely talked about those painful memories, which made her description even more unusual.

All through the summer and well into November, Lurancy continued to have these trances. Each time, she would describe another world, the world beyond the veil of reality. Beyond that curtain that separates life and death, there were angels, spirits, Heaven, and all of the details she attached to it. It seemed surreal. And then on November 27, things . . . well, they took a left turn at Weird and cruised down Crazy Street, if you know what I mean.

The seizure she had that night was extremely violent. She was stretched out on the bed and would violently arch her back with each episode. One report claims that she bent so sharply at the waist that her feet touched her head, though I'm honestly not sure how that's possible. If it happened, I can't imagine a more creepy scene than watching a young woman bend in half backward while screaming in pain.

This wasn't a one-time thing, either. These new seizures went on for weeks, leaving the family distraught and Lurancy exhausted and in pain. This pattern—first seizures, and then visions—repeated itself regularly for nearly three months. Their doctor didn't know how to help. And while the seizures were something that he could at least put a medical name to, her visions of the afterlife—full of spirits and angels and the like—defied his expertise. Members of her extended family were beginning to think that the young woman had lost her mind. They begged the Vennums to send her to Peoria, where there was an asylum well equipped to help treat her illness, but the Vennums refused.

One person who *did* offer them answers was Dr. E. Winchester Stevens. He was a friendly man in his mid-fifties from Janesville, Wisconsin, and he worked as a spiritualist doctor, offering a mixture of medicinal cures and otherworldly solutions to people just like the Vennums.

He'd heard of Lurancy's story through the Vennums' neighbors, an older couple with an interest in spiritualism and the afterlife. But when Dr. Stevens entered her room for the first time on the thirty-first of January, he didn't meet Lurancy. Instead, the voice that came out of the young woman claimed to be that of an elderly German woman named Katrina Hogan.

She'd been sixty-three years old when she passed away years before, and now she was in possession of Lurancy's body. And she wasn't nice, apparently. This elderly spirit, speaking through the young woman's mouth, insulted and verbally abused Thomas and Lucinda Vennum. This went on for a few moments before shifting into another spirit entirely.

This one claimed to be that of a young man named Willie Canning, who'd died after running away from his family. But he, too, vanished after just a few minutes. Dr. Stevens, who'd simply been an observer up until this point, stepped in to help. According to the historical account of the events of that day, Stevens used mesmerism—what we would call hypnosis today—in an attempt to help Lurancy calm down.

And the seizures stopped. The young woman managed to tell all the adults in the room—her parents, Dr. Stevens, and the neighbor who had brought the spiritualist to the Vennum home—that evil spirits wanted to control her. She was afraid, and she wanted help. Dr. Stevens suggested that perhaps she should find a *good* spirit instead. Lurancy nodded, then closed her eyes.

When she opened them again, she smiled. It was as if all the pain and trauma were gone and Lurancy had become whole again. Except she hadn't. Instead, she turned her gaze toward the neighbor standing toward the corner of the room, a look of intense recognition on her face.

"Father?" she said, and then added, "It's me. Mary Roff."

. . . Quite Contrary

Mr. and Mrs. Roff were understandably full of mixed emotions. They'd spent the past twelve years getting over the loss of their daughter. Mr. Roff had even gone to see a medium more than once, hoping for answers or at least closure. In one instance, the medium handed him a note, claiming it had been communicated to her by his dead daughter.

There was a lot of guilt there, obviously; they'd left their daughter alone for three whole days, after all, and when they'd returned from their trip, she was dead. They'd spent years getting over all of that. Mary had been a joy and a challenge and a blessing all at the same time, but for more than a decade she'd been gone from their life.

Until now.

Mr. Roff went home that afternoon and told his wife what had happened. At the same time, Dr. Stevens continued to ask Lurancy questions to get to the root of her morbid role-playing. But every answer just confused the spiritualist more. This young woman was no longer Lurancy Vennum. She was Mary Roff.

And Mary, it seems, wanted to go home. She didn't recognize anyone in the Vennum household at all. They were strangers to her. She wanted to return to the home she knew and loved. So she asked the Vennums if she could go live with her parents at *their* house, and kept repeating this request for days. Finally, after nearly a week, the Vennums relented, and they escorted their daughter out of the house, down the street, and up to the front door of the Roffs' house.

There she immediately fell into a comfortable routine. She used nicknames for her parents and siblings that no one but Mary Roff would have known. She recognized family friends and would mention others from out of town that the Roffs knew, people who had never visited Watseka in all the years the Vennums had lived there. There was simply no way for anyone other than Mary Roff to know these things.

When she did see the Vennums, she treated them as if they were just some nice family she'd only recently met. She was polite to them, sure, but it never evolved into anything more. But Mary knew of Lurancy. In fact, she claimed to understand better than anyone else what was really going on with her. It was just a difficult story to believe.

Mary said that Lurancy was sick. Her seizures were a symptom of that illness. But Mary had gone through all of that in her own lifetime, and she knew how to help. So Lurancy, at least according to Mary, was in Heaven "getting better." And when she'd recovered, Mary would leave and allow the young woman back into her own body.

Look, I get the skepticism. I'm right there with you. This is pretty bizarre stuff, no doubt about it. And these people were obviously primed for this story, too. Spiritualism was hot in 1878. The amazing Fox sisters were three decades deep into their career as world-famous mediums, traveling around performing séances for sellout audiences. It would be another ten years before their act was exposed as a fraud. To the Vennums and the Roffs, and especially to Dr. Stevens, spiritual things were real and possible and undeniable.

To our modern minds, though, there's a lot to question. Lurancy had to have known her neighbors prior to that day. She'd most likely heard the tragic story of Mary Roff, if not from their own mouths then from others in town. Surely at some point in her childhood someone looked at her and said, "Oh, you live next door to the Roffs." It's not a story you forget.

But there were things that are harder to dismiss. Being able to name out-of-town friends was one of them, but the woman claiming to be Mary Roff could do a lot more than that. She had dozens of conversations with old friends—people who had known Mary well before her death—and in each of those chats she mentioned details or events that no one other than her could know.

One day, Mary walked into the Roffs' sitting room and pointed to a velvet headdress sitting on a table. Mrs. Roff had pulled it out of Mary's things and left it for the young woman to discover. When Mary saw it, she lit up and described how she had worn it when her hair was short. Mrs. Roff nodded in disbelief.

Another time, Mary approached Mr. Roff and told him that she had sent him a note once, through a medium he'd gone to see. She told him the date, and he confirmed it with others. How she knew it, though, was a mystery—unless, of course, she really was Mary, back from the dead.

All of this went on for over fifteen weeks. There were periods here and there when Mary seemed to disappear and Lurancy would return to her body. But these were brief moments, and Lurancy never seemed to be fully there. She was confused, especially by her surroundings in the Roff house, and she asked to be taken home. But before anything could be done, Mary would return.

On May 7, Mary announced to the Roffs that Lurancy was ready to return for good. There were more brief switches between the two spirits for another two weeks, and then it was over. On May 21, Mary stood in the parlor of the Roff home and said tearful goodbyes to her family. Then one of the Roff daughters took her by the arm and escorted her down the sidewalk to the Vennums' house. They chatted as they walked, with Mary discussing family matters and giving life advice to the other woman. And then they arrived.

Mary mounted the steps alone and knocked on the front door. When the Vennums opened it, Mary had vanished. Lurancy was in full control of her own body again, awake and aware. She said she felt as if she'd been dreaming, and then embraced her parents. They wept for joy and welcomed her home.

For as long as she lived, she never had another seizure.

VISITATIONS

This is one of those events that are difficult to accept. I fully admit that. Many people believe Lurancy Vennum made the whole thing up. It was a cry for attention, or a youthful prank, or maybe even a stunt put on by both families.

Others, though, think it's possible that she suffered from some form of psychosis, which ultimately manifested itself as schizophrenia. They believe that, had the Roffs not taken her in and given the girl time to recover, the Vennums eventually might have had to send her to a mental asylum, which—in the 1870s—was a one-way ticket to suffering and possible death. According to those who subscribe to this theory, it was the generosity and open-mindedness of her neighbors that saved her.

But too many questions are left on the table for us to sort through. How did symptoms as dramatic and serious as powerful seizures simply vanish after just fifteen weeks? How did she know things about the Roffs that no one else could have known? There was even a moment during the ordeal when Lurancy, claiming to be Mary, told Dr. Stevens that she'd seen his deceased daughter in heaven, and described a cross-shaped scar on his daughter's cheek. Dr. Stevens, amazed, confirmed that the scar was from surgery she'd undergone to stop an infection.

Whatever we end up believing today, back then Lurancy's parents were convinced. They said that their daughter had returned to their home "more intelligent, more industrious, more womanly, and more polite than before." She'd grown up somehow. And she was physically restored. No more seizures, no more random trances. It was all gone.

For a couple of years, though, Lurancy tried her hand at being a medium. Maybe the Roffs talked her into it, or maybe she wanted to see if she could still do the things that she'd become famous for.

Four years later, she married a farmer named George Binning. George, it seems, had no interest in spiritualism, and shortly afterward, her efforts to work as a medium sort of ground to a halt. Two years later, they left town, moving to a farm in Kansas. They raised thirteen kids and, naturally, life got busy. But she stayed in touch with folks back home as best she could.

One of the people who wrote her often was Mr. Roff. It's understandable, really. For a little while, his daughter Mary had come back, and he was attached to Lurancy because of it. And on the rare occasions that she returned to Watseka to visit her parents, she would always make it a point to walk next door and visit the Roffs.

She would knock, of course. It wasn't really her home, after all. But they would always welcome her in. I imagine they'd make her a cup of tea and gather together in the sitting room. I have to wonder if Mary's velvet headdress was still sitting out on the table, and if Lurancy ever felt it looked familiar somehow.

What we do know is that each time she visited the Roffs, she would do them a favor. After a bit of polite conversation, she would sit back in her chair and close her eyes. The clock on the mantel would tick loudly, almost like footsteps approaching from another room. And then her eyes would open again. But it wouldn't be Lurancy.

"Hello, Mother," she would say to them. "Hello, Father. How are you? It's so good to be home."

The Lump

THERE ARE A lot of differences between the northern and southern states in America. The cultures are different. Their citizens behave differently. The climate is vastly different. The way things look and feel . . . just trust me on this, there are big differences. If you spend any time in both regions, you'll feel those differences, too.

So it probably wasn't the smartest idea when Salathiel Stoner married a woman from the South. There was nothing wrong with the act, mind you. And the young couple seemed to love each other. It's just that it didn't seem like either of them weighed those differences carefully enough. They stepped blindly into a life of frustration and broken expectations, and nothing good could ever come of that.

Sal—that's what his friends called him, and it's a heck of a lot easier to say than Salathiel, right?—had gone south, according to the legend, to settle his uncle's estate. I don't know when or why his uncle had moved to Falls Church, Virginia. All I know is that the Stoners had lived in Maine for generations. Right on the coast, actually, near Brunswick. I can only guess that maybe Sal's uncle understood those differences, too, and found the South to be a better home for his sensibilities.

But at the young age of twenty-nine, Sal found himself wrapping up the legal loose ends of his late uncle very far from home.

And it was while he was there that he met a beautiful young woman named Amanda Carter. I'm assuming they were madly in love, because things moved fast and they were married before he returned home.

Maybe, looking back, he had a few regrets about that. I don't know what Sal Stoner was thinking. I don't know what his doubts were, or his regrets, or what kept him up late at night. I can only guess. That's pretty common with history, though; we get stale facts and have to find some humanity hidden among them.

When Sal brought Amanda home, it was to his cold, strict, austere home overlooking the waters of Dark Harbor. Even the name of the place should have been a clue, but Amanda apparently figured it out on her own. New England, and especially the northern half of Maine, was *not* the South.

Maine was cold in the winter. It was dark and stormy most months. The landscape was rocky and harsh and had a way of sucking the cheer out of anything. Modern life might have improved upon that over the years, but in the 1880s, Maine was the polar opposite of Falls Church, Virginia. And Amanda hated it.

At first, the stories say, she was unhappy. And that unhappiness drove the new couple to bickering. Over time, the arguments grew in scope and volume. They would shout and fight, and then avoid each other for days or weeks. You know that cliché about tension you can cut with a knife? It would have felt right at home in their presence, without a doubt.

Twenty years. That's how long this battle between Sal and Amanda went on. I can't imagine the hurt they caused each other, or the things that were said. I can't fathom the regret that Sal might have harbored, or the rage that boiled inside of Amanda. In Sal's mind, he had provided a nice home for an ungrateful woman. To Amanda, it felt like she had been the victim of a bait-and-switch; she'd been promised happiness but had been moved to hell.

The legend tells us that one of those arguments was about the floor in their parlor. It was, as in so many homes in New England, a vast expanse of beautiful hardwood. And of course Amanda hated it. She wanted carpet. So with her birthday approaching, she asked her husband for the thousandth time if he could buy a rug for the room.

This time Sal relented. He traveled to Bangor and came home with an enormous red Axminster rug, imported from England. It was expensive, and it had been a pain to transport back to the house. So when he finally got it inside and unrolled it, he was already frustrated enough.

He retrieved his hammer and a box of tacks, then moved the furniture out of the way to position it properly. He was ready to nail it down when his wife came into the room. She stood over the rug for a moment in silence. Sal probably sat on a chair and watched her, hoping that for once she would be pleased, that she might even smile.

Instead, Amanda spoke. "I hate it," she said coldly. "I hate it as much as I hate you."

To Sal, that was the final straw. He sprang from his seat and raced toward his wife, hammer raised high above his head. And then he beat her bloody. According to the story, Sal then pulled the rug out from under her, placed it over her still-breathing body, and then began to nail it down around her.

Amanda, they say, slowly died under that rug over the next few days. Whether she bled to death or suffocated, the details are as foggy as the coast of Maine. But soon enough, she was dead.

After that, life seemed to return to normal for Sal. It was quiet, there were no more arguments, and he was even seen around town with a smile on his face. But as in all stories of hidden bodies, eventually the truth was uncovered, and so was Amanda's body.

Sal was committed to the insane asylum in Portland and died a few years later. But the mark left by his horrible deed never really faded away. The local stories tell of how the Stoner house was sold after his death and a new family moved in. But right away, things were far from normal.

They would come downstairs in the morning to find that all of the furniture in the parlor had been moved off the rug. At first they assumed someone had broken in during the night, so they began locking their doors and windows, but it didn't stop. If the stories are to be believed, the new owners also found a large blood-stain in the middle of the big rug there in the parlor. They would clean it as best they could, but the stain would reappear later, just as fresh as before. And then one day they came home to find a lump in the middle of the rug.

They say the lump was moving. That it was making *sounds*. The kind of sounds you might expect if someone was alive and trapped beneath it. So, naturally, they pulled the rug up.

But there was nothing there.

Write Me a Letter

WHEN DANIEL HOME was born in 1833, his family was already a mess. His parents lived just outside of Edinburgh and had three other children. Four more would follow Daniel, but he would never meet them. At the age of one, he was adopted by an aunt and removed from what everyone perceived to be an abusive home.

Daniel was a sick child. Mild illnesses would set him back further than most other children. But he did his best to be brave. When he was nine, his aunt and uncle moved to Connecticut in the United States, and they brought Daniel with them.

There he formed a strong friendship with another boy at school—no one remembers his name, sadly—but the two spent much of their time together. They shared an interest in the supernatural, and they made a pact that, no matter how long it took, when the first of them passed away, he would return and tell the other about it.

Daniel didn't grow up in the home of his mother, but he had always been told that she was gifted. Family said she had "the sight," that she was a seer and fortune-teller. She seemed to be able to know when a friend or family member had passed away, even if that person lived hundreds or even thousands of miles away.

So when Daniel had a vision at the age of thirteen that his

friend had died, his sadness was tempered by another emotion: pride. He believed he had inherited his mother's gift. When news came just days later that his friend had indeed passed away, it was all the confirmation he needed.

Daniel's mother died in 1849, and when she did, he had the same type of awareness. This time, though, other events followed: knocking could be heard from distant parts of the house. Daniel's aunt apparently didn't care for this. She believed all of it—the visions, the premonitions, the knocking—to be the work of the devil. And although she tolerated it for a while, she eventually had enough, and when Daniel was eighteen years old she kicked him out.

It was shortly after that, at the age of twenty, that Daniel held his first séance, attempting to communicate with the dead while seated at a table with other participants. The results were so impressive, they say, that word of his abilities spread quickly. This was, after all, the era of spiritualism. The amazing Fox sisters had leveraged the supernatural to turn themselves into superstars, traveling the country and performing séances to huge crowds.

Daniel quickly found himself in high demand. People flocked to see him, and he made predictions and conducted séances for years. Some say he could even heal people, although in the end he was the one who truly needed the healing. The frailty of his youth plagued him even into adulthood, preventing him from pursuing a career in medicine.

Then in 1852 he was invited to the home of a wealthy silk manufacturer named Ward Cheney. Cheney had a great love of the supernatural, and he saw potential in Daniel. Others were invited, one of whom was Franklin Burr, brother of the editor in chief of the *Hartford Daily Times*. Unlike Cheney, though, Burr wasn't there as a believer; he was there to debunk what he perceived to be a fraud.

Daniel was blindfolded, and the séance was conducted in a well-lit room. There would be no tricks, no ropes, no pulleys or hidden levers. Burr wanted this event to be transparent and open. He knew that many other celebrity mediums had already been exposed as frauds, and Daniel Home represented his chance to add one more name to that list.

At first Daniel claimed to be in communication with a number of spirits. Despite the blindfold, he managed to write down their messages using a board with words preprinted on it. Unconvinced, though, Burr asked him to focus on one spirit in particular and go deeper. *Tell us the story. Tell us what they want. Prove that this is real.*

So Daniel told them of the sailor whose spirit was in the room. And as he did, witnesses say that the room filled with the sound of howling wind. It was as if they were on the high seas in stormy weather. As the sounds grew louder, the table itself began to tilt and rock.

Burr looked for signs of trickery. That's why he was there, after all. But he would later claim that, although he had a clear view of the space beneath and around the table, there was absolutely nothing suspicious to be found. The table was just . . . moving.

A moment later, the table stopped tilting and simply rose nearly a foot off the floor. And there it hovered, without explanation. Burr threw himself on the table, as did a few others, but the table would not sink back down.

After a few frustrating moments of wrestling with the floating furniture, Burr cried out a demand for irrefutable proof, a sign that could not be explained away with tricks or sleight of hand. In response, he later wrote, Daniel's body lifted off the chair and rose high into the air—so high, Burr said, that the man's head and hands touched the ceiling of the room. And that was the moment of transformation for Franklin Burr. He entered the home of Ward Cheney as a skeptic that day but left a true believer. Two days later, he published his experience in the newspaper and told the world his story.

Daniel didn't fare as well. His bouts with illness increased, and he was eventually diagnosed with consumption, what we would call tuberculosis today. In an effort to find relief of his symptoms, he boarded a ship and moved back to the United Kingdom. It seems to have worked, for within the year he was healthy again and traveling all across Europe as a celebrity medium. Royalty and the wealthy elite called on him to conduct séances in their grand homes. He even performed more of the levitation that Franklin Burr had witnessed that day in Connecticut. And he did all of this for decades.

One last detail: Daniel had another vision in the spring of 1876. In it, his old friend Ward Cheney had passed away. He sat down that afternoon to write a letter to Cheney's daughter-in-law to express his sadness at her loss.

When the letter arrived weeks later, having been carried across the Atlantic on an ocean liner, Cheney's daughter-in-law was shocked to see the date that Daniel had written at the top of the page: *March 22*, the very day Ward Cheney had died.

The Bank Job

WHEN EUROPEANS DISCOVERED North America in the late fifteenth century, they quickly spread up the eastern coast, up
into what is now modern-day New England and Canada's
Newfoundland. It was probably by accident, but one of the earliest discoveries they made up in those dark, cold Atlantic waters
was fish. Lots and lots of fish.

And it makes sense. It's a unique area up there, where a plateau
in the ocean floor is only about two hundred feet down. Farther
out, of course, the sea floor drops into the depths you might expect. But on that shelf, where the cold Labrador Current mixes
with the warm Gulf Stream, fish would gather by the billions.

One record from 1497 states how there were so many fish in the
water that sailors could just lower a basket over the side and pull
out dozens of them. With actual fishing nets, it was even easier.
And anytime you find a combination of abundance and ease, you're
sure to find humans ready and willing to take advantage of it.

Today, the Grand Banks have been dramatically overfished,
leading to a crazy 99 percent drop in the fish population there. But
in the mid-1800s, fish were still abundant enough to attract hundreds of fishing vessels at a time. The trouble was, when you
packed a hundred or more ships into a small area, storms could do
severe damage to them.

In the sixty years between 1830 and 1890, nearly six hundred ships and three thousand lives were lost to storms in that area. And that meant there were always new ships being built back home. The *Charles Haskell* was one of them. It was a schooner built in Boston in 1869. But even when it was completed, it would take a full year to find someone brave enough to captain it.

It happened during the final inspection. The ship was outfitted for work and ready to go, but it needed to be looked over by an official who would issue an approval. During the inspection, a workman slipped and broke his neck, dying instantly. This was bad. Of course, it's never good for someone to die so tragically. But on a nineteenth-century fishing vessel, the only thing more plentiful than the fish were superstitions. For a brand-new ship to see death and tragedy before it even left port . . . well, that was a bad omen.

It wasn't until 1870 that Captain Curtis agreed to take command of the vessel. That winter, the *Charles Haskell* pulled out of Gloucester and headed east, aiming for the southern edge of the Grand Banks, known as Georges Bank. There they met up with dozens of other ships all trawling the same waters. And that's when the storm blew in.

The waves hammered the ships and pushed them into one another. When the only thing keeping you alive was the ship beneath your feet, nothing could be more dangerous than the risk of that ship sinking, whether from the storm or from being rammed by another vessel. Which is exactly what happened. A schooner called the *Andrew Johnson* collided with Captain Curtis's ship, and both vessels were damaged.

The *Andrew Johnson* went down in a matter of minutes, taking all of her crew with her. Captain Curtis's vessel fared better, but he had to get the ship back to Gloucester for repairs. It was a journey that would take them nearly two days, though, and he had to make the trip with a crew that was even more suspicious of the *Haskell* than before.

Yes, the ship had started life with a tragic death. And though it had just dodged another tragedy when so many ships around it had been lost, the sailors didn't find comfort in that. To them, it only deepened the curse. Despite that, or perhaps *because* of that, Curtis sailed the ship home as fast as possible.

It was during the first night at sea that things started to get odd. At midnight, the two watchmen heard sounds on the outside of the hull that reminded them of sailors climbing out of the water. But of course that couldn't be the case. The ship was moving at a good clip, and there were no other vessels in sight. Still, the sounds continued.

And then, illuminated by the moonlight, shapes began to scramble over the rails. The shapes of men. They were completely silent and moved in eerie slow motion. The watchmen noticed how dark and hollow their eyes seemed to be. They almost seemed . . . dead.

It was difficult to believe. It seemed impossible, really. So the watchmen called Captain Curtis to come see with his own eyes. In all, twenty-six figures climbed onto the deck of the *Haskell,* and then they all sat on the fishing benches along the rails. In utter silence, each of the shapes began to bait invisible fishing lines and then toss them over the side. Once they were done, they stood, climbed the rails once more, and vanished into the water.

Curtis didn't know what to do, so he told the watchmen to keep their sighting to themselves, and he urged the *Haskell* on toward Gloucester. It would take them one more overnight to reach port, and he was eager to be done with a journey as cursed as this one.

The second night, though, mere miles from the coast of home, the strange events happened again. At midnight, the phantom shapes emerged once more, climbing over the rails and going through the motions any fisherman would have recognized. To the watchmen, it was clear that these were dead sailors from a lost fishing vessel, doomed to relive their occupation even in death.

Legend says that this second performance lasted hours. But as it was coming to an end, the *Charles Haskell* slipped into Gloucester Harbor—just as the sun was coming up over the horizon. And as it did, the phantom fishermen stood and climbed overboard once more. This time, though, they didn't slip beneath the cold waves of the sea.

According to the legend, they stood on the surface of the water, and then proceeded to walk in single file away from the ship. They say the ghosts headed in the direction of Salem, or maybe it was Georges Bank they were returning to. Regardless, this silent parade of the dead left its mark on Captain Curtis and his crew.

The *Charles Haskell* never again left port. No crewman was ever willing to set foot onboard after that. It's not that they worried about the phantom sailors returning, or that someday those dead sailors might do more than just bait the line and then return to the sea. No, they feared something worse, because each journey on a fishing vessel was a risk, a period of time when death could have its way whenever it wanted to.

They feared the phantoms, sure. But more than that, they feared becoming phantoms themselves.

Knock, Knock, Knock

IKE A LOT of other homeowners through the ages, Mr. and Mrs. Farrar had a problem with their house. But first let's back up, shall we?

William Farrar graduated from Dartmouth College in New Hampshire way back in 1801. He was a lawyer, and after marriage, he and his wife settled in the nearby town of Lancaster. Life was good for a very long while. His practice was successful, and he served as a deacon at the local Congregational Church.

In 1818, he and his wife realized they needed some help around the house, so they hired a young woman named Hannah Fish to move in and take care of many of their day-to-day needs. She cleaned, she cooked, she took care of the children. In return for her service, she received a small salary and a bedroom on the first floor of the house. The Farrars, along with their children, all slept upstairs.

The day Hannah moved in, something peculiar happened. She had spent the day getting settled, becoming acquainted with the house, and meeting everyone, and by the time dinner was done, she was exhausted. So she retired to her room.

A short while later, she came running back out, screaming at the top of her lungs. Mrs. Farrar came downstairs and scolded the young woman for being noisy. But Hannah insisted that she'd heard something in her room: a knock. Three knocks, actually.

Mrs. Farrar, though, wasn't buying it. Clearly Hannah was an immature girl with an overactive imagination. So she escorted her back into the room. Which is when they both heard it.

Knock, knock, knock.

Both of the women screamed this time, and that, of course, caught the attention of Mr. Farrar, who came downstairs and scolded both of them. But before his wife could explain what had happened, all three of them heard it happen again.

Knock, knock, knock.

After a moment of shock and some whimpers from the ladies, Mr. Farrar puffed up his chest and grabbed one of the pokers from the fireplace. Not to worry, he said; he would take care of the problem. And with that he headed down to the basement.

I imagine he expected it to just be an animal that had gotten into his house. I live in New England, and I know how these old homes can have small gaps or holes in their foundations. Little animals love creeping inside and making nests for themselves. That, he assumed, was the source of the knocking.

But it wasn't. In fact, he found no source for the noise. No evidence of an animal. No explanation at all. The basement was free from rodents or wildlife of any kind. Which, as you can imagine, was pretty frustrating for everyone. So good Deacon Farrar called his minister for help.

When Reverend Joseph Willard arrived, he was led into Hannah's bedroom by the entire group, and all four of them stood in the quiet room for a long while, just listening. And then it happened again.

Knock, knock, knock.

They searched. They looked. Willard offered advice, but nothing came of it. Without finding a source for the noise, the minister left, and the next day he returned with three other upstanding citizens to help him investigate. Still, they were unable to find the answer to the riddle. Who was doing all the knocking?

They tossed around theories, though. A haunting, perhaps. Or maybe it was an omen, hinting at impending disaster. The only thing everyone could agree on was that the knocking only ever happened when Hannah was in the room. So they did the only logical thing they could think of.

They tied the young woman up. They bound her hands and feet, and then laid her out on her bed and set a watch over her for the next twenty-four hours. If she was the real source of the knocking, they said, then either they would catch her doing it or it would fail to happen while she was tied up. Sound logic, I suppose, even if it was a bit drastic and more than a little cruel.

Much to their surprise, though, the knocking *did* happen again. And since it happened while Hannah was bound and imprisoned in her own bed, she was technically off the hook. But the ordeal left an impression on her, and as a result, she informed the Farrars that she no longer wanted to work for them. She quit.

According to a firsthand account, passed on to a historian decades later, as Hannah packed up her room the knocking grew louder and more frequent. Then, as she was carrying her belongings down the hallway toward the front door—*literally* as she was leaving—the knocking transformed into pounding, which seemed to follow her, thumping over and over as she walked away.

Hannah Fish moved on. A couple of years later, she married a man named Israel Nute and gave birth to the first of her six children in 1821. Later, after her husband died in 1835, she moved west, to Michigan, where she died in Saginaw in 1876.

And the house? Well, the Farrars lived there for many more decades. The house was sold in the early 1850s to another family, and everyone expected the stories of the hauntings to end there. But they didn't. The new family often heard pounding and knocking in various parts of the house. Once they described the sound of a log thumping over and over again down their front hall. No source was ever found.

In 1859, they gave up and sold the house. And it was the new owners, the local Catholic Church, who finally took care of the problem for good.

They tore the house down.

Possessed

I N 1671, THE Massachusetts Bay Colony had a devil of a problem on their hands—quite literally. That was the year that the village of Groton experienced something . . . well, *odd*.

Groton, like a lot of the first settlements in New England, was a Puritan town. It was strict and oppressive if you weren't a religious white man. Women worked horrible hours, doing everything from cooking to child care to home repairs. They were often illiterate, and they were treated more like a possession than a partner or equal.

In contrast, the local preacher was a man named Samuel Willard. He was young, Harvard-educated, well-off, and free to experience life. As a Puritan, though, he was known for his fiery sermons and a hard-line stance on witchcraft and devil worship. In fact, when Salem erupted in hysteria two decades later, Willard traveled there to help the community through preaching.

In October 1671—the day before Halloween, in fact—the Willards' household servant, a young woman named Elizabeth Knapp, began to complain about aches and pains. She felt pressure around her neck, as if she were being strangled. She suffered seizures, outbursts of screaming, and fits of deep sadness. And she *saw* things, too.

She said there were people walking around the room. Except there weren't. On another occasion she said there was a man floating above her bed. Now, these might sound like strange things to say, but one of the common beliefs of the time was that witches—men and women who practiced the dark arts—could bilocate themselves, literally be in two places at once. So Elizabeth's *real* accusation was that someone in Groton was a witch.

On the first Sabbath of her illness, Elizabeth's symptoms got worse, and all the while Samuel Willard took notes, observed her with an open mind, and asked questions when he was able to. Once she fell on the floor so violently that she nearly rolled into the fireplace. Or maybe the spirit inside her tried to throw her in; it was hard to say at the time.

She would shout out, too, words that were sometimes unintelligible and broken. Willard said it was almost like the voice of another person projecting out of the young woman's mouth. And sometimes they could be heard when her mouth was closed. When they could be understood, Willard reported, she would scream the phrase "money, sin, and misery," over and over again.

On November 2, just three days after these events began, Willard started to get answers out of Elizabeth. She told the minister that she had been meeting with the Devil for more than three years, and that he had asked her to sign a book. It was full of what she called "blood covenants," and had been signed by dozens—perhaps hundreds—of other people already. And her mission was to destroy men like Samuel Willard.

Her confessions came in bits and pieces over the next few days, but as they did, her seizures and fits increased with them. She spoke of a man in a black robe, and of sealing her pact with the Devil in her own bed. She contorted and sometimes needed to be held down by three, four, or even five grown men. And Willard watched, taking notes and studying the young woman's condition.

On November 28, roughly a month after things began, Elizabeth had the biggest seizure of all—one that lasted more than forty-eight hours—before collapsing into a catatonic state. For ten days she lay silent and unmoving. No fits. No screams. No dark confessions. And then, on December 8, she awoke.

Willard recorded more of the same for another month, and as far as the records tell us, Elizabeth never improved. But on January 15, 1672, Willard made some observations hinting that things had finally come to an end. It was his conclusion that her condition was no act, no trick or performance designed to fool him. It was real and powerful. He also concluded that the symptoms were nothing short of diabolical, originating from dark forces. Even the voices were rooted in the Devil's influence.

But with all of that said, Willard refused to admit that Elizabeth had willingly brought it all upon herself with a pact. There were too many holes in her story, he said. Too many inconsistencies. Which meant, in seventeenth-century language, that she was a victim, not a criminal.

Elizabeth pops up in public records one final time. Two years later, at the age of nineteen, she married a man named (I'm not making this up) Samuel Scripture. And then she disappeared.

I don't see a possession, though. Most historians don't, either. Because when you take in the social climate of the times, the real story can be seen just beneath the surface, like the hint of a mattress beneath a thick sheet. Let me peel it back for you.

In Puritan New England, you stood out only if you bucked the system. We know about Elizabeth Knapp today only because she broke through the barriers around her and left a mark on her community. Elizabeth Knapp, a young, illiterate servant girl working in the house of a wealthy, educated, socially powerful man, took control.

She claimed her own voice. She became the center of conversation in an age when women were ignored and socially oppressed. She was *noticed*. Even if it lasted less than three months, Elizabeth Knapp became someone. She became *powerful*.

And then she disappeared, and that's the truly sad part, isn't it? Because it hints at submission. Yes, she did try to speak out briefly, but in the end she gave up and closed her mouth. She married the male servant of the family next door and assumed her role in society once again.

If we're going to remember Elizabeth at all, let's remember her full of a new voice and a new spirit. She was a bold, nasty, power-ful woman—for a while, at least.

Maybe she really was possessed after all, but it was no demon that took hold of her. No, Elizabeth Knapp, I think, was possessed, if only for a little while, by her true self.

Something I hope we can all aspire to.

ACKNOWLEDGMENTS

Without a small number of very important people in my life, this book would not exist.

At the top of that list is my wife, Jennifer, who not only has supported me and encouraged me to build and dream, but also loves this crazy thing I get to do for a living. And my girls have given me a reason to tell tales and teach lessons. Read and grow, girls . . . read and grow.

My heartfelt gratitude also goes out to the brilliant minds behind the publication of this volume: my editor, Tricia Narwani, and the folks at Del Rey; my agent, Susan Zanger; and the brilliant artist M. S. Corley.

Thanks to Seth for telling me my original idea for Lore was a bad one, and to Chad for providing the soundtrack to my career. And last—but certainly not least—thank you to each and every one of the people who have listened along and shared Lore with their friends and family over the years.

BIBLIOGRAPHY

They Made a Tonic

"Ramanga," Vampire Underworld, n.d., vampireunderworld.com/
african-vampires/ramanga.

Rossella Lorenzi, " 'Vampire' Skeletons Found in Bulgaria," *Seeker*,
June 6, 2012, seeker.com/vampire-skeletons-found-in-
bulgaria-1765817778.html.

Lindsey Fitzharris, "Buried Alive: 19th-Century Safety Coffins,"
The Chirurgeon's Apprentice, June 26, 2013, thechirurgeons
apprentice.com/2013/06/26/buried-alive-19th-century-safety
-coffins.

Paul Snow, "Hunting for Thoreau's Vampire in Vermont," *The
Uncertainist*, October 24, 2013, uncertaintist.wordpress.
com/2013/10/24/hunting-for-thoreaus-vampire-in-vermont.

Deep and Twisted Roots

Abigail Tucker, "The Great New England Vampire Panic,"
Smithsonian, October 2012, smithsonianmag.com/history/the
-great-new-england-vampire-panic-36482878/.

Thomas D'Agostino, *A History of Vampires in New England*
(Charleston, SC: Haunted America/History Press, 2010), 49–50.

Denise Hinckley Goodwin, "Vampires: New England and the
World," *Vermont Dead Line*, October 13, 2014, vermontdeadline
.blogspot.com/2014/10/vampires-of-new-england.html.

Eric Michael Johnson, "A Natural History of Vampires," *Scientific American,* October 31, 2011, blogs.scientificamerican.com/primate-diaries/a-natural-history-of-vampires.

Rosemary Guiley, *The Encyclopedia of Vampires, Werewolves, and Other Monsters* (New York: Infobase, 2004), 107.

David Ono, "Vampires Are Real: David Ono Journeys to Serbia to Find Real Story," KABC-TV, Los Angeles, October 31, 2013, abc7.com/archive/9308452.

Timothy Taylor, "The Real Vampire Slayers," *Independent,* October 27, 2007, independent.co.uk/news/world/europe/the-real-vampire-slayers-397874.html.

Daniel McLaughlin, "A Village Still in Thrall to Dracula," *Guardian,* June 18, 2005, theguardian.com/world/2005/jun/19/theobserver.

Dark Conclusions

Bruce McClelland, *Slayers and Their Vampires: A Cultural History of Killing the Dead* (Ann Arbor: University of Michigan Press, 2006), 97–102.

Asbjorn Dyrendal, James R. Lewis, and Jesper Petersen, *The Invention of Satanism* (New York: Oxford University Press, 2015).

"The Highgate Vampire—How It All Began," *Mysterious Britain & Ireland,* n.d., mysteriousbritain.co.uk/england/greater-london/hauntings/the-highgate-vampire-how-it-all-began-by-david-farrant.html.

Stephen Emms, "Highgate Cemetery—And the Tale of the Highgate Vampire," *Kentishtowner,* October 31, 2016, kentishtowner.co.uk/2012/10/31/wednesday-picture-highgate-cemetery-and-the-tale-of-the-highgate-vampire.

Jennifer Westwood and Sophia Kingshill, *The Lore of Scotland: A Guide to Scottish Legends* (New York: Random House, 2012), 186–87.

Sandy Hobbs, "The Gorbals Vampire Hunt," *Herald Scotland,* June 23, 1989, heraldscotland.com/news/11919192.The_Gorbals_Vampire_hunt.

Brought Back

Mike Mariani, "The Tragic, Forgotten History of Zombies," *Atlantic,* October 28, 2015, theatlantic.com/entertainment/

archive/2015/10/how-america-erased-the-tragic-history-of
-the-zombie/412264.

William of Newburgh, *Historia Rerum Anglicarum* (1567), Book 5,
Ch. 24.

Paula R. Stiles, "Historical Zombies: Mummies, *The Odyssey*, and
Beyond," Tor.com, September 13, 2010, tor.com/2010/09/13/
historical-zombies-mummies-the-odyssey-and-beyond.

Lakshmi Gandhi, "Zoinks! Tracing the History of 'Zombie' from
Haiti to the CDC," *Code Switch*, National Public Radio, December
15, 2013, npr.org/sections/codeswitch/2013/12/13/250844800/
zoinks-tracing-the-history-of-zombie-from-haiti-to-the-cdc.

Patrick D. Hahn, "Dead Man Walking: Wade Davis and the Secret of
the Zombie Poison," Biology Online, September 4, 2007, biology
-online.org/articles/dead_man_walking.html.

Kelly Faircloth, "Zora Neale Hurston, Zombie Hunter," *io9*, July 23,
2011, io9.gizmodo.com/5823671/zora-neale-hurston-zombie
-hunter.

Zora Neale Hurston, *Tell My Horse* (New York: Harper Perennial,
2008), 182, 195.

"The Curious Case of Clairvius Narcisse and Other Instances of
Haitian Zombies," *Kreyolicious*, n.d., kreyolicious.com/the
-curious-case-of-clairvius-narcisse-and-other-instances-of
-haitian-zombies/4005.

Garth Haslam, "1979, April: Francina Illeus, aka Ti-Femme,"
Anomalies, n.d., anomalyinfo.com/Stories/1979-april-francina
-illeus.

Wade Davis, *The Serpent and the Rainbow* (New York: Simon and
Schuster, 2010), 27.

The Trees

Michael E. Bell, *Food for the Dead: On the Trail of New England's
Vampires* (Middletown, CT: Wesleyan University Press, 2011).

Michael E. Bell, "The Vampires," *Food for the Dead* (blog), n.d.,
foodforthedead.com/vampires.html.

John Castellucci, "New England Vampires? Folklore Battled a
Genuine Specter," *Providence Journal*, October 25, 1994, available
at thevampireproject.blogspot.com/2009/03/new-england
-vampires-folklore-battled.html.

THE OTHERS

"The Pygmies," Mythology Guide, n.d., online-mythology.com/pygmies.

"The Legend of Maya Aluxes," Mexico News Network, February 2014, mexiconewsnetwork.com/tv-series/maya-alux/.

"The Trows of Orkney and Shetland," *The Faery Folklorist*, October 15, 2015, faeryfolklorist.blogspot.com/2015/10/the-trows-of-orkney-and-shetland.html.

"The Pooka," Ireland's Eye, n.d., irelandseye.com/paddy3/preview2.htm.

Kathy Weiser, "The Little People of Wyoming and the Pedro Mountains Mummy," Legends of America, last updated March 2017, legendsofamerica.com/wy-littlepeople.html.

UNDER CONSTRUCTION

Emma Jane Kirby, "Why Icelanders Are Wary of Elves Living Beneath the Rocks," BBC, June 20, 2014, bbc.com/news/magazine-27907358.

Ellyn Santiago, "Mohegan Tribe's Cultural Boundary Reduced but Still Could Block Affordable Housing," Patch.com, September 24, 2012, patch.com/connecticut/montville-ct/mohegan-tribes-cultural-boundary-reduced-but-still-cf43f7b1f78.

"Legendary Native American Figures: Squannit (Squant)," Native-American.org, n.d., native-languages.org/squannit.htm.

TAMPERED

Brett Swancer, "The Real Gremlins of WWII," *Mysterious Universe*, July 23, 2015, mysteriousuniverse.org/2015/07/the-real-gremlins-of-wwii.

"Wee Folk and Their Friends," *Encyclopedia of the Unusual and Unexplained*, 2008, unexplainedstuff.com/Mysterious-Creatures/Wee-Folk-and-Their-Friends-Gremlins.html.

"WWII Pilot Speaks Out," *Cryptozoology News*, February 11, 2014, cryptozoologynews.com/wwii-pilot-speaks-out-gremlins-are-real.

"Charles Lindbergh and the Third Man Factor," *Theresa's Haunted History of the Tri-State*, August 4, 2014, theresashauntedhistory

ofthetri-state.blogspot.com/2014/08/charles-lindbergh
-and-third-man-factor.html.

Doing Tricks

"Second Chalk Figure Discovered Near Uffington White Horse,"
National Trust, March 31, 2017, nationaltrust.org.uk/news/
second-chalk-figure-discovered-near-uffington-white-horse.

"Here's All of Google's April Fools' Day Pranks So Far," *Verge*, April
2017, theverge.com/2017/3/31/15140206/google-best-april-fools
-jokes-roundup-2017.

"List of Fictional Tricksters," *World Heritage Encyclopedia*,
n.d. (accessed July 2017), worldheritage.org/article/
WHEBN0012058193/List%20of%20fictional%20tricksters.

Marie Caroline Watson Hamlin, *Legends of Le Détroit* (Detroit:
Thorndike Nourse, 1883).

Christopher R. Fee and Jeffrey B. Webb, *American Myths, Legends,
and Tall Tales: An Encyclopedia of American Folklore* (Santa
Barbara, CA: ABC-CLIO, 2016), 695–96.

"Great Fire of 1805," Detroit Historical Society, n.d., detroit
historical.org/learn/encyclopedia-of-detroit/great-fire-1805.

Lee DeVito, "The Legend of the Legend of Detroit's Nain Rouge,"
Detroit Metro Times, March 16, 2016, metrotimes.com/detroit/
the-legend-of-the-legend-of-detroits-nain-rouge/
Content?oid=2404384.

Alan Naldrett, *Forgotten Tales of Michigan's Lower Peninsula*
(Charleston, SC: History Press, 2014).

Trees and Shadows

"The History of Human-Animal Interaction: Ancient Cultures and
Religions," Library Index, n.d., libraryindex.com/pages/2148/
History-Human-Animal-Interaction-ancient-cultures-religions
.html.

Linda S. Godfrey, *Real Wolfmen: True Encounters in Modern America*
(New York: Penguin, 2012).

Shawn Fields, "13 Questions for 'Beast of Bray Road' Author &
Paranormal Investigator Linda Godfrey," *Unexplained Research*,
March 15, 2011, unexplainedresearch.com/media/13_questions
.html.

Mark Moran and Mark Sceurman, *Weird U.S.: Your Travel Guide to America's Local Legends and Best Kept Secrets* (New York: Sterling, 2009), 122.

OFF THE PATH

Edward Clodd, *Tom Tit Tot: An Essay on Savage Philosophy in Folk Tale* (London, 1898), 200.

Edward Westermarck, "L'Ar, or the Transference of Traditional Curses in Morocco," in H. Balfour et al., *Anthropological Essays Presented to Edward Burnett Tylor in Honour of His 75th Birthday, Oct. 2, 1907* (Oxford: Clarendon Press, 1907), 361ff.

Cora Linn Morrison Daniels and Charles McClellan Stevens, *Encyclopaedia of Superstitions, Folklore, and the Occult Sciences of the World* (Chicago: J. H. Yewdale & Sons, 1903), 1261.

Leslie A. Sconduto, *Metamorphoses of the Werewolf* (Jefferson, NC: McFarland, 2008), 32.

Laurence Marcellus Larson, ed., *The King's Mirror* (New York: Twayne, 1917), 115–16.

THE BEAST WITHIN

Virgil, "Moeris," Eclogue IX, *Eclogues,* trans. J. W. McKail, 1934, available at sacred-texts.com/cla/virgil/ecl/ecl09.htm.

Moonlight, "Ancient Norse Werewolves," Werewolves.com, n.d., werewolves.com/ancient-norse-werewolves.

George Bores, "The Damnable Life and Death of Stubbe Peeter" (London, 1590), in Montague Summers, *The Werewolf* (New York: Dutton, 1934), 253–59, available at pitt.edu/~dash/werewolf.html#stubbe.

Andrew Amelinckx, "Old Time Farm Crime: The Werewolf Farmer of Bedburg," *Modern Farmer,* August 5, 2013, modernfarmer.com/2013/08/peter-stubbethe-werewolf-of-bedburg.

Nathan Robert Brown, *The Mythology of Grimm* (New York: Penguin, 2014), 77.

Dirk C. Gibson, *Legends, Monsters, or Serial Murderers?* (Santa Barbara, CA: ABC-CLIO, 2012), 54–55.

Colin Wilson and Damon Wilson, *Strange: True Stories of the Mysterious and Bizarre* (New York: Skyhorse, 2014).

Samantha Lyon and Daphne Tan, *Supernatural Serial Killers: Chilling Cases of Paranormal Bloodlust and Deranged Fantasy* (London: Arcturus, 2015).

HUNGER PAINS

"Witiko," Native-Languages.org, n.d., native-languages.org/ witiko.htm.

"Chenoo," Native-Languages.org, n.d., native-languages.org/ chenoo.htm.

Andrew Hanon, "Evil Spirit Made Man Eat Family," Canoe.com, August 12, 2008, cnews.canoe.com/CNEWS/WeirdNews/2008/ 07/20/6213011-sun.html.

Thomas Fiddler and James R. Stevens, *Killing the Shamen* (Moonbeam, ON: Penumbra Press, 1985).

James R. Stevens, "ZHAUWUNO-GEEZHIGO-GAUBOW," in *Dictionary of Canadian Biography,* vol. 13, University of Toronto/ Université Laval, 2003– (accessed May 22, 2017), biographi.ca/ en/bio/zhauwuno_geezhigo_gaubow_13E.html.

Ontario Legislative Assembly, "The Killing of Wa-Sak-Apee-Quay by Pe-Se-Quan, and Others," *Sessional Papers: Legislature of the Province of Ontario,* vol. XL, part 4 (1908), 91–120.

A DEEP FEAR

Ian Steadman, "The Bloop Mystery Has Been Solved," *Wired,* November 29, 2012, wired.co.uk/article/bloop-mystery-not -solved-sort-of.

Grace Costantino, "Five 'Real' Sea Monsters Brought to Life by Early Naturalists," *Smithsonian,* October 27, 2014, smithsonianmag.com/science-nature/five-real-sea-monsters -brought-life-early-naturalists-180953155.

David Leveille, "Why There Are Sea Monsters Lurking in Early World Maps," *The World,* Public Radio International, April 11, 2016, pri.org/stories/2016-04-08/why-there-are-so-many-sea -monsters-early-world-maps.

"Sea Monsters," American Museum of Natural History, n.d., amnh .org/exhibitions/mythic-creatures/water-creatures-of-the -deep/sea-monsters.

"The Great New England Sea Serpents," New England Historical Society, n.d., newenglandhistoricalsociety.com/great-new -england-sea-serpents.

Loren Coleman, *Monsters of Massachusetts: Mysterious Creatures in the Bay State* (Mechanicsburg, PA: Stackpole Books, 2013), 39–43.

Jon Nicholls, "The Monster of Massachusetts," *Library, Art, and Archives* (blog), Kew Royal Botanic Gardens, August 4, 2014, kew.org/discover/blogs/library-art-and-archives/monster -massachusetts.

J. P. O'Neill, *The Great New England Sea Serpent: An Account of Unknown Creatures Sighted by Many Respectable Persons Between 1638 and the Present Day* (New York: Cosimo, 2003), 209.

Alisha Morrissey, "Newfoundland Fishermen Snag Sea Monster in Nets," *Telegram*, March 2, 2010.

LOST SHEEP

Mark A. Hall, *Thunderbirds: America's Living Legends of Giant Birds* (New York: Cosimo, 2008), 82–84.

Patty A. Wilson, *Haunted West Virginia: Ghosts and Strange Phenomena of the Mountain State* (Mechanicsburg, PA: Stackpole Books, 2007), 64–68.

ONE WORD

Linda S. Godfrey, *Real Wolfmen: True Encounters in Modern America* (New York: Penguin, 2012).

UNBOXED

David L. Sloan, *Ghosts of Key West* (Key West, FL: Phantom Press, 1998), 5–15.

Christopher Bolzano and Tim Weisberg, *Haunted Objects: Stories of Ghosts on Your Shelf* (Iola, WI: Krause, 2012), 100–109.

DO NOT OPEN

Gerald Brittle, *The Demonologist: The Extraordinary Career of Ed and Lorraine Warren* (iUniverse, 2002), 39–53.

John Harker, *Demonic Dolls: True Tales of Terrible Toys* (n.p.: Black Cat Books, 2015).

A Devil on the Roof

James McCloy and Ray Miller Jr., *The Jersey Devil* (Moorestown, NJ: Middle Atlantic Press, 1976), 24–25.

Charles X. Skinner, *American Myths and Legends,* vol. 1 (New York: Lippincott, 1903), 243.

James McCloy and Ray Miller Jr., *Phantom of the Pines* (Moorestown, NJ: Middle Atlantic Press, 1998), 74.

Over the Top

Jan Bondeson, *The London Monster: A Sanguinary Tale* (New York: Da Capo Press, 2009).

John Matthews, *The Mystery of Spring-Heeled Jack: From Victorian Legend to Steampunk Hero* (New York: Simon and Schuster, 2016).

Missing the Point

Juanita Rose Violini, *Almanac of the Infamous, the Incredible, and the Ignored* (San Francisco: Weiser Books, 2009), 136.

Ken Gerhard, "The Texas-Sized 'Monster' Bird That Created a Huge Flap Back in 1975," *San Antonio Current,* January 20, 2012, sacurrent.com/the-daily/archives/2012/01/20/the-texas-sized -monster-bird-that-created-a-huge-flap-back-in-1975.

Mark A. Hall, *Thunderbirds: America's Living Legends of Giant Birds* (New York: Cosimo, 2008), 89–91.

Pete Brook, "Inside the Eerie TNT Storage Bunkers of West Virginia," *Wired,* March 31, 2014, wired.com/2014/03/joshua- dudley-greer-tnt-storage.

Loren Coleman, *Mothman* (New York: Paraview Press, 2002), 38–44.

Troy Taylor, "Gallipolis's Mothman," *Weird US,* n.d., weirdus.com/ states/ohio/bizarre_beasts/mothman/index.php.

"The Black Bird of Chernobyl," *North Atlantic Blog,* October 31, 2014, northatlanticblog.wordpress.com/2014/10/31/the-black -bird-of-chernobyl.

Sean Alfano, "The Afterlife: Real or Imagined," *Sunday Morning,*
CBS News, October 30, 2005, cbsnews.com/news/the-afterlife
-real-or-imagined/3.

"Dead Spiritualist Silent," *New York Times,* February 8, 1921.

John J. Kucich, *Ghostly Communion: Cross-Cultural Spiritualism in
Nineteenth-Century American Literature* (Hanover, NH:
Dartmouth College Press, 2004), 70–77.

E. H. Britten, *Nineteenth Century Miracles* (New York: William
Britten, 1884), 459.

E. W. Capron, *Modern Spiritualism* (Boston: Marsh, 1855), 132–71.

Joseph A. Citro, *Passing Strange* (Boston: Houghton Mifflin, 1996),
18–32.

Elisabeth Tilstra, "The Eerie Mystery of the Phelps Mansion
Knockings," *The Line-Up,* January 22, 2016, the-line-up.com/
phelps-mansion.

Bela Black, "The Mystery of Phelps Mansion," *American Ghost
Stories,* February 3, 2015, americanghoststories.com/new
-england-ghost-stories/the-mystery-of-phelps-mansion
-stratford-connecticut.

THE BLOODY PIT

Cheri Reval, *Haunted Massachusetts: Ghosts and Strange Phenomena of
the Bay State* (Mechanicsburg, PA: Stackpole Books, 2005), 5–7.

Michael Norman and Beth Scott, *Historic Haunted America* (New
York: Macmillan, 2007), 157–60.

DINNER AT THE AFTERGLOW

Adam Woog, *Haunted Washington: Uncanny Tales and Spooky Spots from
the Upper Left-Hand Corner of the United States* (Guilford, CT:
Globe Pequot, 2013), 112–16.

Richard Walker, *Roche Harbor* (Charleston, SC: Arcadia, 2009), 91–
100.

HOMESTEAD

William Montell, *Haunted Houses and Family Ghosts of Kentucky*
(Lexington: University Press of Kentucky, 2001), 104–6.

David E. Philips, *Legendary Connecticut* (Willimantic, CT: Curbstone Press, 1984), 250.

ADRIFT

Sir Arthur Thomas Quiller-Couch, *The Blue Adventure Book* (London: Cassell, 1905), 320.

Philip Ross, "Oldest Shipwreck In Mediterranean Found? Ancient Phoenician Vessel Contains 2,700-Year-Old Artifacts," *International Business Times,* August 25, 2014, ibtimes.com/oldest -shipwreck-mediterranean-found-ancient-phoenician-vessel -contains-2700-year-old-1668798.

Elwood Walter, "The Dangers of Sailing in High Latitudes," *The Ariel: A Literary Gazette,* nos. 1–2 (1827): 130.

TAKE THE STAND

E. P. Evans, *The Criminal Prosecution and Capital Punishment of Animals* (London: Heinemann, 1906), 143.

Katie Letcher Lyle, *The Man Who Wanted Seven Wives* (Chapel Hill, NC: Algonquin Books, 1986), 63.

Garry Rodgers, "How a Ghost's Evidence Convicted a Murderer," *Huffington Post,* February 2015, huffingtonpost.com/garry -rodgers/how-a-ghosts-evidence-con_b_9252062.html.

Troy Taylor, *No Rest for the Wicked: History and Hauntings of American Crime and Unsolved Mysteries* (Alton, IL: Whitechapel Productions, 2001).

THE DEVIL'S BEAT

"Earliest Music Instruments Found," BBC News, May 25, 2012, bbc .com/news/science-environment-18196349.

Joseph Glanvil, *Saducismus Triumphatus, or Full and Plain Evidence Concerning Witches and Apparitions: In Two Parts; The First Treating of Their Possibility; The Second of Their Real Existence* (London: J. Collins and S. Lownds, 1681).

Michael Hunter, "New Light on the 'Drummer of Tedworth': Conflicting Narratives of Witchcraft in Restoration England," *Historical Research* 78, no. 201 (2005): 311–53.

Michael Kernan, "The Talking Drums," *Smithsonian,* June 2000, smithsonianmag.com/arts-culture/the-talking-drums-29197334.

Harlan McKosato, "Drums: Heartbeat of Mother Earth," *Native Peoples Magazine,* July/August 2009, nativepeoples.com/Native -Peoples/July-August-2009/Drums-Heartbeat-of-Mother-Earth.

MARY, MARY

"For 50 Years, Nuclear Bomb Lost in Watery Grave," *Weekend Edition Sunday,* National Public Radio, February 3, 2008, npr.org/ templates/story/story.php?storyId=18587608.

E. W. Stevens, *The Watseka Wonder* (Chicago: Religio-Philosophical Publishing House, 1887).

Brian Haughton, "Lurancy Vennum," Mysterious People, 2003/2005, mysteriouspeople.com/Lurancy_Vennum.htm.

William James, *The Principles of Psychology* (New York: Holt, 1890), 397–99.

"Mary L. Binning," MooseRoots, n.d., death-records.mooseroots .com/l/208166293/Mary-L-Binning.

THE LUMP

"The Bump in the Carpet," *Fairweather Lewis,* April 25, 2010, fairweatherlewis.wordpress.com/2010/04/25/the-bump-in-the -carpet.

Dennis William Hauck, *Haunted Places: The National Directory: Ghostly Abodes, Sacred Sites, UFO Landings and Other Supernatural Locations* (New York: Penguin Books, 2002), 200.

Joseph Citro, *Passing Strange* (Boston: Houghton Mifflin, 1996), 278.

WRITE ME A LETTER

Diana Ross McCain, *Mysteries and Legends of New England* (Guilford, CT: Globe Pequot, 2009), 98–107.

"A Few Words on an Unpopular Subject," *Hartford Daily Times,* August 10, 1852.

THE BANK JOB

Mary Bolté, *Haunted New England: A Devilish View of the Yankee Past* (Riverside, CT: Chatham Press, 1972), 43–46.

Knock, Knock, Knock

Charles J. Jordan, *Tales Told in the Shadows of the White Mountains* (Hanover, NH: University Press of New England, 2003), 18–22.

History of Penobscot County, Maine: With Illustrations and Biographical Sketches (Cleveland: Williams, Chase and Co., 1882), 413.

Possessed

Elaine G. Breslaw, *Witches of the Atlantic World: A Historical Reader and Primary Sourcebook* (New York: New York University Press, 2000), 230–45.

Sam Behling, "The Possession of Elizabeth Knapp," Ancestry.com, n.d., homepages.rootsweb.ancestry.com/~sam/knapp/elizabeth .html.

"Samuel Scripture," Rjohara.net, n.d., rjohara.net/gen/scripture.

ABOUT THE AUTHOR

One of the most successful podcast producers in the world, AARON MAHNKE began his career in 2015. His first podcast *Lore* has been downloaded half a billion times, adapted for television by Amazon, and published as a major book series from Penguin Random House. Aaron has also produced a number of other wildly popular podcasts, including his chart-topping *Cabinet of Curiosities* and his award-winning supernatural audio drama, *Bridgewater.*

lorepodcast.com
facebook.com/lorepodcast
Instagram: @amahnke & @lorepodcast
Threads: @amahnke & @lorepodcast

ABOUT THE ILLUSTRATOR

M. S. CORLEY is a professional illustrator and book cover designer fascinated by folklore, the supernatural, and all things strange. Besides *The World of Lore: Monstrous Creatures*, he has also created illustrations for *Darkness There: Selected Tales by Edgar Allan Poe*, *Never Bet the Devil & Other Warnings* by Orrin Grey, and others. He haunts Central Oregon with his wife, daughter, son, and cat named Dinah.

mscorley.com
X: @corleyms

ABOUT THE TYPE

This book was set in Tribute, a typeface designed by Frank Heine for the Emigre type foundry in 2003. It was modeled on a printed specimen of typefaces cut in 1544 and 1557 by the French punchcutter François Guyot. While Guyot's approach to the design of his Renaissance Antiquas tended toward the idiosyncratic, Heine enhanced the readability of Tribute by giving it stronger stroke widths and decreasing the overall contrast between the thick and thin strokes.

DISCOVER MORE FROM
DEL REY &
RANDOM HOUSE
WORLDS!

READ EXCERPTS
from hot new titles.

STAY UP-TO-DATE
on your favorite authors.

FIND OUT about exclusive
giveaways and sweepstakes.

CONNECT WITH US ONLINE!
@ ☑ ▾ @DelReyBooks

DelReyBooks.com
RandomHouseWorlds.com